Long Vistas

Long Vistas

Women and Families on Colorado Homesteads

KATHERINE HARRIS

UNIVERSITY PRESS OF COLORADO

Copyright © 1993 by the University Press of Colorado
P.O. Box 849
Niwot, Colorado 80544

The University Press of Colorado is a cooperative publishing enterprise supported, in part, by
Adams State College, Colorado State University, Fort Lewis College, Mesa State College, Metro-
politan State College of Denver, University of Colorado, University of Northern Colorado, University of Southern Colorado, and Western State College of Colorado.

ISBN: 0-87081-288-2

The paper used in this publication meets the minimum requirements of the American
National Standard for Information Sciences — Permanence of Paper for Printed Library
Materials. ANSI Z39.48–1984

∞

10 9 8 7 6 5 4 3 2 1

To the memory of my parents,
Katherine Kemp Stanley and Robert McClaughry Hill,
and of my brother, Peter Stanley Hill

Contents

Preface

Long Vistas is about women and their families, land, and opportunities. It tells the stories of a particular group of women in a particular time and place, and how those women responded to the possibilities land-ownership opened to them.

On another level, *Long Vistas* encompasses two themes now engaging historians of the West. The first of these, the diversity of western populations, emerges primarily by implication. The women of this book are not *the* women of the West. Their stories do not reflect the experiences of *all* western women. But to say that special circumstances produced women homesteaders does not in any way diminish their significance. Their experiences teach many lessons, especially about economics and empowerment. And these lessons still have wide application within capitalist cultures, whether situated in the western United States or elsewhere.

The second theme touches the heart of the debate pitting the West's "mythmakers" against its "realists." I refer to the battle lines drawn by historians, policymakers, western enthusiasts, writers, and others over two huge and amorphous concepts — success and failure. Contention typically centers on such western enterprises as the fur trade, mining, cattle ranching, or water development. Each produced wealth, and each exacted costs. Depending on one's point of view — as industrialist, Indian, or environmental activist (just to name three) — each business rates a label as either a "success" or a "failure." One western enterprise, however, stands outside the debate, thanks to an uncharacteristic unanimity of opinion. Lacking glamour and now quaintly anachronistic, homesteading, all contenders agree, was a failure.

Ever since my student days when I first became acquainted with the 1862 Homestead Act, I learned that homesteading, especially in the arid West, failed its mandate. The 160 acres of the national domain offered by the act fell short of the land required to support a farm or ranch. Home-steaders not only impoverished themselves when they invested all their resources in a doomed enterprise, they degraded the land when they cultivated areas of marginal fertility and low rainfall. Their unwitting abuse of the environment contributed to the dust bowl disasters of the twenties and thirties. Ultimately, the abandonment of homesteads dashed lawmakers' hopes for a West populated by an army of yeomen farmers. From whatever aspect one chooses to look at homesteading — the human costs, the damaged environment, or as national land policy — homesteading failed.

None of these charges is exactly false. Yet taken together they do not tell the whole truth either. Homesteading encouraged millions of people to move west. Their numbers pressured lawmakers to carve states out of the western territories and created a flurry of economic activity benefiting women, men, and families. In time homesteaders, and especially their children, became leading citizens all across the West. Surely, these outcomes count as successes — at least from the viewpoint of settlers and western developers.

The closer the inspection of homesteading, the clearer the picture emerges of a western enterprise more confused than illuminated by labels like "success" and "failure." Whose success? Whose failure? And which time period in the course of the enterprise are we considering? These are questions begging answers.

I came to ponder the meanings of success and failure, especially as functions of time, through personal experience. In recent years, I helped care for my aging parents and watched in distress the slow slide of two vital and competent people into confusion and dependency. Painful though that experience was, it changed the way I look at the disintegration that inevitably overcomes all systems, whether living, inanimate, or abstract. When the energy that creates and maintains systems dissipates, they disintegrate into chaos. Physicists have a word for that disintegration; they call it *entropy*.

Although physicists use *entropy* to describe what happens to matter and energy in the cosmos, I find the term useful for more down-to-earth applications. On the prosaic level of housework and gardening, for example, I know all about entropy. I have been fighting it for years. But what does entropy have to do with homesteading or with human lives? Simply that neither homesteading nor people deserve judgments based on final outcomes. Homesteading, like life, dealt a complex and sometimes subtle mix of successes and failures. *Long Vistas* attempts to demonstrate some of that complexity and concludes that for the women who settled the grasslands of the South Platte valley, homesteading offered more opportunity than pain.

Throughout the preparation of this book, I received help from many people and institutions. *Long Vistas* started life back in the Dark Ages (well, maybe not quite that long ago) as a dissertation at the University of Colorado. Sue Armitage headed me in the direction of Sterling and Akron where I first found primary materials on homesteading women. Margaret Cooley at the Akron Public Library, Betty Kenyon and the staff at the Sterling Public Library, and Phyllis Dollerschell, the Logan County Clerk, were unfailing in their courtesy and helpfulness. Cassandra Volpe guided me through the mysteries of the map collections at Norlin Library's Western History Archives in Boulder. Meg West of the Colorado Historical Society directed me to the homesteading papers of Alice C. Newberry; Margaret Walsh and other members of the staff assisted me in my search for pictures.

I am indebted more than I can say to the people of northeastern Colorado and to the historical societies they support. For family histories they helped preserve and for pictures that do so much to enhance this book, I would especially like to thank L. Scotty and Claretta Odell, Ken and Aladean Cole, Mildred Starlin, and Lucinda Starlin of the Washington County Museum Association; Dorothea Safford, Marvin Gardner, and Ann Withrow of the Crook Historical Society; Florence and William Plank, Sr., Cecelia Nolte, and Helen Lambert of the Fleming Historical Society; Anna Mae Hagemeier of the Overland Trail Museum in Sterling; and Vivien Warren of Fleming. I am particularly grateful to those who personally shared with me, through interviews and letters, their own homesteading experiences or those of family members: Amy Dickensen Worthley, Lois Ervin, Elva Bowles, Olive Ross, Chet Kincheloe, and Ethel F. Yergen. That many of them are no longer living underscores the sad fact that time has just about run out for collecting such stories firsthand.

Gathering together materials is only part of the challenge in creating a book. Analyzing and presenting those materials in a form that readers can follow is at least half the battle. Insofar as I have succeeded, I owe that success in large part to the guidance of others. Lee Chambers-Schiller and Ralph Mann provided much encouragement, advice, and constructive criticism through the first incarnation of *Long Vistas* as a dissertation. Following my graduation and a hiatus of some years, I had the good fortune to meet Patty Limerick. No one could have been more generous to the waif at her door — especially a waif presenting her with a manuscript in need of a great deal of massaging. Lavishing her pen as freely as her time, Patty lassoed fuzzy arguments and slashed through the dreaded "kudzu" (her metaphor) of the passive voice, somehow managing all the while to add words of encouragement. The simple truth is this: Without Patty's help, *Long Vistas* never would have found a publisher. In the final analysis, of course, I alone am responsible for the contents of this book. But I cannot leave Patty without adding this thought: To you, Patty, thanks must be given by me.

If ever I had any delusions about my casting as a rugged individualist, writing this book has utterly dashed them. To the expressions of gratitude in these acknowledgments, I add my thanks to friends and family for their unfailing support. My sisters, Muriel H. Cronin and Susan A. Hill, and my mother-in-law, Lorle K. Harris, "held my hand" through many years of trying to meet the needs of work and family. My brother, Peter S. Hill, assisted me with some of the finer points of the research. I only wish he had lived to see *Long Vistas* published. My twelve-year-old son, Robert, has never known a time when I was not somehow involved with this book. From the toddler who gave new meaning to the word "distraction" as I struggled with the early drafts of the manuscript, Robert has graduated to my valued research assistant and traveling companion. His easy charm broke the ice wherever the pursuit of pictures took us.

As I try to say thanks to Frank, I hardly know where to begin. He has been my best friend, my sounding board, my meal ticket, my unflagging supporter. He appears nowhere in the text, the notes, or the bibliography, but his influence is there on nearly every page.

Katherine Harris
Boulder, Colorado

It seemed to me that the long vistas of green prairie were beautiful.

— Nancy Johnson
Colorado homesteader

Long Vistas

Introduction: Western Women in "Fact" and Fiction

"I think I thought I was rich." Seated in the living room of her home on a hot June day in 1980, Lois Ervin still remembered the thrill she felt nearly sixty-five years earlier upon receiving $1,600 from the sale of her Colorado homestead.[1] And, in fact, Lois was rich by the standards of her neighbors. Yet few of them would have said that Lois's experience was exceptional. Like other settlers on Colorado's plains, Lois's neighbors dreamed confidently of riches they would acquire through their own homesteading ventures. Their dreams took shape either in the commitment to "make a go" of a family farm or in the speculative pursuit of hard cash.

Stories like Lois's validated settlers' expectations and gave some substance to boosters' extravagant claims. But Lois's success carried additional and special significance because of her gender. Prior to the Civil War, federal laws effectively barred women from purchasing or claiming government land. Congress set prices for most buyers at $1.25 to $2.00 per acre and from 1786 to 1830 gradually reduced the minimum size for land sales from six hundred to eighty acres or less. Smaller tracts made government land more affordable for small-scale farmers, but buyers had to pay cash. Few farmers of either sex could scrape together the money to buy land on those terms. Pressures mounted in Congress to grant easier credit terms for purchasers of federal land, eventually resulting in the Preemption Act of 1841. Settlers still had to pay $1.25 per acre for a maximum of 160 acres, but they could make smaller payments over a period of time.

One historian described the Preemption Act as "the most important agrarian measure ever passed by Congress," for the act signaled a change in national land policy.[2] Before 1841 public land sales served primarily as a source of revenue. But with the Preemption Act, the primary objective of public land policy became the division of the public domain into small farms for the greatest number of people. Congress, however, added language

to the act that specifically placed limits on women's land purchase opportunities. Only widows and women who were heads of households (women
who supported children because of divorce, adoption, or the absence or
incompetence of a spouse) were eligible to buy preemptions.

Under continuing pressure to make land available on even better
terms, Congress finally passed the Homestead Act in 1862. The statute
offered government land free to qualified claimants, a category now expanded to include unmarried women. True, claimants paid entry and patent
fees and the expenses incurred making required improvements. But the
land itself, a maximum of one quarter section, or 160 acres, cost nothing.
The Homestead Act's offer of free land distinguished it from most earlier
laws governing the disposal of the national domain.[3] Just as important, and
often overlooked, was the act's dramatic expansion of land ownership
opportunities for women.

Congressional supporters of the Homestead Act had practical reasons
for granting unmarried women the chance to claim land. Such women,
they assumed, would become wives for the single young men drawn west
by homesteading opportunities. Together these young men and women
would create families with racial, economic, and political ties to the white,
abolitionist Northeast. But these national goals did not alter a fundamental
reality: For the first time in the history of the land laws, Congress gave
single women who were twenty-one years of age and older, as well as female
heads of households, the right to claim 160 acres of the federal domain.

The government's creation of a new class of propertied women
through the provisions of the Homestead Act suggests interesting questions. To what extent did women take advantage of land entry opportunities? How did women's landownership affect gender relations in the family
and in the community? And perhaps the most fundamental question, how
did landownership affect women's views of themselves and their perceived
place in society?

The example of homestead settlement before and after the turn of the
century in northeastern Colorado provides us with answers. Significant
numbers of women, as well as men, exploited their homestead entry rights.
Moreover, the proportion of women among homestead entrants increased
over time. Homesteading reinforced and magnified women's influence in
the family. It expanded women's work roles, both in the family and in the
community. Homesteading raised family and community expectations of
women's capabilities. And homesteading reinforced women's own positive
opinions of their capacities to act as independent, self-determining persons.

In the microcosm of homestead settlement, we can see women's empowerment through their own economic development. Homesteading, in fact, serves as a case study that has significance far beyond the immediate story of women in the agricultural West. Similar issues of who controls resources, who has access to property, and who gets to decide how to spend money underlie much of women's history. These issues also inform women's ongoing struggle to reach equality of opportunity in contemporary American life.

The concern here, however, is only indirectly with the modern women's movement and with the full sweep of women's history. The focus centers instead on the broadening horizons of Colorado's women homesteaders and the question of whether their stories are consistent with images of women settlers portrayed in much of the historiography and literature of the West. If we are to believe generations of mostly male historians and novelists, the answer to that question is no. With few exceptions, writers have characterized women as passive or coerced participants in a movement that served primarily men's needs and goals.

The authors who created such images were responding in part to one of western history's truisms, namely, that white women were scarce. And from that source they derived several corollaries: White women were too frail and too refined to thrive in the West. Those women who chose to go west were either bad women (prostitutes) or eccentrics. The few good women in the West were there to provide homes for their men. Good women were lonely, fearful, and overworked.[4]

Plenty of anecdotes seemed to provide proof of the peripheral role women played in western settlement and of the hardships they endured. And yet in the agricultural West, females represented about the same proportion of the population as they did in the East.[5] Many women were, moreover, assertive central actors in western communities. Their significant and active presence notwithstanding, women failed to win recognition because excluding them from full engagement in western history resonated with deeply felt, though largely subconscious, masculine mythologies. Western conquest served as a paradigm for male rites of passage. Daring deeds in savage places offered proof of manhood, as did the sexually analogous acts of penetration into the wilderness and domination over nature.[6] By relegating women to an outsider's role, writers created out of western experience a kind of sacred "men's house" whose membership remained exclusively male.

This "men's West" inspired both longing and apprehension in its creators. Writers celebrated the West as a paradise where men might achieve "total" manhood. But, alas, civilizing angels in the form of white women transformed this manly idyll into "paradise lost." Freedom, after all, is one step removed from license, and authors who sensed the danger laced their scripts with virtuous women whose natural goodness restrained men's equally natural lusts and aggressions.[7]

The helpmates and heroines of western history and fiction endured and conquered great hardships. They unhesitatingly, if not cheerfully, performed "male" tasks whenever the need arose. But the women in these scripts were also victims. Not that men intended to inflict pain on their wives and daughters when they brought them west. It was just that women's natural frailties, specifically their reproductive functions and their emotional sensitivities, made them especially vulnerable to hardship.

Writers' assumptions of female dependency and vulnerability prevented them from probing deeply into women's actual experiences. Why, in fact, question what most white, middle-class Americans of the last century and much of this have taken for granted — namely, that God ordained women as the weaker, though purer, of the sexes?[8] Caught in a web of subconscious cultural prescription, authors substituted belief for knowledge and created a legacy of western "history" written with authority and few footnotes.

In arriving at these conclusions, I followed a long and winding path interrupted by many detours along the way. Although born and raised in Denver, I received little exposure to western history beyond childhood visits to some of the tourist attractions and monuments to pioneers located within easy driving range of my family's home. My parents dutifully entertained our frequent summer visitors with tours of the mountains in the old 1948 Plymouth sedan. These excursions generally included stops at Georgetown, Blackhawk, Central City, and other towns that had gotten their start during the mineral rushes of the past century.

My memories of these expeditions are hazy, but they left impressions of mining towns inhabited almost entirely by men and a sprinkling of a few adventurous and self-sacrificing women. Those women seemed to come together in the legendary image of Silver Heels, the captivating dance hall girl who nursed the miners of Alma during a smallpox epidemic. Although she lost her beauty when she finally fell victim to the disease, she gained the heartfelt gratitude of the miners and eventually everlasting fame as a heroine of Colorado's twentieth-century tourist industry.

If Silver Heels represented one kind of selfless western woman, the bronze pioneer on a downtown Denver monument honoring participants in Colorado's "Wild West" represented another. Alone in a company of

Statue honoring the "Pioneer Mothers of Colorado." Part of the Monument to the Smoky Hill Trail at Colfax and Broadway in Denver. *Photo by author.*

male figures, the woman strikes a resolute yet feminine pose. Cradling a baby in one arm and embracing a rifle with the other, she appears ready for any peril that might threaten her family in their new western home.

Such were my limited visions of western women. And they remained virtually unchallenged through a primary and secondary education in Denver's public schools. An assignment to read O. E. Rolvaag's *Giants in the Earth* did broaden my notion of settlers to include European immigrants.[9] But this story of Norwegian homesteaders, chosen by my high school history teacher to demonstrate the bitter lives of women settlers, merely added bleaker dimensions to an already-accepted "fact": Women sacrificed themselves to the noble cause of helping men tame the West.

Not until I was nearly twenty years older and a graduate student did I encounter a substantially different view of western women. At that time an eye-opening article by Sheryll Patterson-Black, titled "Women Homesteaders on the Great Plains Frontier," appeared in *Frontiers*. Using land records in Colorado and Wyoming, Patterson-Black estimated that 4.8 to 18.2 percent of the land entrants were women and that a higher percentage of women than men succeeded in patenting claims (42.4 percent versus 37 percent). Women's success rate, she maintained, "discounts the theory of woman as helpless, reluctant pioneer."[10]

Patterson-Black also drew on long-forgotten personal narratives, many of them rediscovered and published in the 1960s. One of the narrators, Elinore Pruitt Stewart, enthusiastically boosted women's home-steading opportunities. She urged those who like herself were single women working in cities to give up washing other people's clothes and file on government land. Doing wash, she maintained, was far more arduous than farming. Besides, filing on government land offered a woman the possibility of lasting rewards: "independence, plenty to eat all the time, and a home of her own in the end."[11]

Another of Patterson-Black's narrators, Mary O'Kieffe, was a woman in very different circumstances from those of Stewart. O'Kieffe had left her shiftless husband to begin a new life with her nine children on a Nebraska homestead. According to her youngest son, Charley, Mary "had dreams of a better life" and decided to "start all over in a new country under what she hoped would be more favorable conditions and where at least she would have greater freedom."[12] Mary's life on a homestead, like her earlier existence, followed a cycle of unending labor. Yet she, like Elinore Pruitt Stewart, found a new chance for respectable independence on her own government claim.

These were intriguing revelations: Patterson-Black's documentation of women patenting government land at a higher rate than men and stories of two enterprising women patenting homesteads. But such revisionist images were not to remain unchallenged. A second article soon appeared painting a sharply contrasting picture of western agricultural settlement. In Christine Stansell's view, "Women . . . [were] workers in an enterprise often not of their own making."[13] Men, she contended, exploited women and robbed them of their treasured domestic sphere. Stansell based her argument on newly published research describing "ideal" nineteenth-century, white, middle-class gender relations, particularly the notion that women and men properly occupied distinct spheres of employment.[14]

This culturally prescribed separation of the sexes arose during the 1820s when industrialization began to make a noticeable impact on manu-facturing in the urban East. Men left home to take wage-earning jobs in factories, where they produced more and more of the goods once made by women in their homes. Women found new importance as consumers whose chief concerns revolved around providing comfortable, moral, and healthy homes for their husbands and children. The growing emphasis on women's domesticity perpetuated their economic and political subordination to men. Some women recognized the inequities arising from cultural expectations that confined them exclusively to the home. But most women embraced domesticity because it offered them an important role to play in the family and a measure of freedom from male direction and interference.

Stansell assumed that women in western agricultural settlements also placed a high value on their domestic role. She maintained that the West's labor shortage did not allow women to elaborate a domestic sphere. A coercive atmosphere developed within settlers' families because husbands and fathers required women's help with tasks usually performed by men. Yet men rarely helped with "women's work." Men, moreover, invested whatever surplus the farm produced in new land, seed, and equipment, seldom in housing or improvements to raise the family's standard of living. In sum, women lost almost everything they valued in the move west: homes, friends, relatives, and, perhaps most important of all, their identities as women engaged in womanly (that is, domestic) pursuits.

For the bulk of her evidence, Stansell used secondary sources and western literature — works by historians Everett Dick and Walter Prescott Webb and stories by novelists Hamlin Garland, Mari Sandoz, Willa Cather, and my old high school acquaintance, O. E. Rolvaag. I wondered just how reliable these familiar sources were, every one of them decades old and some bearing the label "fiction."

Everett Dick's *Sod House Frontier,* with a chapter devoted to "Women and Children on the Frontier," first appeared in 1937. In passages resonant with melodrama Dick described the settler's wife as a "frail girl," a "tender clinging vine" who could not adjust to the harsh plains environment, the constant wind, the scarcity of water and trees, the extreme heat and cold. "Some [women] begged their husbands to hitch up the team, turn the wagon tongue eastward, and leave the accursed plains which were never meant for human habitation."

To those women who somehow managed to persevere despite the hardships, Dick accorded neither an independent nor a self-fulfilling role. Only as helpmates, never as speculators or farmers in their own right, could women find the strength to endure the "rude surroundings of the frontier." "Many a member of the fairer sex bore her loneliness, disappointment, and heartaches without complaint. Brushing away the unbidden tear, she pushed ahead, maintaining her position by the side of her hardy husband, a fit companion of the resolute conqueror of the plains." Yet for all his sweeping generalizations, Dick offered his readers but a single direct citation from a bona fide woman settler.[15]

Dick was not alone in offering judgments of western women based on minimal evidence. Walter Prescott Webb merely pointed to the blighted lives of the women characters in *Giants in the Earth* and concluded, "The Plains repelled the women as they attracted the men."[16] Why, I wondered, did Webb place so much confidence in what Rolvaag had to say? I could only assume that he, like Dick, operated under the assumptions that sources were scarce and further research would not produce substantially different results. In any case, I could not escape the fact that Rolvaag's novel kept intruding on the debate. It seemed I was going to have to reread *Giants* with a more analytical presence than my sixteen-year-old self could muster.

Rolvaag, I learned, was himself a Norwegian immigrant to South Dakota, though not a homesteader.[17] As a young teacher among other Norwegian-Americans, he gathered the material for his novels that shaped the images of western settlement held by so many Americans, including Webb, Stansell, my high school history teacher, and me. Rereading *Giants in the Earth* proved an enlightening experience, for I discovered that Webb and the others had read Rolvaag selectively, ignoring the full range of his message. Yes, Rolvaag's women suffered in the settlement of the plains, but his male protagonists suffered and died.

The novel's central character, Beret Hansa, had left Norway with her husband Per to settle in Dakota Territory with a small group of other Norwegian families. Beret hated the treeless prairies, which she regarded as a place of exile. She believed that her journey to this wild and empty land was God's punishment for conceiving a child out of wedlock and marrying in defiance of her parents' wishes. Per, on the other hand, looked forward to the challenge of homesteading in America. Here was a chance to become a respected farmer of substantial means, an opportunity not available to him in the old country.

Per's ambitions were utterly alien to Beret's own feelings. She longed for the familiar people and places she left behind in Norway. Yet Beret knew in her heart that she would never see her old home again and that Per's foolish hopes would end in sorrow and death. Nothing could ease her forebodings, not even the comfort she derived from her children. Slowly Beret descended into madness, threatening the whole family's ability to survive.

Rolvaag further elaborated the theme of female instability when he described a family of home seekers arriving at the Hansa soddy. The husband had tied the wife and mother to a trunk in the wagon. The couple's son had died, and the family was leaving the site of his makeshift grave.

The husband explained that his wife repeatedly tried to return to the boy's body. "Women folk," he said, "can't bear up."[18]

My history teacher pointed to the woman in the wagon and to Beret as the epitome of reluctant and damaged pioneer women. Yet he, like Webb, ignored Rolvaag's treatment of Per and his best friend, Hans Olsa. Both men died in their struggles with the natural environment. Rolvaag conveyed additional, symbolic meaning in the deaths of these two virile young homesteaders when he anthropomorphized various elements in nature by giving them malevolent female personalities. In one startling passage he personified the prairie as an evil temptress: "That night the Great Prairie stretched herself voluptuously; giant-like and full of cunning, she laughed softly into the reddish moon. 'Now we will see what human might may avail against us! . . . Now we'll see!' "[19] Rolvaag rendered the prairie and the moon (itself an ancient female symbol, and "reddish" with menstrual blood?) as malevolent co-conspirators against male domination.

Rolvaag continued the theme of female destructive power when he showed the harm Beret inflicted in her womanly role as nurturer. When Hans Olsa lay dying of complications from exposure during a blizzard, Beret insisted on finding the minister to attend him. Her anxiety convinced Hans of his desperate condition and hastened his death. Beret also became the indirect cause of Per's death when she sent him on a desperate errand to find the pastor for Hans during the height of the storm. Per's body remained hidden in the snow until spring, his face turned appropriately toward the beckoning West. Tonseten, a third male character, survived the storm. But Tonseten could not father the child his wife desperately wanted. With his masculinity diminished by infertility, Tonseten escaped the full force of the prairie's avenging womanhood.

In *Giants in the Earth* Rolvaag portrayed the sufferings of women, but he showed that men, too, suffered in the settlement of the West. Rolvaag stood out among his contemporaries in challenging the usual sexual symbolism in the literature of western conquest. Like others he affirmed the masculine essence of pioneering, but Rolvaag remained virtually alone in questioning the triumph of male pioneers over a female natural environment.

Other writers of western fiction and history depicted the defeat and submission of the land and its indigenous population as inevitable. From the concept of manifest destiny applied to the United States's relentless westward expansion, they inferred the manifest superiority of Anglo-American males. Yet an inescapable irony lay in that victory. Once the pioneer (always male) subdued the land, he risked losing his manhood through the feminizing influences of civilization. Dee Brown demonstrated the enduring power of this belief when he described women as "the most conservative of creatures, hating with a passion those three concomitants of the western frontier — poverty, physical hardship, and danger." He concluded that "to destroy these traditional testers of human endurance [as communities matured and overcame the harsher aspects of settlement] was to destroy something male in the race."[20] The committed pioneer spent his life in an endless, and ultimately futile, effort to preserve his manhood, moving from one unsettled place to the next to escape women's civilizing presence.

But what of the fate of that same pioneer's wife who hated "with a passion . . . poverty, physical hardship, and danger"? Forced to follow her husband from wilderness to wilderness, she sacrificed her woman's needs to his selfish ambitions. It is this scenario that Hamlin Garland explored in novels and short stories inspired by his life as a farm boy on what he called the "middle border" of Iowa and the Dakotas.

Garland, like Rolvaag, believed that all settlers experienced hardship. But women, he said, suffered much more than men. Physically weak and emotionally dependent, women could not endure the wrenching separations and almost ceaseless labor demanded of them as pioneer wives and mothers. In later years Garland wrote of his first book, *Main Travelled Roads* (1891), "Even my youthful zeal faltered in the midst of a revelation of the lives led by the women on the farms of the middle border. Before the tragic futility of their suffering, my pen refused to shed its ink. Over the hidden chamber of their maternal agonies I drew the veil." And with this judgment his mother concurred. "It scares me to read some of your stories — they are so true. You might have said more, but I'm glad you didn't. Farmers' wives have enough to bear as it is."[21]

Both Garland and his mother viewed women as essentially powerless. The elder Garland had, after all, demonstrated to his wife and son an unwillingness to consider any but his own desires. Exuding optimism, strength, and love of adventure, he had moved his family from one farm site to the next in an endless quest for new land. Again and again, the father provided the son with a model for male egotism, coercing reluctant women and helpless children to achieve its own ends. Similarly, the mother set an example of feminine weakness and submission. Copying the pattern of his own family, Garland made these qualities gender specific in his characters.

When Garland described men's coercion of their wives and children, he elaborated a new theme in western literature. Instead of blaming the natural environment for the hardships women suffered, Garland placed the blame squarely on men. The real villains of western settlement were not acts of God or the isolating miles of empty wilderness. They were the men who forced their women to abandon parents, siblings, and friends for a life of lonely desperation in some graceless hovel on the plains. Garland tempered his indictment, noting that many men had taken up pioneering in order to escape landlordism in settled communities. Such men were themselves victims of other men. But in striving to satisfy their own desires for property, self-respect, and new experiences, pioneering men behaved selfishly. They uprooted their wives and children and gambled away the few comforts their families possessed in order to engage in a game of chance few settlers could win.[22]

Garland achieved a narrow realism by describing settlement from childhood memories of his own mother and father. Yet Garland's perspective was in its own way as limited as that of the romantics whose exaggerated western adventure stories he wished to refute. Dime novelists like Prentiss Ingraham and Ned Buntline glorified the West as an arena for white men's deeds of "daring do" and ignored the consequences of those deeds on others, including the wives and children of the adventurers they celebrated.[23] Garland rejected such uncritical fantasizing, but his imagination did not stretch to create characters who challenged his parents' limited gender roles.

Mari Sandoz, like Garland, drew on childhood memories to write novels about the West. Yet her stories portray a much wider range of women's and men's experiences. To a remarkable degree, Sandoz transcended gender stereotypes. Her characters, both male and female, run the gamut of human possibilities from wickedness to nobility. In some of Sandoz's stories, women suffer far worse treatment at the hands of men than Garland's heroines. Take, for example, Sandoz's biography of her father in which she ignored old taboos and explored the subject of wife abuse. As Sandoz described him, Jules was a complex personality capable of touching readers' sympathies and even of exciting their admiration. But his relationships with his four wives and with his children bristled with cruelties. In the isolation of the Nebraska Sandhills, Jules was a law unto himself. His wives and his children escaped his brutalities only by running away.[24]

Jules, however, never became Sandoz's typical western male. Nor did Jules's wives (all victims with varying capacities for resisting their oppressor) become Sandoz's representative western women. Indeed, one of Sandoz's most forceful and abusive characters, Gulla Slogum, was a woman. Consumed by acquisitiveness and a compulsive desire to dominate the people around her, Gulla was herself the oppressor who cast others, including men, as victims. Over the years she accumulated thousands of acres, virtually stealing property through manipulated foreclosures and sheriff sales. She even prostituted her daughters for her own aggrandizement. Nothing satisfied Gulla's greed or tempered her desire for more power. She lived on, despite old age and failing health, for the sake of the one pleasure life had consistently offered her — control over others.[25]

As a foil to Gulla's evil energies, Sandoz introduced the benign strength of Old Moll Barheart. Old Moll homesteaded by herself near the Slogums. "She had kicked her past in the pants and come West, like most of the other settlers, only they wouldn't own up like she did."[26] Old Moll represented women who possessed a different sort of power from Gulla's, women whom Sandoz acknowledged in another work with these words: "Among my acquaintances are many women who . . . made good lives for themselves and those about them. And when they could [leave] they did not turn their backs upon the land they struggled to conquer. They stayed . . . knowing that life there can be good and bountiful."[27]

Such women were neither victims nor exploiters. They made their own choices and worked hard and faithfully to create "good and bountiful" lives. Moreover, they created an image for western women that included qualities of self-direction, strength, and concern — not just a concern for family and neighbors (long a part of women's role) but also a solicitude for the land and the animals in their care.

Sandoz helped project that image through characters like Old Moll. But another woman author, Willa Cather, centered whole novels on such women, granting them an unprecedented visibility within the literature of the West. Of Alexandra Bergson (*O Pioneers!*) Cather wrote, "[The land] seemed beautiful to her, rich and strong and glorious. Her eyes drank in the breadth of it, until her tears blinded her."[28] Cather's words might have applied as easily to Antonia Shimerda (*My Antonia*), just as her portrait of Antonia among her fruit trees might have captured a similar moment with Alexandra: "She had only to stand in the orchard, to put her hand on a little crab tree and look up at the apples, to make you feel the goodness of planting and tending and harvesting at last."[29] The symbols of conquest common to renderings of male pioneers do not suit these women farmers. Instead of images of rape, their husbandry elicits visions of tender midwifery.

Cather drew strong distinctions between men and women farmers. Women coaxed plants and animals to produce and reproduce. They did not seek quick profits at the expense of the natural environment. Alexandra summarized women's attitudes when she explained the illusory nature of landownership: "We come and go, but the land is always here. And the people who love it and understand it are the people who own it — for a little while."[30] Cather implied that men did not understand nature or feel a part of the natural world. Men worked the land simply for a living, for money, and for power.

Cather preached a radical message. Women farmers possessed an inner wisdom that their male counterparts lacked. Nor did men acknowledge their deficiencies. Instead, they raised all sorts of barriers to prevent women from using their innate gifts. Alexandra, for example, reaped the jealousy of her older brothers when she inherited the leadership of the Bergson family after her father's death. Because of her industry and intelligence, the Bergsons prospered. Alexandra divided the land she acquired with her brothers, but the older ones claimed that all the land rightfully belonged to them as males, whatever her legal rights might be.

Although Alexandra did not accede to her brothers' demands, she could not escape the heavy psychological weight of patriarchy. In an immigrant community where custom directed women to submit to men, Alexandra's strength and independence left her increasingly isolated. Yet Cather pointed out that native-born white women also suffered from male dominance. The native-born farmers in Antonia's neighborhood would not allow their daughters to work as domestics in town where they might experience the independence of living away from home. Foreign-born farmers gladly sent their daughters into domestic service; but they also expected to receive the wages their daughters earned.

Cather blamed men for oppressing women. At the same time, she celebrated women who cultivated the mother within themselves to realize the full potential of their womanhood. Indeed, Cather wrote from a feminist viewpoint when she created woman-centered dramas of western settlement. But just as the masculine emphasis of male western authors reinforced one set of gender stereotypes, Cather's feminism reinforced another. Readers of *My Antonia* and *O Pioneers!* might ask themselves whether these stories contain essential truths or whether they merely offer women their own western fantasies to counter those of men.

Christine Stansell credited Cather with showing the brighter side of western women's experience and acknowledged that a few women like Cather's heroines had really existed. She explained their presence in generational terms. Many were daughters who grew up on the plains and "managed to reclaim the land that had crushed their mothers."[31] But without further documentation, her explanation was little more than an interesting hypothesis. Indeed, in 1976 when Stansell and Patterson-Black published the articles that introduced me to the history of women in the

West, the field offered many more hypotheses than facts about the ways women experienced western settlement.

But hypotheses can generate interest and enthusiasm, and by the late 1970s the re-examination of western history using gender as a frame of reference had begun to bear fruit in book-length studies. In the process of creating these books, their authors debunked long-standing notions about the scarcity of sources about western women. Typically, the educated, white middle class left the bulk of the written records used in these studies. But government documents and the diaries, letters, and reminiscences of other groups, mostly European immigrants, proved to be rich sources of information. At last, it seemed we were in a position to learn how white women, at least, fared as participants in western settlement.

Yet the books proliferating in the following decade produced no clear-cut results. "Western women" turned out to be a remarkably heterogeneous group. And that reality, combined with the differing viewpoints of the authors, left open the old argument of whether western women suffered disproportionately relative to men or found opportunity in the West, as did some men.

In 1979 an important book appeared supporting the view that men had exploited women in the process of western settlement. Using diaries, reminiscences, and contemporary folk songs, John Faragher, in *Women and Men on the Overland Trail*, explored the gender relations of mid-nineteenth-century midwestern farm families who joined the westward migration. He found that women in these families related to men in ways typical of earlier, colonial gender patterns. Women had separate work roles — taking care of children, feeding and clothing their families, cultivating a kitchen garden, milking cows, and raising a few chickens — but women did not occupy a separate and autonomous domestic sphere.

In nearly all aspects of everyday life, women deferred to masculine authority. Men directed market transactions of all kinds and decided how to allocate resources. They controlled women's incomes from the sale of eggs, butter, and other products of their labor. In matters of sickness and religion, men did yield authority to women. But the decision to uproot the family for the move to Oregon or California belonged entirely to male heads of households. Men expected women to contribute their labor to the enterprise and to assume male work roles whenever necessary. Yet men almost never helped their wives with cooking, washing, or child care, despite the extraordinary effort these tasks required of women on the trail.[32]

Faragher's extensive use of primary sources made a strong case for the view that women assumed disproportionate burdens in the move west. And the publication, also in 1979, of Julie Roy Jeffrey's *Frontier Women: The Trans-Mississippi West, 1840–1880* gave his case further reinforcement. Jeffrey's subjects differed from Faragher's in important ways. Most of her women had already settled on farms or in towns scattered from Kansas to Oregon in a variety of economic and social settings. Significantly, they were no longer struggling with the rigors of the trail. But more important to Jeffrey's analysis, the majority of women in her study belonged to middle-class families who valued the notion of separate, autonomous spheres for men and women.

Jeffrey argued that women perceived the West as an essentially masculine environment that threatened their position as wives and mothers, whose duties and interests centered on the home. Consequently, when women moved to the West they clung to their domestic duties more tenaciously than ever and rejected opportunities to develop skills beyond the confining strictures of gender roles. Women devoted their energies to re-creating and reinforcing the domesticity they had practiced before migrating west. This preoccupation became an overriding goal that "helped women bear what they hoped were temporary burdens and reestablished their sense of identity and self respect. It served as a link with the past."[33]

The quantity of women's writings gave weight to Jeffrey's thesis. However, the great variety of Jeffrey's subjects, from Mormon wives in Utah to mining town prostitutes, precluded an in-depth analysis of any single group. Still, the emphasis Jeffrey placed on women's alleged deep-seated identification with domesticity challenged others to address the issue: Just how important was a separate domestic sphere to the white women who settled the West?

Confronting this question, Glenda Riley compared the diaries, letters, and reminiscences of women living on the prairies of Illinois, Missouri, Iowa, and Minnesota with similar records left by women who settled the western plains. Domesticity, she concluded, directed the lives of white women and black, native-born and foreign-born, in both regions. "Despite locale or era, women's experiences exhibited a remarkable similarity, which was shaped largely by gender and its associated concept of 'women's work.' "[34]

Riley reasoned that the expansion of women's activities in the West followed from a perceived threat to their domestic sphere. Women worried that the great need for labor as well as the absence or weakness of institutions like churches and schools would diminish the importance of their domestic role. Ironically, this concern for protecting home and family (not a changing self-identity) led women to engage in nontraditional work roles on farms, in business, in reform movements, and in politics.

Like Jeffrey, Riley attempted to use domesticity as a theme unifying women across a broad spectrum of backgrounds. But grouping so many different kinds of women in so many different settings obscures important differences in economic opportunities, religious attitudes, work roles in urban and rural locales, and social interactions shaped by race and ethnic origins. No one would deny that western women assumed responsibility for their families' home life. (When and where have women *not* assumed responsibility for domestic duties?) But Riley's view left little room for variation in the ways women valued and practiced domesticity in different communities, places, and times.

One writer who did acknowledge the variations among the women she studied was Sandra Myres. Some women, she said, adopted new ways of acting, whereas others rigidly clung to eastern notions of womanliness and "failed to take advantage of the frontier experience as a means of liberating themselves from constricting and sexist patterns of behavior." Those who "survived . . . adjustment to frontier conditions and changed roles for women tended to ignore, or at least not slavishly strive toward, Eastern-dictated models of femininity. . . . [They] stepped out of woman's place with few regrets."[35] Myres particularly criticized "radical feminist" historians (namely, Faragher and Stansell) who in her view incorrectly "pictured Western women as exploited downtrodden drudges deprived of the liberating virtues of the West." The reality for western women, she maintained, was much more complex than "militant" feminists portrayed it, given the great variety of women's backgrounds and their differing circumstances in the West.[36]

In *Westering Women*, Sandra Myres offers a treasure trove of sources and stories describing women and incidents during a period of 115 years across much of the trans-Mississippi West. But inevitably, so diffuse a focus presented daunting interpretive problems. In the end, Myres came down gingerly on the side of the West's liberation of women.[37] Yet Myres did not closely examine the variations she found or apply them in a systematic way to her analysis.

John Faragher, whom Myres criticized for depicting western women as "downtrodden drudges," did a far more complete job of describing and analyzing his subjects. The women he studied belonged to native-born, white, rigidly patriarchal, pre–Civil War midwestern farm families. And Faragher made a good argument that these women were, in fact, drudges. But Faragher then abandoned the case for variability implied by his many identifying details. He concluded that the women in the families he studied experienced the West in ways that were typical for farm women of other regions who accompanied their husbands and fathers on the westward migration. In making this leap, Faragher came dangerously close to slipping into the category of historians who overlooked or minimized the differences among western women.

Nonetheless, Faragher's example in defining his subjects by race, place, ethnicity, national origin, occupation, class, and (of course) gender led others to these and new categories of analysis. Lillian Schlissel, for example, examined women's diaries from the overland migration and analyzed the importance of generational, or "life cycle," differences. She discovered that wives, often pregnant and usually caring for small children, experienced trail life entirely differently from girls and unmarried young women. Burdened with extra work, worried about the safety of their families, and grieving for people and places left behind, married women found little to like about the trip west. Their daughters, on the other hand, often relished the journey. They enjoyed the unfamiliar landscapes, the occasional glimpses of Indians, and (much to their mothers' dismay) the relaxation of rules governing young women's dress and behavior. Schlissel explained, "It is in the diaries of the *younger* women that one finds the willing — sometimes the eager — acceptance of new roles and a broader definition of what a woman might effectively do."[38]

Both Schlissel and Myres argued that the West offered at least some women a measure of opportunity and fulfillment. Yet similarly ambitious studies by Faragher, Jeffrey, and Riley confirmed the view of women's loss and hardship in the West. How can we reconcile these differences? I believe that the explanation for the confusion lies in the authors' use of sources. Faragher and Schlissel looked at fairly discrete populations. Myres, Jeffrey, and Riley studied large and diverse populations. This latter approach necessarily obscured the experiences of certain groups of women. The fact is, some women prospered in the West, and some did not. To understand the reasons for the differences, we need to learn more about smaller, more homogeneous populations of western women.

Happily, two books set a curative example. Paula Petrik, in *No Step Backward*, and Sarah Deutsch, in *No Separate Refuge*, concentrated their efforts on narrowly defined populations of women — "postholing," as some have labeled the process. Postholing, or in-depth analysis, is somewhat like trying to solve a physics problem. One must try to take into account all the forces acting on a given object. In this case, the object is a particular group of women. The forces include such intangibles as religion and culture, as well as specific qualities and conditions often overlooked, such as wealth, health, and marital status.

Petrik devoted most of her book to tracing the evolution in attitudes of middle-class women in Helena, Montana, between 1865 and 1900. These women, she demonstrated, adapted to life in a western mining town by redefining womanhood to include expanding public roles and increasing independence for women within marriage. But I would like to single out, as a particularly instructive example of in-depth analysis, Petrik's chapter on Helena's prostitutes, "Capitalists with Rooms."

Using demographic data from a number of sources, Petrik reconstructed prostitutes' living arrangements, financial activities, mobility, and other indicators of life-style over a period of about four decades. She found that in Helena's early years many prostitutes accumulated sufficient capital to invest in a variety of enterprises. As the town became more "respectable" and as the economy faltered toward the end of the century, prostitutes lost their economic advantage and fell under the control of pimps, creditors, and municipal officials. But for a brief time, at least, they had enjoyed the entrepreneurial opportunities available to enterprising men in a western boom town.[39]

The links between economic power and personal autonomy among Helena's prostitutes parallel issues of landownership and influence among another narrowly defined group: Hispanic women in the Southwest. Sarah Deutsch traced the migration of villagers from Mexico and northern New Mexico to southern Colorado coal mining towns and northern Colorado beet fields, and examined the disruptions in traditional Hispanic culture — particularly the effect of those disruptions on women. In the villages, women owned land and cultivated gardens, providing themselves and their families with food and homes. These women operated outside the cash economy, exchanging work, favors, and even children. In the process, they created powerful bonds of obligation and affection reaching all members of their families and communities.

In time, Hispanic women left their villages to join relatives in Colorado. But the cash they could earn as domestics or as workers in the beet fields did not fulfill their needs. They contributed to the bare survival of their families but rarely had any surplus to share (as they formerly had from their gardens) with friends and more distant kin. On what Deutsch called the "frontier" between the Hispanic and Anglo cultures, Mexicans and Mexican-Americans suffered exploitation at the hands of the more numerous and economically dominant Anglos. All members of the Hispanic migrant community, regardless of gender, lost the security they once had in their villages. But migrant women lost even more, namely, their central roles in production and in family and community life.[40]

Important to Deutsch's story were the reform efforts of particular groups of Anglo women who tried to "Americanize" Hispanics through the education of wives and mothers. Missionaries sponsored by the Presbyterian Board of Home Missions and women agents of the coal companies reached out to Hispanas, hoping to instill in them Americanized habits of dress, food, and housekeeping. The Anglo women, and the men who employed them, believed that women were the arbiters of behavior in both cultures and that exchanges between women were the most efficient means of transmitting "superior" Anglo customs. When such efforts were successful, as in the training of coal miners' wives to a narrow and economically dependent domestic role, Hispanic women lost power in their own families and communities.

Ironically, the Presbyterian women missionaries, who lived sometimes for years in New Mexican villages, internalized Hispanic culture to a greater degree than they succeeded in Americanizing their hosts. In retrospect, this unwanted outcome is hardly surprising given the circumstances under which the Presbyterian women had entered the mission field. Their choice of careers suggests, in fact, a subconscious protest — although a mild one — against women's prescribed role in Anglo culture. As independent spinsters removed from the sight of family and friends, these missionaries pushed at the boundaries of normally accepted behavior for Anglo women.

From the point of view of the New Mexican villagers, these women filled time-honored female roles as healers, "witches," and nuns. By a happy accident, many missionary women found a greater degree of acceptance and prestige in the village than they had ever known at home. Conversion, as these missionary women experienced, can operate in both directions.

Taken together, Deutsch's and Petrik's books hold important lessons for studying the West's impact on women. First, they illustrate emphatically the diversity of western women. From Hispanic villagers and migrant women, to Anglo missionaries and social workers, to mining town prostitutes and middle-class wives and daughters, these women stand as examples that dramatize the folly of trying to lump western women into a synthetic whole. Clearly, women's life experiences depended on many variables; among them racial identity, marital status, life stage, relative conditions of comfort or poverty, the presence or absence of emotional support systems, and prevailing religious and cultural definitions of women's proper roles.

The general case for diversity, however, does not deny that threads of common experience run through women's lives. Domesticity in one form or another is certainly one of those common experiences.[41] Another is the relationship to economic independence particular groups of women shared. Deutsch and Petrik wrote about women who controlled some area of production (land, property, gardens, or wages). Such women exercised real power in their families and in their communities. When they lost control of production, they also lost power. They learned, like many other economically dependent women, that persuasion and influence are nearly always poor substitutes for the power of self-direction that goes with economic self-sufficiency.

Long Vistas is my contribution to what I hope will be the continuing exploration of women's economic activities in the West. Through a close examination of a limited population, I acknowledge the diversity of western women and underscore the importance of economic power in determining the quality of women's lives. Among the homesteaders of northeastern Colorado, women's autonomy grew along with their expanding economic and community roles. And I see links between these roles. I agree with Glenda Riley that women's deepest loyalties typically belonged to home and family. I acknowledge that women's concern for their domestic role motivated them to enter the public sphere. These circumstances persist to this day. And yet they alone cannot account for either the continuing restrictions or the expanding choices that homesteading women experienced.

The waxing and waning of women's economic power in relation to men's has had a significant impact on women in all eras. The Homestead Act of 1862 began a unique period of opportunity for women when Congress offered free government land to spinsters, widows, and female heads of households under the same terms it extended to men. Homesteading opened up a whole new area of power for single women, and their successes enhanced the status of wives and daughters involved in family homesteading enterprises. Women's economic prominence, in turn, shaped community institutions and affected the ways in which men and women related to each other.

As homestead entrants, women (like men) achieved varying degrees of success. Prior to 1900 spinsters and widows who filed on land in Washington and Logan counties (the principal locales for this study) accounted for up to 12 percent of the total entrants. After 1900 the proportion of women entrants increased to 18 percent. Their patent rates (measured as the percent of title deeds issued relative to the total number of claims) also rose over time. These rates remained nearly identical to men's — in the neighborhood of 50 percent.

Single women, like single men, rarely homesteaded alone. If not participants in their parents' homesteading enterprises, they settled with siblings, cousins, or friends. Those women who proved up and gained title to land in order to increase family holdings retained the right to their patents. In other words, fathers and brothers did not assume "ownership" of patents held by female members of the family. Men often had the use of their female relatives' land, frequently through leasing arrangements, sometimes without cost. But the women patent holders retained the proceeds from sales of their homesteads.

What about the wives of men who claimed land? Did husbands exploit their labor? Did wives have a voice in decision making? Did homesteading represent opportunity or loss for them? Overwhelmingly, the evidence throughout the period of this study suggests that women married to homestead entrants regarded themselves as partners in a joint venture.

The testimony of both women and men reveals no pattern of rigid patriarchy. On the contrary, many husbands expended their labor and resources to reduce their wives' drudgery and improve the family's standard of living. Work roles remained largely gender specific, but when the need arose, both men and women assumed tasks usually performed by the opposite sex. Women created female networks through family ties, friendships, clubs, and church groups, but they did not necessarily invest their emotional lives in other women. Social occasions of all kinds, as well as life crises of death and illness, included entire families and whole communities, with both men and women taking part.

A number of writers have argued that the needs of women as individuals are incompatible with the needs of families.[42] Certainly, married women by law did not have the same freedom to patent land as spinsters. Homesteading, however, provided single women with the opportunity to achieve a degree of economic independence that was not "at odds" with family obligations and interests. Here was an instance, in fact, where the family assisted rather than impeded the self-realization of its female members. The interdependence of homesteading women and men shaped my approach to *Long Vistas*. Although my primary focus is women, *Long Vistas* is also a book about men and children, families and communities. In my view, to talk about women homesteaders apart from the men and children in their lives is to distort their stories. What is more, the experiences of men and children serve as "controls" for evaluating the experiences of women. If we do not know what men and children in homesteading communities were doing or not doing, how can we fully judge the impact of homesteading on women?

Long Vistas borrows from the collections of energetic local historical societies in Logan and Washington counties. The Washington County Museum Association, the Crook Historical Society, and the Fleming Historical Society have published histories of hundreds of homesteading families written by the children of land claimants or, in some cases, by the homesteaders themselves. The histories document the process of settling the plains and provide family and individual statistics: the ages at which homesteaders married, migrated, entered claims, and died; the sizes of homesteaders' families; and the homesteaders' places of origin. Some of the histories include hints or statements reflecting the participants' feelings about homesteading. These testimonies I treated with caution, knowing that memory can distort or exaggerate events and emotions that occurred in the distant past.

Oral histories, letters, diaries, and financial records fill many gaps in the reminiscences. Particularly valuable are the papers of a Kit Carson County homesteader, Alice Newberry. Alice left a record of homesteading and its impact on her life in a series of letters and documents spanning more than fifty years. Her story is uniquely complete and merits its own chapter.

Government land transactions recorded in the federal tract books yielded another rich lode of information. These records indicate home-steaders' names (usually gender specific), whether or not entrants received patents, and the dates and locations of claims. The beginning time limit for this study marks the date (1871) when William S. Hadfield filed the first homestead claim in present-day Logan County.[43] The earliest claim entered by a woman in my sample belonged to Benona Prewitt (1874), also within the boundaries of present-day Logan County. The concluding date for this study does not mark any specific event but reflects the fact that by 1920 claimants had filed on virtually all exploitable government land. Entrants continued to make homestead claims for another decade or more but in insignificant numbers.

Homesteaders in northeastern Colorado were mostly white and American-born. This group never composed less than 83 percent of the entire population of the area and finally accounted for a high of 94 percent in Washington County. The numbers of nonwhites (especially blacks, Asians, and Indians) remained tiny during the years of this study.[44] I capitalized on the overwhelming presence of white, native-born Americans by deliberately excluding (when their identity was clear) foreign-born and nonwhite homesteaders from my analysis. Why did I do this? Because I wanted to examine a population that was as homogeneous in its cultural attitudes and experiences as possible.

We know quite a bit about how middle- and upper-middle-class American white women were supposed to behave, according to nineteenth-century notions of ideal femininity. We also know that this ideal spread beyond the eastern urban populations where it originated. During the post–Civil War years, white farm families received through the press and other agents of popular communication an intense education in women's proper domestic role.[45] Of course, the relation of cultural prescription to behavior is a problematic one. Ideals can reflect societal fears concerning changes away from the ideal. Yet ideals also shape behavior, especially gender roles. Northeastern Colorado provides a good laboratory for examining the interplay of cultural prescription and the actual behavior of American-born, white women within the context of a particular kind of economic activity.

In a further effort to limit the variables, I confined this study to homesteaders and eliminated from consideration buyers, renters, and those who filed on government land through statutes other than the homestead laws. The original Homestead Act of 1862 underwent several revisions, generally making government land entry more attractive by shortening the length of time required for proving up and by increasing the amount of land an individual could patent. My analysis includes entrants, and wives and daughters of entrants, under acts passed in 1909, 1912, and 1916, as well as those filing under the original law.[46] I did not include as homesteaders those who entered claims only under Preemption, Timber Culture, or Desert Land acts.

Between 1877 and 1891 (when all these laws were operative), a homesteader could prove up on a total of 1,120 acres of government land by claiming 160 acres each by homestead, preemption, and timber entries and 640 acres through the Desert Land Act. The several land acts had different criteria for compliance, making comparisons between categories of entrants difficult, if not meaningless. How could one compare, for example, the success rates of homesteaders with those of desert land entrants when the latter had to build irrigation systems in order to patent the land they claimed? The homestead records by themselves provide a reasonably accurate picture of land entries and patents, especially after 1891 when the Revision Act repealed most alternatives to homestead entry. In the interests of both consistency and manageability, I restricted this study to entrants under the homestead laws and to the immediate families of those entrants.

"For American women, as individuals," historian David M. Potter once wrote, "opportunity began pretty much where the frontier left off" and cities began.[47] The example of Colorado's women homesteaders runs counter to Potter's statement. Land entry itself bestowed a degree of autonomy and prestige, even when women filed claims to expand family holdings. The award of a government patent gave further tangible evidence of accomplishment. Married women, who were (with rare exceptions) ineligible to claim land in their own right, also experienced expanding options. Homesteading wives and husbands engaged in a partnership, and both expected women to exercise a large degree of control over family resources they had helped build. Few wives saw life on a claim as a kind of exile or as a threat to their womanhood.

Homesteading, moreover, had the potential to plant other, more disruptive, seeds in the social order. Not that the framers of the homestead laws had any such intent. They merely wanted to encourage the settlement of western lands by white American families when they gave single women, as well as men, the right to claim government land. Spinsters, however, did not always quickly trade their new-found opportunities for the retiring domesticity that the sponsors of the homestead laws assumed they would prefer. Instead, many women enjoyed the excitement and adventure of learning to live on their own, removed from close family scrutiny. Controlling their own real estate for the first time, women also discovered that homesteading opened up a hitherto unknown spectrum of choices. As farmers, speculators, and investors, women homesteaders pursued a measure of personal and financial independence. And in that pursuit they created a tantalizing example — one that other American women would want to follow.

1

Getting Rich Quick in God's Country

God's Country or Great American Desert? Different minds dreaming different dreams have applied both labels to the high plains of eastern Colorado. As long as Anglo-Americans had discovered no use for the grasslands, official maps branded them "desert." But when arable free land to the east became scarce, the West's abundant acres — and new technologies developed for farming the arid regions — eroded that stigma. Whites came instead to dream of the plains as the Great American Garden.[1] In fact, the plains were neither desert nor garden. Great wealth was never a likely consequence of ranching or farming the grasslands. Modest prosperity, on the other hand, might reward careful planning and diligent effort when good weather and favorable market conditions prevailed. With characteristic optimism, Americans flocked to the South Platte River valley in two separate land rushes, one before and one after the turn of the century. As homesteaders, they claimed millions of acres of government land.

The first land rush, in the 1880s, followed more than a decade of economic decline and stagnation along the South Platte Trail. Gone were the stage stops and ranches that had once done a brisk business serving the hordes of prospectors on their way to Colorado's gold fields. Their ruins gave mute testimony to the Indian wars of the 1860s. Construction of the transcontinental railroad, also during the 1860s, diverted traffic to the north across Wyoming, and inevitably the trade, which had provided the underpinnings for white settlement along the river, disappeared.[2]

For a number of years the valley was almost deserted. The Indians who had once roamed along the South Platte were gone by the end of the 1860s. They had surrendered to army troops, who promptly hustled most

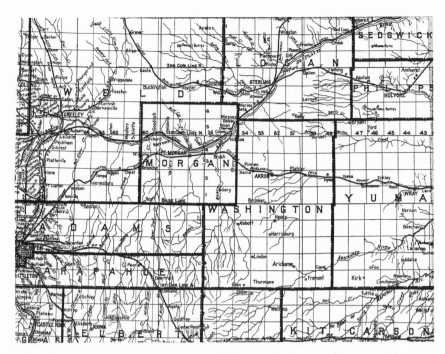

Northeastern Colorado. "Reference Map of the State of Colorado" (Denver: Williamson-Hafner Co., 1910). Western History Archives, Norlin Library, University of Colorado, Boulder.

of the native inhabitants off to reservations. The remaining residents, led by men like John Wesley Iliff and Jared Brush, worked chiefly in the cattle industry. Iliff ranged his cattle mostly to the north of the river, Brush to the south.[3] The Iliff and Brush outfits played a particularly crucial role for the small groups of settlers who began taking up land in the early seventies, for these large operations provided some economic stability in what was otherwise a highly speculative environment.

The earliest land entrants followed, on a small scale, the example of Iliff and Brush by making their claims the nuclei of cattle-ranching operations. William S. Hadfield, who settled on an island at the confluence of Pawnee Creek and the South Platte River in 1871, earned himself future distinction as Logan County's first permanent resident. Within five years about a dozen families intent on farming settled near Hadfield's Island — much to the annoyance of Hadfield himself, who predicted the "hayseeds" would fence the land and ruin it for cattle ranching.[4]

The South Platte River as it looks today at Sterling. Early travelers commented on the absence of trees along the river's banks. *Photo by author.*

Other newcomers founded the community that came to be known as "Old Sterling," about twelve miles to the northeast and four miles north of present-day Sterling. Early in the spring of 1873, a group of southerners, families and single men from the states of Tennessee and Mississippi, arrived in Greeley hoping to join the Union Colony. Finding the better locations already taken, some of them decided to investigate the possibilities down the South Platte. They selected the Old Sterling site both for its irrigation potential and for its location in line with the Colorado Central Railroad's roadbed, then under construction between Julesburg and LaSalle. Four families and a single man made the move that first autumn. Other families continued to trickle in, from Greeley and from southern and eastern states, and by 1875 Old Sterling could claim twelve houses, some of sod and others of adobe, each on 160 acres of land.[5]

Lacking railroad connections and markets where they could sell their produce, early settlers practiced little more than a subsistence agriculture. They kept chickens, cattle, and milk cows, and some tended plantings of wheat, oats, and even watermelons. One enterprising woman gathered and hatched wild goose eggs. Another resident recorded his experiments with irrigation farming along the newly dug South Platte Ditch. He and three companions raised corn, squash, potatoes, and "garden stuff," by which he probably meant lettuce, onions, and beans. He maintained that planting extensively was "useless," for there was no way to market the harvest. Besides, range cattle broke through settlers' smooth wire fences, wreaking havoc on many crops. Yet this man and his neighbors persevered, believing prosperity would surely arrive in just a year or two when the railroad came through. And while they waited, farmers could still get a "good" return on squash and potatoes selling at two and one-half cents a pound to the Colorado Central's construction crew across the river.[6]

The settlers' expectations suffered a blow in April 1873 when they heard the disheartening news that the Colorado Central had halted construction on its track. Financial panic in investment markets had eliminated the capital necessary to build the line.[7] The stop-work order destroyed prospects for easy access to farm customers, including the railroad building crew, and wiped out one of the few sources of cash income in the community. Construction jobs had paid well: $3.75 per day for twelve to fourteen hours of work. The loss of the railroad discouraged further settlement, and the population actually declined as established settlers lost hope and moved away.[8]

As if settlers needed more reasons to leave, Indian scares surfaced off and on through the decade of the 1870s. One rumor had as many as twelve hundred Sioux camping around Old Sterling and other white settlements. True, Indians did occasionally leave the Red Cloud Agency in Dakota Territory, with permission, to hunt buffalo. Sometimes they let themselves into settlers' houses and demanded food — an unnerving experience for some women at home alone or in the company of small children. But, generally, whites had no real justification for their fears. Some said that ranchers had started the rumors in order to discourage settlement.[9]

In the face of so many doubts about the future, a few settlers reacted with an irrepressible boosterism. Residents of the tiny community of Buffalo (later known as Merino) sent letters throughout the United States and even abroad advertising their town's charms. Recruitment was concentrated in the southern states, where the community's founders had many relatives and friends. Buffalo's promoters further reasoned that former Confederates might be receptive to the idea of building new lives on Colorado's grasslands. The boosters, however, miscalculated. No quantity of promising advertisements could hide from prospective residents their first disenchanting view of the town: a combination sod house and dugout that provided Buffalo with its only landmark.[10]

A small herd of buffalo owned by an early-day rancher. In naming the town of Buffalo, settlers memorialized the wild buffalo that were fast disappearing from Colorado's grasslands during the 1870s. *Courtesy of the Washington County Museum, Akron.*

Among Buffalo's boosters, none was more enthusiastic than Sid Propst. Propst raved about Colorado's climate, and from the moment he arrived in the little community in 1873, he never lost faith in the South Platte valley's potential. He did, in fact, succeed in capturing the attention of a number of friends and relatives back home in Alabama. Susan Powell, Propst's sister-in-law, was a young girl of about sixteen when she visited Colorado in 1876. A half century later she reflected on her brother-in-law's powers of persuasion: "Mr. Propst [told] . . . such thrilling enthusiastic stories about the country and its possibilities as to climate, prospects of 'getting rich quick' etc. — all was there for the asking. In fact he orally painted the country as an Eldorado and inspired many war-ridden inhabitants whom he knew in Alabama with the desire to emigrate to 'God's Country.' "[11]

Susan Powell did not number herself among the inspired. But doubters only seemed to renew Propst's commitment to his one-man promotional campaign. Like the angler who knows that only a hook in water is going to catch fish, Propst dangled lures before any audience that would listen. His stage service, which he started in 1876 between Julesburg and Greeley, proved particularly useful for advertising purposes. Few passengers escaped

Propst's lectures on the South Platte valley's healthful climate and the golden opportunities awaiting anyone who wanted to acquire land.[12]

Sid Propst was himself a good example of the fact that most settlers made ends meet by combining farming with other occupations. Besides his stage business, Sid, like many other men, found paying jobs with the big ranches. His wife, Missouri, complained in a letter home that Sid had left her a "widow" to work the roundup. He sweetened the rough job of cutting out his own cattle by collecting and branding his employer's stock for a salary of thirty dollars a month.[13] Other settlers earned cash and filled their larders by hunting buffalo. Fresh meat sold for two cents a pound; tongues for $6.50 a dozen. After the mid-1870s, buffalo hunting declined sharply with the diminishing herds. In this money-poor economy, barter remained the primary route for exchanging goods and services. Still, settlers found creative ways to earn a little hard cash. Mrs. A. J. Cheairs, the owner of the only piano in Old Sterling, gave lessons at twenty-five cents a session to aspiring musicians in the community.[14]

Whereas most settlers perfected the art of working different kinds of jobs whenever opportunities presented themselves, one family managed a prosperous subsistence based solely on mixed crop and livestock farming. S. D. and Belle Clanton raised cattle, turkeys, chickens, and pigs; they also cultivated corn, alfalfa, potatoes, and cabbage. The Clantons had many helping hands in their large family of girls and one boy. They also had another, more unusual asset: The Clantons knew how to produce and process many different kinds of farm commodities. Their neighbors, who lacked that knowledge or maybe just the energy and willingness to carry on a Clanton-style operation, needed income beyond their farming to survive.[15]

Ironically, the most important source of outside income came from large-scale ranchers, who perhaps logically should have given farmers every incentive to leave. After all, small farming operations, if allowed to become numerous, would ultimately destroy the open-range cattle industry. But the ranchers, who often believed that Colorado's plains would never develop into farming country, ignored that possibility. Instead, ranchers and settlers alike accepted and used each other to their mutual advantage. The settlers provided a labor pool for the ranches and received in return much-needed cash. They also gave cowboys food and shelter, saving many a life in a storm. For their part, the cowboys let the settlers have motherless calves. Many struggling farms received a boost in the form of a donated calf from a nearby ranch.[16]

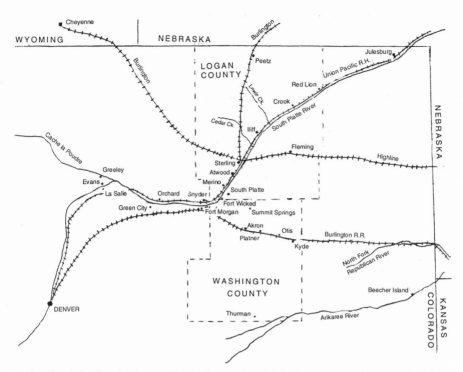

Railroads of the South Platte valley. Adapted from U.S. Department of Interior, Land Office, Map of the State of Colorado, 1905. Western History Archives, Norlin Library, University of Colorado, Boulder.

Social gatherings further broadened relations between cattle ranchers and small landholders. The influx of farm families brought a major benefit for all those bachelors living on isolated ranches. "Families" in their lexicon translated into "women" and, in some cases, marriageable young women. Any excuse for a dance would do. Even a corn shucking could turn into a party for both ranch hands and settlers.[17] Ranch owners might have remained aloof from such gatherings, but the cowboys and farmers, who sometimes shared overlapping identities (as in the case of Sid Propst), fraternized. This kind of interaction suffered when settlement greatly increased in the following decade, but by then other factors, like the introduction of purebred stock and a new emphasis on protecting herds from winter storms, were also modifying the cattle industry and its reliance on the open range.

In the early eighties, economic conditions significantly improved. The Colorado Central resumed, and finally completed, construction of the Julesburg cutoff through the South Platte valley and on into Denver.

The first Burlington train to arrive in Akron, 1882. *Courtesy of the Washington County Museum, Akron.*

Beginning in 1883, the Union Pacific leased and operated this line and eventually gained ownership. At about the same time, the Burlington and Missouri route (later the Burlington and Quincy) laid track through northeastern Colorado. Entering the state about seventy miles south of its competitor, this road crossed the plains to Akron and Fort Morgan, then angled south toward Denver. Later in the decade (1887), the Burlington added another route from Nebraska to Cheyenne, Wyoming, through Sterling. Known politely as the "High Line," the local population dubbed this road the "Jerkwater."[18] A fourth route, built in 1900, linked Sterling and Nebraska through the present town of Peetz near the northern Colorado border. The Denver and Montana Railroad Company leased this line to the Burlington until 1908, when the latter bought the road.[19]

With the coming of the railroads, the South Platte valley received a new lease on life. Old settlements revived and new ones sprang up. Sterling moved to its modern site on the Union Pacific tracks, where it soon became a transportation hub for the Union Pacific and Burlington railroads. As a marketing center for local farmers and ranchers, Sterling dominated the economic life of the valley.[20] At some distance from the river itself, settlements clustered around the Burlington's two east-west routes. Fleming was a creation of the company on the High Line. Akron, Platner, Otis, and Hyde ("Skintown," the locals nicknamed it) dotted the railroad's more southerly route. Akron's development as a supply and shipping point was second only to Sterling's.[21]

Boosters expected the valley's growth to mushroom once the trains started rolling in the early eighties, and their predictions proved accurate. By 1886 the boom was on as land seekers poured into northeastern Colorado. S. S. Worley, a claim locator, described the hubbub created by crowds of newcomers in "Denver Junction," the local name for Julesburg: "It seemed as though everybody wanting a home was coming west. Every train from the east to Denver Junction brought would-be homesteaders. Some rode in Pullmans, some in day coaches, some on top of the coaches, some on the bumpers, some in wagons, some on foot — some had money and some had none." Worley added, "The hotels and restaurants were all crowded day and night . . . [with] new settlers [coming] in from Nebraska, Kansas, and even from Missouri and Arkansas by the wagon load." Another old-timer recalled, with some exaggeration, that "practically all of eastern Colorado was homesteaded."[22]

The railroads had initiated the land rush with the completion of lines through northeastern Colorado. With their ongoing promotion of settlement, they intended to keep the boom going. Both the Union Pacific and the Burlington created subsidiary companies for marketing railroad-owned lands along their tracks. These land companies published pamphlets and sponsored traveling agricultural exhibits to stimulate interest in Colorado. Reaching European as well as American audiences, these advertising brochures offered inducements that many found irresistible. Prospective buyers of railroad real estate, and even homesteaders planning to settle near the routes, could get free or reduced-rate tickets to their destinations. Special trains transported carloads of settlers' belongings.[23]

The railroads continued to assist farmers after they had relocated. The Burlington supplied well water to the towns of Otis and Hyde. Water users paid forty cents a barrel for the service. The lines also provided employment, a crucial economic boost for some homesteading families. To settlers in real distress, the trains brought direct relief in the form of clothing, food, and fuel. During the hard winter of 1890, trainmen even butchered steers killed by the locomotives. Mary Clark Peterson recalled, "The section men had the task of skinning the cattle that were killed by the trains. They sometimes cut off pieces of the best of the beef and buried it in the snow. They would tell us [children] where to find it."[24] Train kills, of course, represented losses to other settlers or to cattle ranchers. No doubt these unwilling donors had their own views on the subject of the railroads' generosity. Families in need, however, certainly welcomed any additions to their cooking pots.

By offering so many services to settlers, the railroads ultimately promoted their own interests. To stay in business they needed to sell company-owned land and transportation services, and they were willing to lose money to see settlers through the initial, difficult stages of settlement. In the long run, the more people who took up land along the tracks and stayed, the better the prospects for future profits. Yet to assume that every act of assistance bore the taint of calculated self-interest on the part of the railroads would be wrong. Some of the trainmen, after all, were homesteaders who had taken railroad jobs to subsidize farming ventures. For them settlers in need were "neighbors," whether in fact they knew them or not. Who could say when the trainmen might find themselves in a similar fix and on the receiving end of railroad charity? Such men did not care why the rail lines helped settlers. They would have agreed with one historian's contention that the railroad was "the indispensable institution which made possible the general settlement of the grassland." Long before freight revenues became significant, the railroad was a lifeline for homesteaders and other settlers along the tracks.[25]

The extension of train service in the 1880s coincided with two other developments that also funneled would-be settlers into northeastern Colorado. Just as cheap land in Kansas and Nebraska was becoming a thing of the past, the plains experienced unusually wet weather from 1885 to 1887.[26] Never had Colorado's empty spaces looked greener or more inviting to the land hungry.

Newcomers with money to spend might buy land from the railroads or from earlier settlers. Under the terms of the Preemption Act of 1841, they could also assert first purchase rights on as much as 160 acres of federally owned land for the rock-bottom price of $1.25 per acre. Free government land, however, had obvious attractions, and during the land rush of the 1880s, settlers acquired free land by one or more of three methods: homesteading, timber entry, and desert land claim. Under the terms of the 1862 Homestead Act, claimants could acquire 160 acres (a quarter section) of the public domain "free" by paying about $26 in filing and patent fees and by making improvements while living on the land continuously for five years. Homesteaders could "commute" their claims and patent their land after six months' residence if they had made the obligatory improvements and if they paid $1.25 an acre for their claims.

The Homestead Act initiated a policy of permitting spinsters twenty-one years of age and older, as well as single men, widows, and heads of households, to file on federal land. The Timber Culture Act, passed in 1873, also allowed single women to claim land under its terms. By growing forty

The "city" of Thurman, 1892. Homesteaders could obtain water at town wells like the one in Thurman marked by the windmill in this photograph. *Courtesy of L. Scotty Odell, Akron.*

acres of trees in good condition for ten years, a claimant could receive title to an entire quarter section. In 1878 Congress reduced the requirement to ten acres because so few timber claim entrants succeeded in cultivating forty acres of trees on the arid and naturally treeless plains. A few women and men also filed on an entire section (640 acres) through the 1877 Desert Land Act. But the difficulty of meeting the conditions set forth in the act, especially irrigating the land within three years after filing, made this a workable option only in areas bordering the South Platte River.[27]

Obtaining water loomed as the settlers' first and most pressing problem. Before the 1880s, no one attempted to farm at any distance from a stream. But the great majority of newcomers staked claims wherever they could, relying on nature and neighboring wells until the time came when they could dig their own. Lacking special drills and often the horsepower to run them, settlers dug into the ground with tools as basic as picks and shovels. A descent of forty feet or more to reach water was not unusual. In the meantime, settlers hauled water from some distant source, usually a well located in town or on a neighbor's claim. In the absence of windmills, they pumped or raised water by hand, a time-consuming and strenuous task. From hard experience, high plains farmers soon learned to appreciate a dependable water supply. With a well and a windmill, they could keep stock; and stockraising proved a crucial hedge against failure. By combining crop culture with keeping small numbers of horses and cattle, a cow for milk and butter, and a few pigs and chickens, a family had a better chance of hanging onto their land through the droughts that lay ahead.[28]

The settlers' standard of living depended largely on the ease or difficulty of obtaining water for domestic use and for a garden. Nearly everyone put in a vegetable patch, but the need for hand irrigation meant that kitchen gardens varied widely depending on the circumstances and enthusiasm of the individual cultivator. Field crops like corn, wheat, oats, and rye grew without irrigation. After harvesting the grain heads, farmers used the rest for animal fodder. Combined with hay cut from native grasses and Russian thistle, crop refuse contributed to the survival of livestock over the harsh winters.[29]

Farmers with irrigation systems enjoyed some advantages over their dryland counterparts, but irrigation presented its own problems. In the absence of dams on the South Platte, the increasing number of diversion ditches upstream reduced the volume of water downstream during the critical summer months and deprived some cultivators of their water rights. The prevailing "doctrine of prior appropriation" granted water rights to users in the order of their claims over time. But inadequate policing of irrigators, as well as evaporation and seasonal lulls in the river's flow, limited the doctrine's regulating powers over plains water users. True, shallow wells, one to twenty feet deep, in the river's dry bed produced a virtually limitless supply of water, but the costs of pumping made its distribution to large fields impractical. In practice, the irrigation and dryland farmers shared many of the same problems when the South Platte's flow dwindled to small channels after the spring runoff from the mountains. The irrigator, moreover, faced the peril of flooding in those years when the annual melt turned into a raging torrent.[30]

Questions of too little or too much water had little effect on the tide of "nesters" invading Colorado's eastern plains. Their surging numbers began to antagonize the open-range cattle ranchers accustomed to unlimited and free exploitation of the national domain. The ranchers' alarm intensified in light of federal land policy that favored small farming operations. Lawmakers consistently refused to comply with demands from western cattlemen to grant ranchers the right to acquire title to large tracts of the national domain. In the arid West, where fattening one steer required ten to thirty acres of forage, land laws limiting claimants to a section or less appeared punitive to ranching interests.[31]

The cattlemen, in self-defense (by their reasoning), devised their own "doctrine of prior appropriation" in regard to the grasslands. In so doing they simply applied local custom as "law" in an area where federal legislation did not allow the acquisition of sufficient land for grazing large numbers of cattle. Although a single person could claim 1,120 acres of government land through preemption, homesteading, and desert land and timber entries, that amount still failed to meet the needs of a ranch grazing hundreds or thousands of cattle. But when a number of cowboys working for the same employer all entered similar claims (with the private understanding of the boss's control and option to buy any patented land), the total acreage a rancher could "own" was considerable. The rancher's effective ownership further increased through locating claims on and around water sources, making contiguous lands virtually worthless to anyone without the means to dig a well. But even with these methods for securing the range, ranchers feared losing land they used (but to which they had no legal title) to homesteaders and other claimants. As soon as barbed wire became available in Colorado in the late 1870s, ranchers began fencing the national domain.[32]

Hollywood and pulp westerns have popularized the notion that settlers' fences hastened the end of the open-range cattle industry. But in northeastern Colorado, it was the ranchers who did most of the fencing. The majority of farmers simply could not afford fences, and their claims remained unenclosed until well past the turn of the century. When President Grover Cleveland issued an executive order in 1885 demanding that fences on the public domain be removed, most of the offending cattlemen reluctantly obeyed. Occasionally, homesteaders salvaged fence originally put in place by ranchers. Abe Ingraham profited from his timely interception of the cowboy assigned the task of removing American Cattle Company fencing from the border of his claim. The cowboy was happy to get out of the extra work, and Abe acquired a valuable improvement free for the asking.[33]

The open, unfenced range allowed small farmers as well as the big ranchers to pasture their stock on public land. But that same lack of fencing exposed farmers and their families to the whims of the longhorns. Today we rarely see long-horned cattle, except in pictures. Occasionally, they turn up in zoos or at rodeos celebrating the "Old West." Seeing these large, half-wild cattle with their enormous horns up close is really the only way to appreciate how imposing these animals must have been to the people who had to live around them. Settlers complained with good reason about cattle invading their fields, eating and trampling crops. Sometimes herds clustered around homesteaders' sod houses or barns and, in milling about, tore the buildings apart with their horns. Mary Wright described how she confronted a "bellowing" herd that gathered around her soddy. "I was greatly alarmed. . . . Suddenly, I remembered that Mr. Ross [a neighbor] told us the cattle were afraid of an umbrella. Fortunately, I had one. I grabbed it and opened the door just enough to slip it outside and quickly hoisted it. You should have seen those cattle turn and run. It was a real stampede." Bad-tempered steers made virtual prisoners of less resourceful settlers, forcing them to hide in their houses or dugouts until the animals tired of threatening the occupants. This danger especially traumatized children, who frequently had to walk miles to get to school.[34]

Many settlers believed that the large cattle outfits deliberately turned their cattle loose to drive the farmers away. And some families did leave because of the damage done by the longhorns. The Iliff Ranch cowboys, however, drove their steers west of Sterling and Akron to stay clear of the homesteaders. Iliff and other ranchers found that when their herds ranged on settlers' claims, cattle mysteriously disappeared. On such occasions, as one woman put it, farmers' "stew kettles seemed to contain an unusual amount of beef." Homesteaders usually tried to keep their own cattle from trespassing in their neighbors' fields. Mrs. Henry Deering observed, "There was a tacit understanding among the people that each should guard his own crops from possible depredations [from cattle], but it was considered neighborly for each to try also, as far as possible, to keep his stock from bothering the unfenced crops."[35]

Despite the friction created between cattlemen and "nesters" over the issues of longhorn management and theft, violence rarely erupted. The two groups continued to have many areas of common interest because both ran cattle, and some cattlemen as well as settlers also kept sheep. Ranchers often bought vegetables and hay from farmers, in some cases the same farmers who doubled as part-time cowboys in order to earn extra cash.[36] Both ranchers and farmers, moreover, had to contend with bad weather. Neither group could afford to completely ignore their status as neighbors who might need each other's help.

Several natural disasters struck Colorado's grasslands in the 1880s, some severe enough to wipe out whole herds of animals and alter forever cattle raisers' business practices. The bitter winter of 1880–1881 produced an extensive cattle kill, leading many ranchers to diversify into sheep raising as a means of recouping losses. Stockmen's troubles multiplied when drovers from Texas trailed their herds to the new railheads. Tick fever, a disease to which the Texas herds had developed immunity, fatally infected thousands of Colorado cattle. The Colorado Assembly, in 1885, passed legislation requiring that cattle entering the state should have been free from contact with any diseased animal for at least ninety days. In effect, this law separated the northern and southern herds and encouraged the upgrading of Colorado livestock. Ranchers began to replace their long-horns with better, beef-producing breeds. And to protect their investment, cattlemen cultivated and harvested hay crops, raised shelters against the weather, and erected legal fences to prevent interbreeding.[37]

The winters of 1885–1886 and 1886–1887 added new urgency to these changes in stock management. With the range already in poor condition from overgrazing, terrible blizzards in these years assured the end of the open-range cattle industry. Devastating stock losses wiped out the investments of many speculators. Clearly, cattle raisers could no longer afford to gamble on the weather and expect their animals to survive without protection from cold and hunger. The developing techniques of cattle ranching once again brought the industry closer to farming practices, further expanding areas of mutual interest between rancher and farmer.[38]

Cattlemen, nonetheless, persisted in seeing settlement as a threat. Settlement, after all, diminished the national domain used by stockmen for grazing their own herds. In the view of many ranchers, the one favorable aspect of the blizzards of the eighties was the resulting negative advertising for the area.[39] But land seekers turned a blind eye and a deaf ear to bad news. Much more important to them were the bountiful crops produced during these relatively wet years. With abundant free land still waiting for claimants, immigration continued unabated.

Then a new series of natural disasters struck. Coming on the heels of the panic of 1893, these blows inflicted widespread ruin on farmers and cattlemen alike. The bleakest years were 1894 and 1895. As the nation's economy plunged, drought conditions on the high plains intensified. Around Akron and Sterling only six inches of rain fell in 1894 instead of the usual fifteen.[40] Many homesteaders suffered complete crop losses the following summer when clouds of locusts, thick enough to block out the sun, descended on parched fields and consumed everything in their path. Trains and horse-drawn wagons and buggies spun their wheels on tracks and roads slippery with crushed insects. Mary Wright recalled that grass-hoppers "were so thick on the ground we could not step anywhere without crushing them at every step. The railroad rails were so slick and slimy that sand had to be used to keep the drive wheels from slipping." Ernest Lewis added his own recollections of the grotesque scene confronted by his family. "About half a mile north of our homestead, [grasshoppers] died by the millions . . . and piled up in drifts, broiling in the sun. The stench was . . . terrible. . . . They piled up in the wheel tracks of the trails so thick that the horses would not stay in the track, and the wheels of the wagons and buggies dripped with the slimy mess." Settlers who somehow managed to weather that summer of the grasshopper plague suffered still another blow the following April when a howling blizzard swept across the plains, toppling farm buildings and killing livestock.[41]

Most heavily hit by the hard times were those who had taken out loans for new McCormick harvesters and other machinery bought in the optimism of the wet years. Irrigators faced additional problems because of debts incurred putting in irrigation systems and paying for high-priced land. Many ranchers confronted ruin from losses sustained in the cattle market.[42]

Bankruptcies affected all segments of the farming and ranching economy. Even big outfits like the Iliff Cattle Company went out of business. Settlers sold out for next to nothing or simply abandoned their property. Those who held onto their claims often found themselves forced to find temporary employment elsewhere. One settler remembered that homesteaders hauled vegetables from Greeley to augment their meager winter food supplies. Another recalled with some sense of shame the "black eye" the area received when the railroads delivered clothing and food for relief of the residents. "For several years . . . [Washington County] was alluded to as the part of Colorado where so much aid was sent."[43]

Many of those who stayed simply lacked the resources to leave. They sometimes still managed, however, to buy out their departing neighbors. One man acquired a homestead in exchange for a wagon. Another paid for a quarter section with a two-year-old steer. His son recalled that "most homesteads were simply abandoned. We would probably have left, too, but Dad couldn't get money enough together for train fare for all of us, and Mom declared that she wouldn't trail out of the country in a covered wagon, no matter what. So we hung on and ate beans!" Through persistence and similar opportunistic buy-outs, some settlers accumulated several hundred acres of land.[44]

Additional acres often became pasture for more animals. Farmers who could not have grown a marketable crop ran a few more horses and cattle to meet their expenses and supply their tables. Ranchers, who also increased their land holdings in the exodus, sometimes expanded the scope of their operations by raising sheep as a hedge against the falling cattle market. Overall, the population of range animals rose dramatically. In the decade between 1890 and 1900, cattle increased five- to sixfold; sheep counts doubled and even tripled in some areas.[45]

The competition for range created by burgeoning populations of cattle and sheep divided stockraisers into two hostile camps. On one side were the sheepmen and those who ran sheep as well as cattle. Confronting them were the ranchers who ran cattle exclusively. Convinced that close-cropping by sheep was ruining the grasslands, a few cattle-only ranchers became openly hostile. On one occasion, unidentified men shot two hundred sheep.[46] Although this incident underscored tensions between different groups of stockraisers, it did not lead to extensive open warfare. So many ranchers ran both cattle and sheep that most rival range interests grudgingly learned to tolerate each other.

Injuries to livestock and humans resulted far more frequently from causes other than shootings. Unseen perils lurked in the ground itself. Abandoned wells, a legacy of the human departure, regularly trapped range stock and a few settlers, sometimes with fatal results. Other hazards, largely economic, sprang from the increase in rustling. With more cattle and fewer people to police the range, stock thieves moved in like flies at a picnic. Unlike the occasional harvesting of individual steers by hungry or disgruntled settlers, cattle thieves turned rustling into an organized business. It was a business, however, with significant risks. During the early 1890s, one judge sentenced more than sixty rustlers to the penitentiary.[47]

Whereas rustlers may have applauded the boom in livestock populations, promoters of northeastern Colorado as a farming region viewed this development with some alarm. Because a farm typically required less land than a ranch, they reasoned that farming would attract more people. Farm families would create stable communities, and their activities as producers and consumers would stimulate business and prosperity. This scheme had shriveled in the drought. But determined agriculturalists, as well as a few enterprising confidence artists, offered hope that homesteaders could adjust their farming methods and overcome dryland conditions.

Desperate settlers initially hired rainmakers. One so-called rainfakir toured the countryside around Julesburg, Holyoke, and Fleming. He promised to produce no less than one-half inch of precipitation by burning "chemicals on a raised platform in the open country." Farmers were to pay him six cents for every acre receiving rain.[48] At that rate farmers had nothing to lose. But of course this and other rainmaking projects failed, giving settlers added incentive to listen to the advice of more conventional farming experts.

Agronomists hired by the railroads conducted much of the initial experimental work on dryland farming. Back in the early 1870s, the Kansas Pacific Railway had employed R. S. Elliott to test the feasibility of cultivating a variety of crops on the plains of western Kansas. Elliott grew wheat, rye, barley, potatoes, and several species of trees without irrigation. But these experiments remained largely unknown to homesteaders, who in any event usually preferred to grow corn. A drought-sensitive grain, corn was a staple of the midwestern and eastern farms where most settlers had spent their formative years, and they were more comfortable following familiar farming methods from the past. Besides, Elliott had done nothing to develop new approaches to farming under arid conditions. He had simply shown that certain crops grew in areas receiving less than twenty inches average annual rainfall.[49]

Elliott's work, however, inspired other agronomists. Hired by the railroads or by increasingly active government farm agencies, investigators continued to experiment with growing crops under arid conditions. "Dryland farming" developed from the collective results of their efforts. Farmers who followed the new techniques plowed deeply and harrowed their fields after rainfalls to trap moisture under a dust mulch. They practiced summer fallowing, crop rotation, and diversified farming that combined stockraising with crop culture. Dryland farmers also turned to newly developed varieties of drought-resistant Russian wheat.

The State Agriculture College at Fort Collins, with support from the U.S. Department of Agriculture, bred new wheat hybrids and tested their suitability to eastern Colorado's climate. The railroads, meanwhile, established their own experimental farms with subsidies from the state legislature. Individual farmers supplemented these institutional programs, offering their own experiments with wheat production for public scrutiny. An early local celebrity of the dryland farming movement, Phillip Held, successfully grew winter wheat in fallow fields that he had first plowed and harrowed to destroy weeds and retain moisture.[50]

The example of farmers like Phillip Held raised hopes that Colorado's high plains could develop into farming country, but farmers still needed more water if those hopes were ever to develop into reality. In the early 1870s, Nathan Meeker, founder of the Union Colony at Greeley, had launched an educational campaign to encourage colonists to install windmills. Meeker believed that only wind power could pump enough water to ensure the success of mixed livestock and crop farming on Colorado's grasslands. Meeker also understood that windmills could greatly enhance settlers' standard of living by providing a ready supply of water for domestic needs, vegetable and flower gardens, lawns, and trees. But Meeker was ahead of his time. Most early settlers regarded windmills as nonessentials, luxuries they could ill afford. A change in attitude became widespread only after the severe drought of the early 1890s, and by then manufacturers started marketing windmills with new designs for efficiently exploiting the steady winds characteristic of the high plains. Adopted as an integral part of dryland farming methods, windmills gradually became a standard feature of the grasslands landscape.[51]

Windmills and new farming methods were powerful tools for the boosters of settlement, but by themselves they could not create a new land rush to Colorado. The repopulation depended ultimately on the weather. Starting in the mid-1890s, the drought began to moderate, giving way to an extended period of wet years after the turn of the century. Coincidentally, the nation's economy revived, encouraging investments in new businesses by large and small investors alike. Some of those investors turned to Colorado's wide-open spaces. Thousands of small-time speculators, families as well as individuals, decided to take up homesteads or buy small farms. A few investors with a lot of money to spend put their resources into promising business ventures then beginning to take shape. Their capitalization of extensive irrigation projects and of the embryonic sugar beet industry drew additional thousands of settlers to the South Platte valley.

Sugar beets came to occupy a dominant place in the region's economy after the turn of the century. A few farmers had experimented with the cultivation of sugar beets during the early 1870s, and Meeker himself promoted sugar beet culture, as well as the use of windmills. In response to his urgings, a few Greeley colonists grew sugar beets for stock feed. Meeker, however, had no more luck "selling" sugar beets than windmills because the underlying conditions for their optimal cultivation had yet to develop. Sugar beets require irrigation and labor-intensive cultivation. Efficient processing of the beets into sugar requires centrally located factories. As a capital-devouring crop, sugar beets failed to attract many growers, and not until 1888 did the State Agriculture College even begin to test seed. Agronomists gradually expanded their testing, and in 1897 they conducted field experiments on five hundred pounds of seed received from the Department of Agriculture in Washington. They distributed an additional two hundred pounds to interested farmers around the state.[52]

By the end of the century, sugar beet fever was sweeping the investment markets. Denver capitalists underwrote construction of Colorado's first factory, located in Grand Junction on the western slope. Meanwhile, boosters from northeastern Colorado towns rushed to compete for their own facilities. Loveland became the first South Platte valley community to have its own factory, and within a few years processing plants opened up in neighboring towns all along the river.

Sugar beets soon became the chief cash crop of the South Platte valley. The beet boom, however, could not have happened on a large scale without the development of massive irrigation systems. In 1902 federal

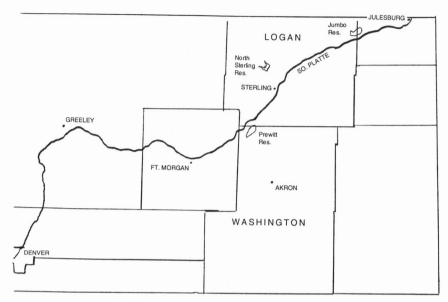

Reservoirs in northeastern Colorado, 1912. Adapted from U.S.G.S. Map, State of Colorado, 1927. Western History Archives, Norlin Library, University of Colorado, Boulder.

surveyors looking for suitable dam sites proposed three reservoirs for Logan and Washington counties. Beet growers and sugar producers immediately set about making these reservoirs a reality, and within just ten years, workers finished construction on all three. The Jumbo (later renamed Julesburg) Reservoir, completed in 1906, straddled the Logan-Sedgwick county line near the Nebraska border. A second reservoir of approximately the same size crossed the Logan-Washington county line south of Merino. Named for a local rancher, L. H. Prewitt, it started operations in 1912. The largest of the three, the North Sterling Reservoir, was ready to begin receiving water at about the same time.[53]

The reservoir construction camps had much the same wide-open atmosphere as the camps spawned by western mining and railroad booms. Men lived in company barracks and spent much of their free time in a combination dining and recreation hall. Wages amounted to $3 a day, less charges taken out for room and board. But if the men preferred, they could receive their pay at the end of each day in liquor, drugs, or poker chips. Drunken carousing reverberated through the nights, driving at least one earnest young man back to his "soft" ranch job where "18 hours of work per day was all that was expected of him."[54]

Promenading along the top of the North Sterling Reservoir dam shortly after its completion. *Courtesy of the Overland Trail Museum, Sterling.*

This young defector had few followers. The construction companies hired enormous work forces, though they sometimes competed with each other for labor. Building the Prewitt required five hundred workmen and an equal number of horse teams to carve out the basin needed for containing its waters. The North Sterling project gave employment to some five hundred transients in addition to every available local man. Four hundred teams of horses worked the site during the earth-moving operations. The dam itself measured nearly a mile long when completed and reached a height of eighty-five feet.[55] These numbers testify to the boomers' intense interest in developing beet culture along the South Platte River. The promoters' ultimate success affected not only the manner and extent of future economic growth but also the size and ethnic mix of the incoming population.

The expansion of the sugar beet industry changed the ways many stockgrowers and farmers managed their animals. Beet tops and the pulp left over from beet processing proved to be nutritious feed for dairy cows, beef cattle, and other livestock. Sugar factories became magnets for feedlots, where stockraisers fattened their cattle before sending them to market. Beet growers used feedlot manure to fertilize their fields. Farmers added more nutrients to the soil by rotating beet plantings with nitrogen-rich alfalfa. When harvested and cured, alfalfa became fodder for cattle and other livestock. This intertwining of beet culture with the dairy and livestock industries expanded the long-established trend toward mixed farming and ranching operations.[56]

The beet boom also attracted foreign immigrants, especially ethnic Germans from Russia,[57] to work the beet fields (Table 1.1). In the early years, German-Russians did most of the backbreaking labor of thinning seedlings and hoeing weeds. At harvest time the work intensified as laborers pulled and topped beets, then loaded them on wagons for hauling to the factory. Few American-born workers would submit to the demands of the job. The Germans from Russia were hardworking and ambitious, and they saw their labor in the beet fields as a way to earn money toward the day when they could buy their own land. They had left Russia because of adverse political and economic pressures, and as refugees they were willing to perform tasks shunned by groups with a larger range of options.[58]

At first the German-Russians ("Rooshuns," the locals called them) accepted jobs on a temporary basis. During the six-month growing season, they lived in shacks or tents supplied by the growers. But in time many German-Russians acquired the means first to rent, and then buy, the land they worked. Families saved every penny and put all family members to

Table 1.1. Origins of the Foreign-Born, 1890–1920

	Logan County				Washington County			
	1890	1900	1910	1920	1890	1900	1910	1920
Total Population	3,070	3,292	9,549	18,427	2,301	1,241	6,002	11,208
Total Foreign-born	523	540	1,344	2,298	319	159	502	675
Austria	5	75	48	21	1	1	29	13
Canada-English	na[a]	69	91	105[b]	na	3	43	13
Canada & Newfoundland	86	na	na	na	22	na	na	na
Denmark	na	20	37	49	na	4	47	29
England	59	61	81	68	42	7	30	37
Germany	136	124	183	238	89	78	138	184
Ireland	43	23	40	37	23	18	35	28
Italy	na	3	93	126	na	0	27	2
Japan	na	0	79	67	na	na	na	na
Mexico	1	1	11	152	0	0	0	44
Russia	na	66[c]	503[c]	1174[c]	na	18[c]	44[c]	131[c]
Other	193	98	178	261	142	30	109	194

Sources: U.S. Census Office, *Compendium of the Eleventh Census: 1890*, part 2 (Washington, D.C.: GPO, 1894), 616–617; U.S. Census Office, *Twelfth Census of the United States, Taken in the Year 1900: Population*, part 1 (Washington, D.C.: GPO, 1901), 740–741; U.S. Bureau of the Census, *Thirteenth Census of the United States, Taken in the Year 1910: Abstract of the Census With Supplement for Colorado* (Washington, D.C.: GPO, 1913), 600, 604; U.S. Bureau of the Census, *Fourteenth Census of the United States, Taken in the Year 1920*, vol. 3, *Population* (Washington, D.C.: GPO, 1922), 139, 149.
[a]na = not available.
[b]May include French Canadians.
[c]Virtually all were German-Russian.

work in the fields, sometimes even requiring children to forgo schooling. Men often earned additional cash by hiring out for haying and other farm work. The sugar factory owners encouraged this transformation from beet "laborers" to beet "growers" by making company land available for rent or purchase under easy credit terms. So successful were the Germans from Russia that, according to the estimates of one historian, they operated 75 percent of the irrigated farms between Denver and Sterling by 1910.[59]

As landowners and operators, German-Russians no longer filled the need for stoop labor, and growers looked for replacements from other foreign-born groups. Of the more than 10,000 beet workers in the South Platte valley in 1909, nearly 20 percent were Japanese immigrants from California.[60] But the Japanese, like the German-Russians, regarded field-work as a temporary expedient. They too wanted to rent and eventually buy land. Mexican workers increasingly filled the need for field labor simply because many Mexicans had no interest in permanent settlement.

Modern cropland near Akron. Although the vegetation has changed, the landscape retains much the same look it had in the early days of settlement. *Photo by author.*

They merely wanted to take home U.S. dollars worth twelve times their nominal value south of the border. Only eleven Mexican-born residents appeared in the 1910 census of Logan County; none appeared in the Washington County Census, though Hispanic beet workers in 1909 numbered slightly over one thousand. In subsequent years, migrant labor from Mexico supplied a growing proportion of beet field labor, and eventually more Mexicans established permanent homes in the area.[61]

Although foreign-born immigrants flooded into Colorado after the turn of the century to take jobs in the beet industry, their percentage of the total population actually declined. The rush of American-born whites nearly eclipsed the presence of other groups. In Logan County the percentage of American-born whites grew from 83 in 1890 to 87.5 in 1920. In Washington County, where the sugar beet industry gained a smaller foothold, the discrepancy became even more pronounced. Fully 94 percent of the population were American-born whites in 1920, up from 86.1 percent in 1890.

When the new rush of homesteaders arrived in the South Platte valley, they discovered that sugar beet growers already monopolized much of the irrigable land. But many settlers actually preferred to claim free homesteads on the dry lands. They had heard the optimistic prognostications of locators, colonizers, railroads, and the state board of immigration assuring newcomers of a secure future on Colorado's plains.[62] Land companies like the Colorado Colony Company and the Platte Valley Land Corporation lured customers with flowery advertisements. "Buy a farm — be your own lord and master and live sumptuously in your declining years." Such admonishments, even taken with a large grain of salt, still rang inviting to renters and young people looking forward to owning their first farm. They responded in droves, traveling by wagon and by rail. In 1909 alone, the Union Pacific and the Burlington lines scheduled a daily total of fourteen passenger trains to the South Platte valley to accommodate the traffic.[63]

The railroads, through their immigration and colonization departments, continued to subsidize settlement as they had in the earlier land boom of the eighties. As a service to newcomers, they sidetracked carloads of homesteaders' goods until the owners could construct shelters to house their belongings. Company policies directed sectionmen to assist struggling farmers. Railroaders distributed damaged ties for use as fence posts or fuel. They offered settlers free coal if they wanted to gather chunks that had fallen along the rights-of-way.[64]

Changes in government land policies also enhanced settlement by ultimately making homesteading on the plains easier and more rewarding. But these changes were slow in coming. For years Congress debated ways to tighten up the land laws in order to discourage speculation and fraud. The original Homestead Act of 1862 allowed a claimant to receive a land patent after living on a claim continuously for five years and making specified improvements (building a house and plowing fields). Alternatively, after living on a homestead for six months, the homesteader could "commute" his or her claim and receive a patent by paying $1.25 per acre. In practice, local custom amended these rules. Before the turn of the century, according to a woman whose family homesteaded in Washington County, "a visit of once in six months to the land was considered legal residence for unmarried people, male or female."[65] Although such local and private understandings did not trouble Congress, lawmakers were concerned about ending land grabs by professional speculators.

In 1891 Congress passed the Revision Act, which repealed a number of laws allowing claimants to acquire government land and amended several others. Gone were the Timber Culture Act and the preemption laws. The amended Homestead Act required an additional eight months before a claimant could commute a claim. Congress theorized that speculators would not want to homestead land if they had to wait an extra eight months for a patent.[66]

For nearly two decades no further changes in homestead legislation occurred. Meanwhile, western ranchers and farmers lobbied Congress to increase the size of claims. They argued that the West's low rainfall reduced forage and crop production, making larger homesteads necessary. But Congress listened to dryland farming promoters whose propaganda portrayed the standard 160 acres as sufficient for a family farm. High plains ranchers and farmers strongly objected, and eventually their demands prompted a grudging Congress to pass the Enlarged Homestead Act of 1909 and later the Stockgrowers Homestead Act of 1916. The first allowed claimants to patent 320 acres of arid land providing that they cultivated one-fourth of their claims. The second permitted homesteaders to acquire 640 acres classified as grazing or forage crop land. Both acts encouraged homesteading in northeastern Colorado and contributed to the patenting of virtually all productive government land in much of northeastern Colorado by 1920.[67]

One other law gave a boost to homesteading. The Three Year Homestead Act (1912) shortened the residence requirement from five to three years and allowed entrants to absent themselves from their land for five months out of the year. By easing the problems of living on claims through the winters, the Three Year Homestead Act permitted settlers greater freedom in taking cash-paying jobs at some distance from their homesteads. The act also had the positive effect, as far as the government was concerned, of discouraging speculation. In requiring only twenty-one months of actual residence, the act made commutation, allowed after fourteen months of living on the claim, considerably less attractive.[68]

The whole issue of land speculation already had a long history for both Congress and the American public by 1912, when the Three Year Homestead Act passed. During the early years of the Republic, individual speculators and companies gained control of large tracts by taking advantage of federal land laws. "Speculator," in the vocabulary of most Americans, became synonymous with "villain," even though some of the United States's most venerated heroes, including George Washington, were among the nation's greediest land grabbers. Yet influential individuals (most notably Thomas Jefferson) promoted an agrarian ideal centered on the settlement of the United States's hinterlands by hardy Anglo-Saxon farmers and their families. According to Jeffersonian reasoning, these independent yeomen formed the backbone of virtuous, republican government. Speculators, on the other hand, contributed nothing of value to the country, for they were interested only in making money and not in developing homes for honest citizens.

The Homestead Act of 1862, passed after decades of protest against speculators who could afford to buy up large areas of government land, was supposed to end speculation by giving quarter sections to citizen farmers. But the Homestead Act simply democratized speculation by allowing small-scale capitalists to claim quarter sections of the federal domain. In fact, many if not most settlers, female and male, were speculators. They hoped to gain a few hundred (or a few thousand) dollars through the eventual sale of their homesteading enterprises. But Congress chose to condemn the speculative impulse driving homesteading, though it rewarded that same impulse in other western business ventures. Generous government land subsidies had encouraged the construction of western railroads, yet Congress balked at allowing the small-scale speculations of homesteaders. The eagerness of many entrants to sell their claims for profit threatened to concentrate land titles in the hands of absentee landlords. To believers in the Jeffersonian ideal, this possibility perverted the intent of homestead legislation and placed the nation's virtue at risk.

Settlers, on the other hand, saw their own government land acquisitions and sales (if they even recognized the speculative nature of such transactions) as innocent efforts to improve their individual and family fortunes. Colorado homesteaders were no different in this regard from settlers in other homesteading areas. And so, following the western tradition of self-promotion, they vigorously pursued their rights to enter and sell claims.

Few if any Colorado officials raised objections to the land speculation frenzy taking place on the grasslands after the turn of the century. Nonetheless, the very number of claimants inevitably created frictions. The wet years following the drought had made stockraising, as well as farming, profitable once again, and new ranching enterprises organized to exploit the range.[69] Some old-time ranchers, however, refused to recognize the "nesters' " legal entitlement to the land, claiming instead their own right by prior custom and use. Under these circumstances, clashes between the two groups escalated. Ranchers taunted the "wrinkle bellies," predicting the farmers' certain starvation once another dry cycle hit the plains. Occasionally, more serious attacks occurred. One man who recalled his father's homesteading experience wrote that "relations between the settlers and cattlemen worsened until several members on both sides were killed in gun battles." A rancher complained that the new wave of settlers "did not take time to fence their land and would shoot the legs of the stock that got onto their property."[70] A homesteader became the butt of some cowboys' "fun" when they shot holes through his new hat and then "took aim" at his stock water tank. "He wasn't very friendly afterwards with these cowboys," observed his son. Other conflicts arose from Nebraska's herd law. The statute allowed the state's farmers to hold any stock that had drifted onto their property until the animals' owner paid seventy-five cents per head to the aggrieved farmer. Some Colorado ranchers accused Nebraska farmers of driving loose cattle onto their land where they held them for "ransom."[71]

The rush to Colorado also created other, more subtle kinds of conflict than arguments between ranchers and farmers over land use. The boom affected land values, and as prices rose, the democracy of land ownership began to fade. Tenancy increased, at first slowly and unevenly, then sharply after 1910.[72] This development signaled declining opportunities, especially for those settlers arriving with more hope than capital to underwrite their new lives. Yet for many of at least modest means, life's horizons had begun to expand in dramatic and novel ways.

Making their appearance around the turn of the century and beyond, telephones, electric lights, cars, automated farm machinery, and rural free delivery eased the burdens of country living. For the first time technology made possible the connection of far-flung farms and ranches with urban centers all across the nation. These changes proceeded gradually and did not affect everyone equally. Residents of towns generally benefited from the spread of technology first, sometimes decades before their country neighbors. Nonetheless, the changes touched everyone — both those who adopted the new ways and those who gazed from the sidelines at the alterations in others' lives.

Sterling became a hub for new technologies. As early as 1902, the town's power plant supplied electricity to a few customers. Expansion of service temporarily halted in 1905 when the plant burned down, leaving Sterling without electric lighting until 1909 when a new power station began operations. Even so, Sterling enjoyed electric service years before the nearby town of Merino, where residents had to wait for electricity until 1918 when workers completed a line from Sterling's generators.[73]

Telephone service developed in a similar, piecemeal fashion. But in contrast to electric service, telephone lines often showed up in rural neighborhoods before they appeared in town. Groups of homesteaders sometimes banded together to form companies, stringing barbed-wire lines on insulators mounted on the tops of fence posts. These local systems transmitted poorly and provided no privacy. Everyone connected to the line considered listening in on conversations a form of free entertainment. But with all its drawbacks, a telephone could be a lifesaver when a

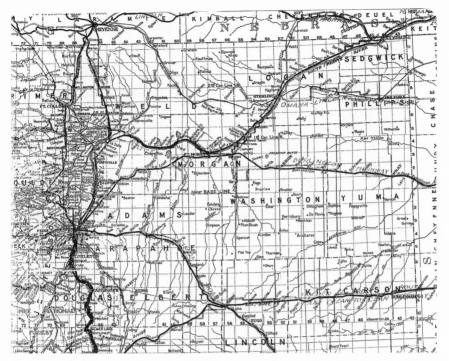

Highways of northeastern Colorado, 1920 (Denver: Clason Map Co.). *Year Book of the State of Colorado, 1920.*

rattlesnake bit little Alice or when the baby caught pneumonia. In town, telephone service seemed less urgent. To be sure, Sterling had telephone lines strung in 1900. But the town of Peetz in northern Logan County managed with only one phone, located in the general store, until 1918 when the Peetz Cooperative Telephone Company organized. Other towns went without service until well into the 1920s.[74]

The automobile, perhaps the most revolutionary technology of all, became commonplace only in the 1910s. The "movers and shakers" of Sterling again led the way when a Ford sales and repair business started operating in 1908. Sales were brisk, considering the novelty and unreliability of those early machines. By 1912 Logan County residents owned about two hundred cars; the following year, nearly five hundred. In neighboring Washington County, only two or three individuals had bought cars by 1910, and one of these belonged to a livery stable owner who rented it out as "auto livery." Driving even short distances was likely to damage tires, and any jaunt through the country could mean a day spent fixing flats until the

Bill Plank pictured in 1923 with his team pulling the water wagon for a steam threshing machine. *Courtesy of William Plank, Sr., Fleming.*

patches ran out. But who could resist the magic of the horseless carriage? By 1920 cars in Washington County numbered about one for every six persons; in Logan County, about one for every five.[75]

To accommodate the traffic, county, state, and federal governments embarked on patchwork programs of road construction after 1910. Builders laid out four major east-west arteries that connected with numerous smaller roads running in all directions. The Platte Valley Highway paralleled the river northeast of Sterling. It joined a branch of the Lincoln Highway, angling down from Wyoming, near Julesburg. The Omaha-Lincoln-Denver road duplicated roughly the present-day route of U.S. 6. The Burlington Highway to the south lay generally along the Burlington Railroad right-of-way, passing through Washington and Yuma counties. Today U.S. 34 approximates its route.[76] A fourth road, the ambitiously named Ocean to Ocean Highway, cut through the middle of Kit Carson County, anticipating the route of Interstate 70.

These highways eased the burdens of immigration, putting out the welcome mat for thousands of newcomers. Latter-day homesteaders sometimes drove the family car to Colorado, perhaps transporting their belongings by rail. But many, probably the great majority, continued to immigrate as others had in the past. If by train, the men generally stayed with the family possessions and farm animals in an "immigrant car." The women and children rode only slightly more comfortably by coach. Many other families still traveled by covered wagon, a practice that extended into the twenties. At least as late as 1929, a man moved his possessions from Nebraska to Washington County in a horse-drawn covered wagon.[77]

A similar pattern of old technologies surviving alongside the new characterized farm machinery. Walking plows, manually operated planters, and horse-powered headers and threshers remained standard equipment through the second decade of the twentieth century. As a rule, one man owned the thresher and hired out or traded services with his neighbors during the harvest. This arrangement continued when some farmers ac-quired gasoline-driven tractors, using them to break sod on their own and nearby quarter sections. By the late 1910s, the owners of new steam-powered threshers also traveled about, selling or bartering their services. World War I accelerated the spread of mechanization as production goals jumped to meet the nation's demands. Farmers believed they could make payments on new machinery with the profits they earned from inflated wartime prices and higher crop yields.[78]

World War I, in fact, proved to be a watershed. It spurred the expansion of laborsaving technology and encouraged the cultivation of marginal land. Eventually, the push to increase production led to a damaged environment and farm failures once the war ended and markets declined. But in the short run, the war brought a change in outlook to residents of Colorado's grasslands as newspapers, magazines, and other transmitters of patriotic opinion established a new emphasis on a national identity.

Sometimes this identification with the nation at large encouraged bigotry by focusing attention on "foreigners" within the community. Ger-man-Russians suffered discrimination and even violence from some of their American-born neighbors caught up in the chauvinistic fever of those years. In other instances, nationalist impulses turned inward, affecting the ways native-born Americans looked at themselves and each other. One woman described the changing attitudes she sensed among her friends on a visit in 1918 to Briggsdale, Weld County, where two years earlier she had taught school. "After the days of labor and tranquility . . . a certain prosperity had come to everyone. Prices for their products had been lucrative and a feeling of unrest and dissatisfaction seemed to be in . . . [their] hearts."[79] Colorado's settlers were reaching out not only for the material goods that could improve their standard of living but also for the symbolism behind those goods: integration with nationwide values and social norms. Grasslanders wanted to share with other Americans the status of a people whose prosperity and technological ingenuity led the world.

The war, to be sure, had not introduced rural Coloradans to city-produced goods and services. Telephones, electric lights, cars, and other kinds of automated machinery predated the entrance of the United States into World War I, in some cases by nearly two decades. Rural free delivery, moreover, had earlier linked farm families with urban centers, permitting buyers, by means of mail-order catalogs and newspaper advertisements, to obtain merchandise from stores in Denver and other cities across the nation.[80] Nonetheless, World War I, or rather the prosperity and patriotism it generated, did raise the standards by which homesteaders and other rural residents measured their material well-being. People no longer considered as toys or luxuries mass-produced items from department stores. Nor did they regard new machinery as an extravagance. These items had become necessities as indicators of one's American identity.

By 1920 "free" land, and the opportunity it offered homesteaders, no longer represented a significant theme in northeastern Colorado's development. Although sparse settlement continued to characterize large areas inhabited by fewer than five persons per square mile, settlers had taken up most of the patentable federal domain.[81] The value of real estate had risen, leaving room for only those farmers and ranchers who could afford to buy their land. Opportunities still existed, but they differed neither in kind nor extent from those in many older U.S. communities.

The integration of northeastern Colorado into the nation's rural and small-town landscape carried for the residents a double significance. Although it brought a higher standard of living, it also signaled the end of homesteading's boomer magic. Sometimes illusory and sometimes fulfilled, that magic had once lured thousands of women and men to the South Platte valley in search of new lives.

2

Plain, Everyday People

Who exactly were the women and men who homesteaded Colorado's grasslands and how did they fare? Jessie Hassig Challis described her homesteading parents and neighbors simply as "plain everyday people [who] enjoyed simple things and took time to live."[1] However apt her description, it leaves us wishing for more information. We could turn to other homesteaders' stories, reminiscences, diaries, and letters to expand on Jessie's observations, but anecdotes by themselves offer an incomplete picture of settlement on the plains. To fill in the blanks we need "hard facts," or demographic profiles, to give us a broad view of homesteaders that includes such details as origin, age, sex, marital status, size of family, and health.

In the following pages, I will attempt a description of homesteaders and their homestead ventures using a notoriously unappealing tool: statistics. Numbers can suggest possible adaptations in family relationships, as well as differences in the ways men and women experienced living on a claim. Numbers, moreover, are essential to any understanding of the economics of homesteading. To be sure, anecdotes have the power to touch us far more forcefully than figures ever can, but the fact is that numbers can reveal much that would otherwise remain obscure or hidden.

The statistics gathered here come from a variety of sources. Census returns and federal land records make up the more "conventional" demographic documents. But a careful combing of family histories, written by homesteaders and their relatives, also produced a wealth of numerical information. Because of the comparatively small sample sizes, data from the family histories are less accurate than those from government records. In some cases, family sources suggest rather than confirm a particular point. Still, the narratives contain material about homesteaders that is unavailable elsewhere. When considered together with data from census and land records, they present a broad abstract of homesteaders and homesteading on Colorado's eastern plains.[2]

Homesteaders' geographic origins offer a logical beginning for our investigations. The narratives show that most homesteaders in north-eastern Colorado hailed from locations in the Midwest and the East. They were familiar with eastern institutions and modes of behavior, and this familiarity influenced the directions in which western institutions and customs later developed (a theme to which I will return in Chapters 3 and 4). Furthermore, these same geographic origins indicate, somewhat para-doxically, that many settlers came prepared with some previous knowledge of how to live and farm on the plains. Historian James Malin, who studied homesteaders in Kansas, observed that his pioneers emigrated primarily from nonadjacent states further east. He concluded that "the adjustments necessary to so marked a change in environment were substantial."[3] But Malin's Kansans represented early generations of grasslanders. Even before the Civil War, settlers had pushed into Kansas and Nebraska — decades before the land rushes in northeastern Colorado. Colorado homesteaders drew on the experiences of these earlier waves of homesteaders, some of whom were their parents or grandparents.

Colorado homesteaders, moreover, frequently lived in Nebraska, Kansas, and Colorado before claiming land in the South Platte valley. Over 50 percent of those immigrating to Colorado before 1900 had previously lived in Nebraska, though the greatest proportion of them had been born in Ohio (followed by New York, Illinois, Iowa, and Indiana). Obviously, a high degree of mobility characterized these immigrants. Mobility also marked the lives of twentieth-century homesteaders, but these later land claimants more often began their lives in locations nearer Colorado. The birthplaces of later settlers concentrated in the two states of Nebraska and Iowa, whereas their most recent previous residences clustered in Nebraska, Iowa, and Colorado itself (Tables 2.1 and 2.2).

Homesteaders' occupational backgrounds also prepared them for settlement. Over 80 percent had either farmed or grown up in farming families (Table 2.3). True, some brought with them the methods and crops of midwestern prairie agriculture. For them prior experience may have slowed their acceptance of new techniques developed to deal with the arid plains environment. But they and most homesteaders were well acquainted with farming, with both its uncertainties and its labor-consuming demands. In this they differed from the Kansas pioneers described by John Ise as inexperienced farmers who had previously worked in the trades: "The fact

Table 2.1. Homesteaders' Birthplaces

State/Territory	Claims Entered Before 1900		Claims Entered After 1900	
	N	%	N	%
Ohio	17	18.7	8	5.8
New York	14	15.4	3	2.2
Illinois	14	15.4	14	10.1
Iowa	13	14.3	29	21.0
Indiana	11	12.1	6	4.3
Missouri	2	2.2	13	9.4
Nebraska	2	2.2	36	26.1
Other	18[a]	19.8	29[b]	21.0
Total	91	100.1	138	99.9

Source: Family histories.
[a]Wisconsin, Maine, New Hampshire, Virginia, West Virginia, Pennsylvania, and Minnesota. Early immigrants to Logan County from Alabama and Mississippi do not show up in these data.
[b]Minnesota, Kansas, Wisconsin, Colorado, Pennsylvania, Maryland, the Dakotas, Tennessee, and New Hampshire.

Table 2.2. Homesteaders' Most Recent Prior Homes

State/Territory	Claims Entered Before 1900		Claims Entered After 1900	
	N	%	N	%
Nebraska	80	52.3	97	29.5
Iowa	27	17.6	79	24.0
Illinois	19	12.4	7	2.1
Colorado	6	3.9	44	13.4
Kansas	5	3.3	30	9.1
Missouri	5	3.3	34	10.3
Dakotas	0	0.0	11	3.3
Other	11[a]	7.2	27[b]	8.2
Total	153	100.0	329	99.9

Source: Family histories.
[a]Indiana, West Virginia, Pennsylvania, Michigan, and New York.
[b]Texas, Indiana, New York, Minnesota, Ohio, Pennsylvania, and Oklahoma.

that so many of the settlers knew little or nothing about farming was one of the reasons for the large percentage of failures among them."[4]

Settlement came late on the high plains. In northeastern Colorado almost three-quarters of the homesteaders entered their claims after 1900, with the peak of homesteading activity occurring in 1910[5] (Tables 2.4 and 2.5). Higher rainfall and more trees, as well as the proximity of markets and transportation routes, had long favored the agricultural development of the

Table 2.3. Homesteaders' Occupational Backgrounds

Occupation	N	%
Farming[a]	216	80.9
Skilled trade[b]	24	9.0
Business	13	4.9
Unskilled trade[c]	13	4.9
Profession[d]	16	6.0
Total	282	105.7[e]

Source: Family histories.

[a]Includes women and men who grew up in farm families. N=216 is probably an undercount because of incomplete information in the reminiscences.

[b]Skilled trades represented here are butcher, painter, decorator, printer, carpenter, mason, cooper, chef, circus entertainer, milliner, seamstress, and blacksmith.

[c]Includes employment at a livery stable, sawmill, creamery, and in railroading, mining, domestic labor, freighting, and the militia.

[d]Includes nursing, teaching, journalism, accounting, and the practice of pharmacy and the law.

[e]This number is greater than 100.0 because the percentages are based on the total number of persons in the sample (267). The same person might work at two or more occupations.

Table 2.4. Homestead Entries by Century, Before and After 1900[a]

	Logan County		Washington County	
	N	%	N	%
Before 1900	1,558	26.4	2,679	29.7
After 1900	4,350	73.6	6,349	70.3
Total	5,908	100.0	9,028	100.0

Source: Federal land records.

[a]Where the same person entered claims both before and after 1900, I counted only the earliest claim.

Midwest and the East. But with the turn of the twentieth century, the West's grasslands began to look more attractive to farmers. Where else but on the western plains could they still find free or cheap farmland? Advances in technology and dryland farming methods and a wetter period in the weather cycle muted many of the problems encountered by earlier settlers who had taken up western homesteads.

For women, opportunities to homestead in the twentieth century came at a particularly favorable time. With the advancing decades of the nineteenth century, middle- and upper-middle-class white women gained more freedom to participate in activities outside the home. Many joined reform movements or engaged in "good works" through women's clubs. A small but growing number of middle-class women found wage-earning jobs; a few even pursued professional careers. By the end of the century, these

Table 2.5. Homestead Entries by Year From 1906 to 1917

Year	N	%
1906	47	4.8
1907	118	12.1
1908	107	11.0
1909	124	12.7
1910	147	15.1
1911	62	6.4
1912	62	6.4
1913	60	6.1
1914	103	10.6
1915	79	8.1
1916	42	4.3
1917	25	2.6
Total sample	976	100.2

Source: Federal land records for Logan and Washington counties.

changes within society had helped loosen whatever inhibitions women settlers felt about entering their own homestead claims. And as attitudes more congenial to women's business ventures spread, the proportion of women land claimants in northeastern Colorado increased substantially. Before 1900 women accounted for about 12 percent of Logan County homestead entrants and 10 percent of Washington County entrants. After 1900 women accounted for nearly 18 percent of the entrants in both counties[6] (Table 2.6).

Women's participation in land entry opportunities was greater than these percentages indicate. We need to remind ourselves that only a small fraction of adult women were unmarried (spinsters, widows, or divorcees) or heads of households and therefore eligible to enter claims. In fact, sample populations in the federal population census schedules for 1910 show that only 15 to 16 percent of white women twenty-one years of age and older and living in Logan and Washington counties were legally qualified to claim homesteads[7] (Table 2.7). Moreover, within the white adult populations I sampled, men outnumbered women. Sex ratios ranged from 116.8 (that is, about 117 men for every 100 women) in the Logan County sample to 150.3 (about 150 men for every 100 women) in the Washington County sample. These sex ratios mean that even if *all* white women twenty-one years of age and older could, and did, claim homesteads in 1910, we would still find fewer female than male land claimants if *all* white men twenty-one years old and older had also entered claims. In this scenario, based on the

Table 2.6. Gender of Homestead Entrants

	Logan County		Washington County	
	N	%	N	%
	Claims Entered Before 1900			
Female entrants[a]	38	12.1	62	10.0
Male entrants	276	87.9	561	90.0
Total[b]	314	100.0	623	100.0
	Claims Entered After 1900			
Female entrants	198	17.5	257	17.8
Male entrants	932	82.5	1188	82.2
Total[b]	1,130	100.0	1,445	100.0

Source: Federal land records.
[a]I determined gender by first names. I did not count names commonly given to both sexes.
[b]Sample sizes are approximately 20 percent and 23 percent, respectively, of all Logan and Washington county entrants before 1900; and 26 percent and 23 percent, respectively, of all Logan and Washington county entrants after 1900.

Table 2.7. 1910 Population Statistics by Age, Marital Status, and Gender for Selected Precincts[a]

	Percentage of White Women Eligible to Enter Homestead Claims			
	Eligible Females (21 & older, single)[b]	Ineligible Females (21 & older, married)	Total Females (21 & older)	%
Washington County	29	162	191	15.2
Logan County	27	140	167	16.2

	Sex Ratios of Whites Ages 21 and Older[c]		
	Men (21 & older)	Women (21 & older)	Sex Ratio
Washington County	287	191	150.3
Logan County	195	167	116.8

Source: Federal population census schedules.
[a]All sampled precincts (5, 8, and 9 in Washington County and 10 in Logan County) were rural.
[b]Married female heads of households could also claim homesteads, but none of the women in the samples fit this description.
[c]Ratios indicate males per 100 females.

sex ratios, forty out of every one hundred entrants in Washington County and forty-six out of every one hundred entrants in Logan County would have been women. But only 15 to 16 percent of the adult women sampled in the federal census schedules qualified as claimants in 1910. Consequently, only seven out of every one hundred adults entering claims in 1910 in Logan County, and only six out of every one hundred adults in Washington County, could have been women — if we assume that all eligible white persons of both sexes entered claims.

How then do we explain the fact that nearly 18 percent of entrants in both counties after 1900 were women? The 18 percent represents cumulative entries over two decades. For example, many women who were wives in 1910, and therefore unqualified to enter claims, homesteaded as spinsters at an earlier date. Some wives later homesteaded as widows. Moreover, not all men used their homestead rights. The data, in fact, suggest the interesting though unprovable possibility that on a percentage basis more women than men exercised their homestead rights. At the least, we can confidently conclude that a high percentage of the women who qualified under the homestead laws entered claims.

But what about the period before 1900, when 10 to 12 percent of the entrants were women? What fraction of adult women were eligible to enter claims then? Unfortunately, the 1890 federal census schedules burned, leaving us with no record of women's eligibility during the first land boom. We can infer from census abstracts, however, that sex ratios for adult whites in Logan and Washington counties were probably lower in 1890 than in 1910 (Table 2.8). Lower sex ratios mean a higher percentage of women in the population. However, if we were to assume that the percentage of women eligible to enter claims remained unchanged between 1890 and 1910, then we might plausibly expect a highter percentage of women among homestead claimants in the period before 1900. On the contrary, the land records show a higher percentage of women (almost 18 percent of all entrants) among claimants in the period *after* 1900. I interpret these data to mean that with the passage of time more and more women recognized and pursued the opportunities open to them as individuals through the homestead laws until, in the twentieth century, a large majority of eligible women entered claims.

Homesteading, however, never qualified as an exercise in freewheeling individualism. Women entrants, like men, usually homesteaded with family members present or nearby who could help in the homesteading venture. Women entrants' last names in the land office tract books often match those of neighboring claimants, implying ties between probable kin.

Table 2.8. Sex Ratios of American-born Whites in Logan and Washington Counties, 1890–1920[a]

Census Year	Logan County		Washington County	
	All Ages	21 & Over	All Ages	21 & Over
1920	108.5	115.8	114.0	124.5
1910	(127.1)[b]	na[c]	(122.3)	na
1900	130.9	na	118.0	na
1890	111.3	na	112.4	na

Sources: U.S. Census Office, *Compendium of the Eleventh Census: 1890*, part 1 (Washington, D.C.: GPO, 1894), 588–589; U.S. Census Office, *Twelfth Census of the United States, Taken in the Year 1900: Population*, part 1 (Washington, D.C.: GPO, 1901), 576; U.S. Bureau of the Census, *Thirteenth Census of the United States, Taken in the Year 1910: Abstract of the Census With Supplement for Colorado* (Washington, D.C.: GPO, 1913), 601, 605; U.S. Bureau of the Census, *Fourteenth Census of the United States, Taken in the Year 1920*, vol. 3, *Population* (Washington, D.C.: GPO, 1922), 144, 146.
[a]Ratios indicate males per 100 females.
[b] Figures in parentheses are ratios for the entire white population. Statistics for American-born whites are not available for 1910. Foreign-born white ratios are usually higher than ratios for American-born whites.
[c] na = not available.

Table 2.9. Kinship Ties Between Women Homestead Claimants and Neighboring Land Entrants[a]

	Claims Entered Before 1900		Claims Entered After 1900	
	N	%	N	%
Women matched to probable kin	40	50.0	196	51.6
Total	80		380	

Source: Federal land records for Logan and Washington counties.
[a]I did not count illegible names or common names such as Brown or Smith.

Indeed, when one systematically matches names, the records reveal that at least 50 percent of women's claims, both before and after 1900, were in some way connected to a family enterprise (Table 2.9). These percentages undoubtedly reflect a large undercount. In-laws' last names, for example, probably differed from those of neighboring relatives. Daughters who homesteaded years after their parents claimed land could easily appear unattached to families. Those women with families living on adjacent land *purchased* from other settlers would also appear unattached in the record books. Taking into account all these possibilities, we can safely assume that a substantial majority of women entrants homesteaded with family members close by.

Table 2.10. Homestead Entries, by Couples, Single Men, and Women

	Claims Entered Before 1900		Claims Entered After 1900	
	N	%	N	%
Couples	77	78.6	141	58.0
Single men	14	14.3	72	29.6
Women[a]	7	7.1	30	12.3
Total	98	100.0	243	99.9

Source: Family histories.
[a]The more accurate federal land records are several percentage points higher. The percentages calculated from the family histories approximate trends within the homesteading population.

The presence of families stands out as one of the overriding features of agricultural settlement. If the tract book records hint at the extent of family participation by repeated entries of the same last names, reminiscences offer a much clearer picture. Data culled from narratives show that claims entered by married men far exceeded those entered by either single men or women. Before 1900 couples held nearly 79 percent of the claims, though only the husband's name appeared in the government land records. After 1900 the portion of such claims dropped significantly to 58 percent, but they still represented the great majority of entries (Table 2.10). The land entry data yielded by the reminiscences are not exact. But the percentages of women entrants before and after 1900 do follow the upward trends indicated by the more precise tract book records[8] (Table 2.6). We can believe, therefore, another trend revealed in the family history data; namely, the high representation of couples among early-day homesteaders and the percentage drop in their numbers over time. Higher sex ratios (that is, greater numbers of men relative to the numbers of women) recorded in the federal censuses of 1900, 1910, and 1920 support this conclusion (Table 2.8).

The federal census schedules of 1890 show sex ratios for all American-born whites in Logan County of 111.3, and in Washington County of 112.4. Ten years later the two counties had sex ratios of 130.9 and 118.0. This change developed as a consequence of severe drought and economic depression, and the in-and-out migration patterns these events produced. In 1910 the ratios remained high (127.1 and 122.3). By 1920, however, the sex ratio for Logan County dropped to 108.5, although the population aged twenty-one and older retained a larger disparity between males and females

(115.8). In Washington County the sex ratio for the older population registered at an even higher level (124.5).

Increasingly complicated population dynamics account for the 1920 figures. By that date urbanization across the state had begun to draw young, unmarried women searching for jobs away from rural areas. At the same time, the growth of Sterling, Akron, and other towns tended to lower composite sex ratios because populations of males and females in urban settings generally remain more evenly divided than in rural areas.[9] But if we focus on the data from 1890 to 1910, the implication remains that family groups were most prominent among the earliest settlers. Later immigrations had higher proportions of single men. This disproportionate increase in white males arose from several causes. The departure of families during hard times in the 1890s began changes that became more pronounced in the early twentieth century. Jobs in the sugar beet industry, dam construction, and in farm labor attracted many unattached men from distant places. Homesteading opportunities drew many others. In fact, family narrative histories show a doubling in the percentage of single male homestead entrants after 1900 (Table 2.10).

Family histories also shed light on the ages of single males and females at the time they entered claims, and in the case of women, on their marital histories as well. Single male homesteaders were generally young. Eighty-seven percent were between the ages of twenty-one and twenty-nine. The age distribution for women entrants presents a similar pattern, despite the many references to widows in homesteaders' reminiscences. A close reading of family histories reveals that the great majority of women entrants were young, and most of them had never married before they homesteaded. Eighty-eight percent of women entrants were between the ages of twenty-one and twenty-nine, and about 78 percent of women entrants were spinsters[10] (Tables 2.11 and 2.12).

The percent distribution by age of married homesteaders peaked in the twenty- to twenty-nine-year-old group, with one exception (Table 2.13). The exception occurred in the period before 1900 when most husbands' ages ranged from thirty to thirty-nine. A much greater spread in age characterized married homesteaders than single women and men. The median age of husbands who entered claims before 1900 was forty. Wives' median age was thirty.[11] Husbands on claims entered after 1900 had a median age of thirty-eight; wives had a median age of thirty-one. Men's ages approached those James Malin found for male settlers on the dry lands of Kansas, where medians ranged over time from forty to forty-four years. The median ages of Kansas women, thirty-seven to thirty-nine years, were

Table 2.11. Age at Which Homesteaders Entered Claims[a]

Age Cohort	Men		Women	
	N	%	N	%
21–29	60	87.0	22	88.0
30–39	3	4.3	1	4.0
40–49	2	2.9	0	0.0
50–59	3	4.3	1	4.0
60–69	1	1.4	0	0.0
70–79	0	0.0	1	4.0
Total	69	99.9	25	100.0

Source: Family histories.
[a]Ten men and three women entered claims before 1900.

Table 2.12. Marital Status of Women Homestead Entrants[a]

	N	%
Widows	7	18.9
Spinsters	29	78.4
Divorcees	1	2.7
Total	37	100.0

Source: Family histories.
[a]Only seven of the thirty-seven women entrants entered claims before 1900. The total sample of women entrants is higher here than in Table 2.11 because the family histories identified marital status more often than age.

notably higher than those of their counterparts on Colorado's eastern plains.[12]

Like women settlers in other areas, homesteading wives on Colorado's grasslands followed contemporary eastern marriage patterns. Generally, they did not enter into early unions. True, more women married at a very young age than did men, but the median age for wives at their first marriage was twenty-one. Husbands' median age was twenty-five, dropping to just over twenty-four after 1900 (Table 2.14). These ages ranged slightly lower than those reported for Dakota Territory's population in 1885, where the median age for women at first marriage was 21.7 and the median age for men was 26.4. Both the Colorado and the Dakota data approximate contemporary statistics for the country as a whole.[13]

Typically, married homesteaders had started families before they settled on claims. Before homesteading with their husbands, wives aged

Table 2.13. Age at Which Married Homesteaders Entered Claims

	Husbands[a]		Wives[b]	
	N	%	N	%
Age Cohort	Claims Entered Before 1900			
15–19	0	0.0	3	8.8
20–29	12	28.6	15	44.1
30–39	14	33.3	6	17.6
40–49	9	21.4	6	17.6
50–59	6	14.3	3	8.8
60–69	1	2.4	1	2.9
Total	42	100.0	34	99.8
	Claims Entered After 1900			
15–19	0	0.0	5	6.3
20–29	39	39.8	36	45.6
30–39	26	26.5	20	25.3
40–49	15	15.3	12	15.2
50–59	15	15.3	5	6.3
60–69	3	3.1	1	1.3
Total	98	100.0	79	100.0

Source: Family histories.
[a]Median age of husbands for claims entered before 1900 was 40.0; for claims entered after 1900, 38.0.
[b]Median age of wives for claims entered before 1900 was 30.0; for claims entered after 1900, 31.0.

twenty to twenty-nine had borne, on average, 1.9 children. Wives between the ages of thirty and forty had borne 3.3 children; between forty and fifty, 5.2 children. Among the sample of very young wives, none had any children (Table 2.15). The narratives suggest that completed fertilities of wives on homesteads claimed after 1900 were higher than those of contemporary, rural, American-born white women in the north central states — the region from which most homesteaders had emigrated. Twentieth-century homesteading wives each bore on the average a total of 4.78 live children. Midwestern wives with the highest fertilities (4.12 children per woman) were twenty-eight years old between 1894 and 1903. Midwestern women who reached this "approximate mean age of childbearing" at a later date bore progressively fewer children. The data further suggest that wives on homesteads claimed *before* 1900 had marginally *lower* fertilities than wives in the Midwest. Every wife who homesteaded in Logan or Washington county prior to 1900 bore, on average, 4.84 children. Her midwestern counterpart bore 5.04 to 5.24 children[14] (Tables 2.16 and 2.17).

Table 2.14. Homesteaders' Age at First Marriage

| | Wed Before 1900 | | Wed After 1900 | |
	Men	Women	Men	Women
Average age	25.1	20.8	24.5	20.7
		21.0		
Median age	25.0		24.3	21.0
Number	51	36	24	21

Source: Family histories.

Table 2.15. Children Born to Homesteading Wives Before Homestead Entry[a]

Wives' Age Cohort (at time of entry)	N Wives	N Children	N (Children)/ N (Wives)
15–19	10	0	0.0
20–29	33	63	1.9
30–39	24	79	3.3
40–49	18	94	5.2
Total	85	236	

Source: Family histories.
[a]Twenty-seven wives homesteaded with their husbands before 1900; fifty-eight homesteaded after 1900.

Table 2.16. Completed Fertilities of Homesteading Wives[a]

N Wives	N Children	N (Children)/N (Wives)
Claims Entered Before 1900		
89	431	4.84
Claims Entered After 1900		
126	602	4.78

Source: Family histories.
[a]Wives were of childbearing age (forty-five and under) when they homesteaded.

Table 2.17. Completed Fertilities, as Reported in the Censuses of 1910 and
1940, for White, American-Born Farm Women in the North Central States[a]

Age Cohorts	Women Aged 28 Between:[b]	Percent Childless	Children Ever Born/1,000 Women Ever Married	Children Ever Born/1,000 Mothers
(in 1940)				
445–49	1919–1923	14.8	3,684	4,077
50–54	1914–1918	15.9	3,749	4,172
55–64	1904–1913	15.7	3,886	4,325
65–74	1894–1903	14.6	4,121	4,497
(in 1910)				
45–49	1889–1893	10.8	5,040	5,355
50–54	1884–1888	10.5	5,239	5,574

Source: U.S. Bureau of the Census, *Sixteenth Census of the United States: 1940, Population, Differential Fertility: 1940
and 1910, Women by Number of Children Ever Born* (Washington, D.C.: GPO, 1942), 126, 134.
[a]North Dakota, South Dakota, Nebraska, Kansas, Minnesota, Iowa, Missouri, Illinois, Michigan, Indiana, and Ohio.
[b]Twenty-eight is "the approximate mean age of child-bearing." Donald J. Bogue, *The Population of the United States*
(Glencoe, Ill.: Free Press, 1959), 298.

Table 2.18. Percent Distribution of Homesteading Wives,
by the Number of Children They Ever Bore[a]

Number of Children	Claims Entered Before 1900		Claims Entered After 1900	
	N	%	N	%
None	0	0.0	3	2.4
1	8	9.0	8	6.3
2	7	7.9	17	13.5
3	13	14.6	13	10.3
4	16	18.0	17	13.5
5 or 6	22	24.7	40	31.7
7 to 9	20	22.5	23	18.3
10 or more	3	3.4	5	4.0
Total	89	100.1	126	100.0

Source: Family histories.
[a]Wives were of childbearing age (forty-five and younger) when they homesteaded.

We could conclude from these data that the fertilities of wives on northeastern Colorado homesteads remained almost constant before and after 1900, while the fertilities of wives on farms in the north central states dropped over the same period. But the fertility statistics extracted from the family histories probably reflect significant omissions from the historical record. The likelihood is high that the reminiscences overrepresent large families: The more children born, the greater the chance that at least one remained to record the family saga. Hard evidence supports this supposition. The number of childless women in the reminiscences is very low: only 3 out of 215 wives, or 1.4 percent. In contrast, the percentages of childless women in the federal census groupings from 1884 to 1923 range from 10.5 to 15.9 (Tables 2.17 and 2.18). Moreover, the percentages of homesteading wives having five or more children are high: 50.6 percent on entries made before 1900 and 54.0 percent on twentieth-century claims (Table 2.18). Federal census data for *all* women show only the earliest birth cohorts (that is, women who reached their twenty-eighth birthday in the years between 1863 and 1887) having as high a percentage with five or more children. Among the cohort of women aged twenty-eight between 1918 and 1922, only 23 percent had such large families.[15]

The overrepresentation of large families in homesteading narratives implies that the fertilities of twentieth-century homesteading wives may not have differed significantly from those of rural women in the north central states. This overrepresentation also implies that nineteenth-century homesteading wives bore substantially *fewer* children than their contemporary north central sisters. In light of studies showing elevated fertilities among women settlers,[16] a lowered birth rate within northeastern Colorado's nineteenth century homesteading population is somewhat puzzling. Couples may have wanted to avoid the burden of taking care of infants during the process of early settlement. Perhaps they lacked privacy for lovemaking. I can only speculate that one-room soddies and a terrain that harbored no shadows conspired against physical intimacy. Husbands who worked away from home at wage-paying jobs, or a high rate of miscarriages, could have produced similar results. Information on miscarriages, however, is almost entirely lacking.

Fertility rates had an enormous impact on homesteading wives for a variety of reasons. Older children could help with the chores, but young children placed a substantial drain on their mothers' energies. Living in a confined space with no running water or other conveniences increased the work of women with infants and toddlers. Nonetheless, the evidence is unclear whether the burden of child care was greater for mothers on homesteads than for women living in settled rural areas farther east. Certainly during the initial phase of settlement, child care presented difficult problems. But as the standard of living on homesteads improved with time, domestic chores may not have required significantly more effort than they did on farms in more "civilized" parts of the country.

Illness and accidents could add staggering physical and emotional demands to the routine burdens of child care. The narrative record contains many anecdotes of childhood injuries and disease. Parents agonized over children suffering and dying from measles, diphtheria, smallpox, and typhoid fever. A daughter in one homesteading family recalled that two of her brothers came down with polio and three contracted rheumatic fever. "The usual family upsets," she said. But others testified to the good health their families and neighbors enjoyed. Glen Durrell, who grew up on a homestead in Lincoln County between 1908 and 1916, remembered "no deaths in the community and I can recall no serious illnesses. Accidents, too, were rare and usually not severe." In the face of such conflicting anecdotal evidence, only a close reading of the family histories can reveal the extent of illness and injuries among homesteaders' children.[17]

If we use mortality as the measure, the cumulative evidence from family narratives indicates that children on northeastern Colorado homesteads really were relatively healthy. Of 431 children born to wives who homesteaded before 1900, 47, or 10.9 percent, died before reaching the age of eighteen. Among a sample of 602 children born to wives homesteading after 1900, 46, or 7.6 percent, died before their eighteenth birthdays (Table 2.19). These figures compare favorably with statistics in The United States Life Tables for both rural and urban populations around 1901 and 1910. The lowest percentage of deaths among white children up to the age of eighteen occurred among rural females in 1910. Mortality for this group reached 14.4 percent. Urban youths suffered the highest rate of fatalities: 26.2 percent of boys living in cities at the turn of the century did not survive to their eighteenth birthday.[18]

The impact of children's deaths is difficult to measure, but such losses surely affected the whole homesteading community. Among 89 mothers on nineteenth-century homesteads, about 37 percent experienced the loss of one or more children. Mothers on homesteads claimed after 1900 were more fortunate. Among 123 mothers, 26 percent lost at least one child (Table 2.20). When about two-fifths to one-quarter of parents suffered the death of a child, many more in the community shared the grief. Ties of kinship or friendship linked most homesteaders with bereaved families, and those parents who managed to raise all their children to maturity did not

Table 2.19. Survival Rates of Children Born to Homesteading Wives

	Claims Entered Before 1900		Claims Entered After 1900	
	N	%	N	%
Children surviving to 18	384	89.1	556	92.4
Children deceased before 18	47	10.9	46	7.6
Total	431	100.0	602	100.0

Source: Family histories.

Table 2.20. Homesteading Wives Who Experienced a Child's Death[a]

	Claims Entered Before 1900		Claims Entered After 1900	
	N	%	N	%
Mothers losing 1 or more children	33	37.1	32	26.0
Mothers whose children all survived to age 18	56	62.9	91	74.0
Total	89	100.0	123	100.0

Source: Family histories.
[a]Mothers were of childbearing age (forty-five and younger) when they homesteaded. Deaths occurred before, during, and after homesteading.

entirely escape the traumas that such losses created. Nonetheless, the reverse of these statistics remains an important positive fact: three-fifths to three-quarters of homesteading mothers and fathers did not have to endure the grief of losing one of their own young children.

Relatively low childhood mortality complemented a low reported incidence of maternal deaths. Only 2 of 110 homesteading women whose deaths appeared in the family histories died following childbirth or of causes probably related to childbearing (Tables 2.21 and 2.22). On the basis of 1,033 children born live to homesteading mothers (Table 2.16), the maternal death rate (deaths per 10,000 live births) was 19.4. By comparison, the death rate for all white mothers in the United States in 1915 was 60.1.[19] Family histories probably do not reflect the actual extent of deaths due to childbirth. No doubt many families faced with the loss of a mother moved away, leaving no one to relate their story. Still, we can reasonably conclude that the death rate from maternity for homesteading women did not exceed

Table 2.21. Age at Death of Homesteaders Living on Homesteads
Claimed *Before* 1900

Age Cohort at Death	Women[a]		Men	
	N	%	N	%
20–29	0	0.0	0	0.0
30–39	1	2.7	3	6.0
40–49	1	2.7	1	2.0
50–59	5	13.5	7	14.0
60–69	4	10.8	10	20.0
70–79	12	32.4	9	18.0
80–89	11	29.7	12	24.0
90–99	3	8.1	7	14.0
100 and over	0	0.0	1	2.0
Total	37	99.9	50	100.0

Source: Family histories.
[a]"Women" includes both entrants and homesteading wives.

Table 2.22. Age at Death of Homesteaders Living on Homesteads Claimed
After 1900

Age Cohort at Death	Women[a]		Men	
	N	%	N	%
20–29	2[b]	2.7	1	1.1
30–39	2[c]	2.7	2	2.1
40–49	3	4.1	4	4.2
50–59	8	11.0	7	7.4
60–69	12	16.4	19	20.0
70–79	13	17.8	22	23.2
80 and over[d]	33	45.2	40	42.1
Total	73	99.9	95	100.1

Source: Family histories.
[a]"Women" includes both entrants and homesteading wives.
[b]One death followed childbirth.
[c]One death may have resulted from childbearing. The woman was the mother of eleven children.
[d]Seven women and four men were still living when their family histories were recorded.

the rate for other white, American-born mothers, and it may have been much lower.

Mortality statistics for all adult homesteaders also indicate a low death rate. But the same reservation that pertains to maternal mortality applies to these figures; that is, the death of a spouse of either sex might have caused a family to move and subsequently disappear from the historical record. The family histories may well overrepresent homesteaders of both sexes who lived a long time. Calculations based on samples of 37 women and 50 men (aged twenty and over) who lived on homesteads claimed before 1900 show that about 38 percent of the women and 40 percent of the men survived beyond the age of eighty. Among 73 women and 95 men on homesteads claimed after 1900, about 45 percent of the women and 42 percent of the men lived past their eightieth year (Tables 2.21 and 2.22).

Comparative data are difficult to evaluate because of the dramatic drop in death rates generally in the twentieth century. But "selected life table values" from 1919 to 1967 for white males and females from ages twenty to sixty-five indicate that only females aged sixty-five in 1967 had an "average expectation of life" exceeding eighty years. The lowest expectancy, 65.6 years, was for males aged twenty between 1919 and 1921.[20] Measured against these standards, homesteaders on Colorado's grasslands racked up a respectable record for longevity. And if that record was skewed in favor of long-time survivors, at least we have no reason to believe that homesteading was a particularly life-threatening occupation or one that affected the longevities of women and men to significantly different degrees.

Low mortality rates coupled with the probable low incidence of divorce imply both stability and long duration of marriages and family units. Many homesteaders rejected divorce as unthinkable. Sometimes families and "entire communities entered a pact of silence" when a marriage dissolved. In one case, the children of a later union remained unaware for years that a parent had been married previously. Some husbands and wives separated but never formally dissolved their marriages and remarried only when the estranged spouse died.[21] Such practices undoubtedly account for my failure to find more than two divorces and one separation among the hundreds of family narratives I reviewed.[22] But if divorce and separation were subjects that many chose to bury in silence, that choice in itself has significance. Loyalty to marriage vows and family cohesion were ideals worth maintaining, even at the cost of some subterfuge. Religious and social teachings upheld these values, while the economy of farms, based on the contributions of all family members, underscored their importance. The loss of a spouse through marital discord might have had the same outcome as a loss through death: the end of the farming operation and perhaps removal to some distant, even urban, location.

For a homesteading wife, divorce and separation were options of last resort. Or perhaps they were not options at all but impositions forced on her by a husband's decision to leave. If faced with the need to support herself and possibly a number of children without the economic advantage of a man's labor, a woman's task was indeed difficult. Her husband, too, might think twice about ending a marriage if he intended to continue farming. His wife's labor as well as the labor of the older children often made the difference between a bare subsistence and modest comfort. But acknowledging the economic ties that bound wives and husbands together should not mislead us into concluding that marriage was a form of endurance contest. Homesteaders' stories describe many unions where wives and husbands regarded each other with affection and loyalty. Certainly, we cannot quantify the quality of married and family life, but we can say, based on statistical evidence, that homesteaders lived a long time and that they stayed married to the same person. Both conditions contributed to stable families.

In the numbers relating to homesteaders' families and personal histories, nothing indicates that homesteading in northeastern Colorado placed overwhelming burdens on settlers. Homesteading did require adjustments in farming skills, but it presented comparatively few risks to lives and marriages. In light of these circumstances, both women and men measured their success not against mere survival but rather against economic prosperity. Some homesteaders made money by selling their unpatented claims as relinquishments. Such transactions could become quite lucrative for those who claimed and sold one quarter section after another. As long as the entrant neither received a patent nor claimed more than one homestead at a time, she or he could file an unlimited number of claims. Indeed, "relinquishment" is a common designation in the tract book records. But we have no way of knowing, in most cases, how much relinquishers received for their claims. Some certainly profited; others did not.

Given the uncertainties, we cannot reliably measure success by counting cash returns. But we can measure another kind of economic success by counting the number of homestead patents issued relative to the number of individuals who entered claims. Of course, the long-term value of patents varied considerably depending on land prices and the total number of years a family or individual either directly made a living off the land or received income from renting the use of the land to someone else. The sale of a claim could net thousands of dollars during the boom years or virtually nothing during the worst years of the farm depression in the late 1920s and early 1930s. Many depression-era farmers had no choice but to forfeit their land as payment on defaulted bank loans. But such unhappy outcomes had no place in the hopes and dreams of homesteaders, who valued the receipt of a patent as a tangible asset. We, too, can count patents as real property, even if the eventual value of some patents disappointed their owners.

Using samples of 1,425 and 2,030 homestead entrants whose claims appear in the tract book records for Logan and Washington counties, I calculated the patent rates for women and men before and after 1900. In nineteenth-century Washington County, 45 percent of the women claimants and slightly over 46 percent of the men received patents. In Logan County the percentages were higher: Over 51 percent of the women and 55 percent of the men succeeded in patenting land. After the turn of the century, women entrants in Logan County actually fared a little better than the men, with success rates of 54.4 percent compared with 52.0 percent. In Logan County the portion of claimants receiving patents remained relatively static over time. But in Washington County entrants achieved a considerably higher patent rate after 1900 than before. Fifty-five percent of women claimants and over 58 percent of men in the later period patented their claims (Tables 2.23 and 2.24). Compared with a national patent rate of about 50 percent, only Washington County homesteaders before 1900 had a lower rate. Otherwise, homesteaders in Washington and Logan counties exceeded the national average for the percentage of claimants who received deeds to government land.[23]

Women and men succeeded about equally in patenting their claims. This balance reflects the overwhelming presence of families in homesteading settlements. Family members helped each other, rendering the receipt of a patent a reward not just for the efforts of an individual but for the cooperative labor of a whole family. Still, a patent and the use of the land it covered counted as a material asset of the individual woman or man whose name it carried. Clearly, many women as well as men enjoyed this distinction. Many more women (and many men, too) benefited secondhand from patents they helped relatives acquire. These secondhand beneficiaries enjoyed the use of land not actually their own, and they shared in the status attached to landownership. Many settlers had spent their whole working lives as renters, as had their parents and grandparents before them. For these homesteaders, a government patent marked their family's rise out of the laboring and lower-middle classes and into the ranks of the landed middle class.

Table 2.23. Logan County Homestead Entrants and Patentees:
Their Percent Distribution by Gender

	N (Entrants)	N (Patentees)	% Successful
		Claims Entered Before 1900	
Female	37	19	51.4
Male	276	152	55.1
		Claims Entered After 1900	
Female	195	106[a]	54.4
Male	917	477	52.0

Source: Federal land records.
[a]In addition to these women, eleven female heirs patented claims entered by males who died before proving up. Because only those heirs who patented land appeared in the records, I could not count the total number of deceased entrants or the total number of women heirs.

Table 2.24. Washington County Homestead Entrants and Patentees:
Their Percent Distribution by Gender

	N (Entrants)	N (Patentees)	% Successful
		Claims Entered Before 1900	
Female	60	27[a]	45.0
Male	557	258	46.3
		Claims Entered After 1990	
Female	249	137[b]	55.0
Male	1,164	679	58.3

Source: Federal land records.
[a]In addition to these women, sixteen widows and female heirs patented claims entered by men who died before proving up.
[b] In addition to these women, sixteen widows and female heirs patented claims entered by men who died before proving up.

When we consider the patent data and the numbers extracted from family histories together, we find many more bright than somber strokes in the picture of homesteading on Colorado's grasslands. Vital statistics relating to marriage, divorce, separation, fertility, and mortality sketch the outlines of individual longevity for both sexes and the long-term stability of families. Homesteaders' occupational and residential backgrounds show that previous work and living experiences provided useful patterns for settling Colorado's high plains. The tract book records supplemented by manuscript census returns redraw the stereotyped image of homesteading as a landowning opportunity exploited almost exclusively by males. The documents reveal instead a landscape filled with homesteads whose claimants included a significant proportion of women. To the personal stories and anecdotes that follow, these numbers add a depth and perspective that might otherwise elude us.

3

At Home on the Plains

June 1910 arrived in Vermillion, South Dakota, and with it the letter that Ruth Schooley had been anxiously awaiting. The soddy was finished, Orrin wrote, and he was ready to make her his bride. During the following weeks as Ruth busied herself with preparations for leaving, she pondered her decision. Was she making a mistake giving up a good teaching job for an uncertain future on a homestead? Ruth's misgivings persisted as she rode the train to Sterling, Colorado. She wondered what Orrin's sod house would look like. "Watching out the window of the coach, seeing the lonely little homesteader shacks built here and there, I grew more and more unsure of my own feelings. Why did people come out to the flat monotonous land to live?"[1] Eleven more days passed after Orrin met her at the Sterling depot, and still Ruth hesitated. Should she stay or not? In the end, her attachment to Orrin and the shared dream of owning their own farm prevailed. On July 7, 1910, Ruth Schooley became Mrs. Orrin Hall. Her life as a homesteader began.

Ruth's decision to homestead rested on motives common to many settlers. First, as a married woman, she would follow her husband. If he wanted to homestead, she would homestead, too. But Ruth also wanted a farm that she and Orrin could call their own. Owning a farm offered a degree of security and a level of respectability for which many couples were willing to work and sacrifice.

Other settlers homesteaded in Colorado for different reasons. Perhaps they had suffered a personal crisis: a job gone sour or the death of a child. Many of the earliest white residents of the South Platte valley, immigrants from Mississippi and Alabama, were looking for physical and psychological distance from the scenes of the recent war. Still others came for their health. The dry Colorado climate offered relief from malaria, rheumatism, asthma, and tuberculosis. Some invalids, in fact, did make remarkable recoveries; the most dramatic being those of sufferers who arrived on stretchers and within a week or two were walking unassisted. They and their families needed no further inducements to stay.[2] But of all the motives attracting settlers to northeastern Colorado, the most compelling was simply the desire to own land.

Free government homesteads and cheap land sometimes available from the railroads or as homestead relinquishments lured tenant farmers living in the settled areas to the east. Many renters, chronically in debt and short of cash, regarded the opportunity to homestead in Colorado as their only hope for patenting land. Other farmers who already owned farms in the Midwest did not have enough land, or money, to set up their sons on midwestern farms. These landed farmers sometimes temporarily rented out the home place and came to Colorado in order to claim land for their sons. Another group of landed midwestern farmers moved to Colorado in the illusory hope of finding better land. With 20/20 hindsight, we can only feel a sense of loss for some of these speculators, like the Nelson family who sold their Illinois farm in 1890 for fifty dollars an acre and settled on a relinquishment near Fleming. How they must have regretted selling that rich Illinois farmland when the dry years of 1893 and 1894 left them struggling to make ends meet.[3]

Still another category of settlers viewed homesteading as a form of insurance. The Nolan family in Washington County returned to Boone, Iowa, almost immediately after proving up their claim, never to occupy their homestead again. Yet the land, according to one of the Nolan daughters, remained in the family for decades, a "cherished Colorado possession, with President Woodrow Wilson's signature on the final papers" — as much symbolic as "real" estate.[4]

In Colorado, as in other areas of homesteading settlement, many entrants — heads of families and single women and men — had no intention of staying after they proved up their claims. But unlike the Nolan family, who kept the title to their land, they planned to sell out as soon as possible. Relinquishment (selling one's right to an unpatented homestead) was even more desirable, because the entrant did not have to go to the trouble and expense of establishing ownership, yet still retained the right to make another homestead entry elsewhere. Speculation of this sort contributed to the impermanence of towns like Abbott in Washington County, where only a small collection of stores marked the townsite in the 1880s. The land speculations of the town's "residents" required them to live on their claims while they commuted to their businesses in town.[5]

A significant number of settlers entered claims to enlarge a family farming operation. Widows figured prominently in this group. In fact, probably most widows who immigrated with their married children's families claimed homesteads for this reason. Younger widows with small or half-grown children usually homesteaded in order to support their families, hoping either to sell out at a profit or to develop a farm as the children matured and could assume more of the work.[6]

Many young spinsters and young single men also homesteaded as part of a larger family enterprise. We should not consider these daughters and sons as mere pawns of the older generation, however. In general, this younger generation of homesteaders profited from the proving up experience in ways that were both material and intangible, and consequently they contributed willingly to the family fortunes. Rarely, a parent did resort to some coercion, as the story of one dutiful young man illustrates. He came to Washington County only at the insistence of his father. The older man had claimed a half section, which he relinquished to the son despite the young man's feelings that the country was "desolate" and "not for me."[7]

Probably the majority of young single women and men found the prospect of proving up a claim attractive, because homesteading fulfilled needs felt by maturing adults of both sexes.[8] For a male it marked the beginning of independence from parental supervision — a period of preparation for the approaching responsibilities of marriage and fatherhood. The receipt of a patent, even if in connection with a larger family operation, not only increased a young man's "net worth," it bestowed the prestige associated with landownership. Homesteading, moreover, offered adventure in the excitement of new challenges confronted in "wild" surroundings. The novel experience of living alone or in the company of a friend or sibling provided the opportunity to reflect and plan for a lifetime of hard work and commitment as a respectable family man.

For a single young woman, homesteading met similar needs, needs that in other settings often went unmet. Typically, a young woman of the middle class (including many a young farm woman) moved out of her father's house only when she became another man's wife. Homesteading offered an alternative pattern: a period of independence before marriage, a distancing from parental authority, and an adventure before settling down. But underlying gender differences did distinguish the roles homesteading played in young entrants' lives. Some women homesteaded for the purpose of finding a husband. One who admitted as much was Effie Mae Garrabrant, who filed a claim outside Akron in order to be near an attractive bachelor. After her marriage in 1914, she made no further effort to prove up. In later life she regretted this failure, believing it was "poor business to let a farm go just to get married."[9] Other women were already engaged when they entered a claim. Anna Weir homesteaded a quarter section adjacent to her fiancé's claim just two months before their wedding. As a married couple, they doubled their holdings.[10]

Young women who taught school while proving up a homestead claim followed a common pattern for their age and gender. Most of these claimant teachers made a self-conscious choice to exploit the economic opportunity homesteading offered. No teaching job provided much more than basic support, but landownership represented a "nest egg" that could finance future enterprises. Lucy Bigler Wilson, who taught in a rural school, recorded how she got the idea to file a claim: "While here in this community I saw that everybody lived on the free land, and I thought 'Why can't I have some, too?' " Lucy's brother helped her locate and homesteaded with her.[11]

Sometimes one woman teacher received encouragement from another. Amy Dickensen Worthley recalled meeting a young teacher who urged her to take advantage of her homestead rights. Amy eventually did just that, claiming 320 acres next to her parents' ranch. Together with her brother's and sister's claims, their homesteads extended the family's grazing land by one and a half sections. Amy continued to teach in Sterling while she proved up, spending the nights on her claim. In later years she acknowledged the role the family's need for pasture had played in her homesteading venture. But she also placed a high value on homesteading as an "experience" (her word) and as an opportunity to acquire property. After Amy's marriage, she and her husband moved to Syracuse, New York, where Amy became president of the local chapter of the National Woman's Party. Amy looked back on campaigning for the NWP and on proving up a homestead claim as complementary activities: the one political, the other economic, and both advancing the cause of equal rights for women.[12]

When families and single women and men made the decision to homestead, they signed up, in effect, for an extended course in problem solving. Moving from a former home, locating a claim site, building a house, finding fuel, and assuring a food supply were some of the practical needs requiring immediate attention. The weather inevitably contributed additional difficulties. Newcomers struggled to adapt to the plains environment and relied on each other for material and moral support. Ultimately, the success or failure of homesteading enterprises depended on the assistance of family and friends, the state of the economy, and such intangibles as attitude and the ability to acquire new skills.

In anticipation of the journey to the claim, homesteaders had first to assemble food, clothing, furniture, farm animals, and equipment. If the journey was short, as it was for the homesteading children of established settlers, the job of moving demanded no extensive preparations. But if settlers immigrated from some distant place, then the move clearly required more planning. Families usually organized various aspects of relocating along gender lines. Men took responsibility for farm stock and machinery; women, for food and clothing. Husbands and wives together decided what furniture to take, keeping in mind how much freight a wagon or a railway boxcar could accommodate.

Over the years women changed the kinds of goods they prepared for the journey. Only the earliest women settlers spun and wove cloth to take with them to the claim. Georgia L. McRoberts, herself a "pioneer" ranch woman, described how her mother had readied the family for the long move from Mississippi to the South Platte valley in 1876. "Mother dried bushel after bushel of fruit and sweet corn; got cotton and wool which she carded, then spun; dyed and wove yard after yard of sheets, bed spreads, dress goods and even 'jeans' for men's pants. My mother also took all of the old clothing and made it into rag carpets; cured a lot of pork and brought that along."[13]

Later accounts hardly mention clothing. Merchants sold yard goods in Greeley even in the 1870s. By the turn of the century, ready-made garments, as well as all sorts of other merchandise, were readily available at local stores. "At the LeRoy Store you could buy lumber, nails, groceries, clothing and about anything else that was needed, just name it," according to an early resident.[14] Women still fashioned and sewed apparel, but preparing clothing for the trip west was no longer the same kind of major undertaking that Georgia McRoberts's mother faced.

McRoberts's mother had also cured meat to take to Colorado. Traveling from Mississippi to Julesburg by train, the family did not eat much during the few days of the journey itself. Rather they needed food to tide them over the days and weeks following their arrival. In 1876 newcomers could not count on finding supplies to buy or borrow. Only after rail services extended into the South Platte valley in the early 1880s did the need to include preserved food diminish. But just because merchants in Akron, Sterling, LeRoy, and other towns had staples to sell, immigrants did not necessarily have money to spend. Most travelers brought along one or more cows and some chickens as a guarantee of milk, eggs, and perhaps a little meat on arrival.

Women immigrating in family groups by covered wagon had a fairly elaborate larder to supervise, regardless of the year they arrived. An account of this aspect of the journey detailed the food consumed by two generations of the Jones family as they moved from Missouri to a claim southwest of Akron in 1887. During the three-week-long trip, the family lived off its provisions of ham, bacon, potatoes, apples, sauerkraut, and dried corn. Stores of cornmeal and flour allowed the Jones women to bake frequent batches of biscuits, pancakes, and corn bread. Crates of chickens tied to the underside of two wagons supplied fresh eggs, and two cows provided milk. The family made butter from cream churned by the motion of the wagon.[15]

Immigrating by railroad clearly lightened the burden of preparation for women but, to some extent, had the opposite effect for men. With an entire "immigrant" boxcar reserved for freight, men brought much more in the way of farm and household goods than a wagon could accommodate. The load typically included the wagon itself, a team of horses, cows, chickens, a breaking plow, a harrow, a tent (for temporary shelter), a shotgun, some tools, and perhaps a few "extras" like a buggy or a supply of lumber. One man, with the help of three grown sons, brought along "several tons of bailed hay."[16] Traveling by train took only a fraction of the time and involved less labor in transit compared with the journey by covered wagon. Considered together, these advantages compensated men for the additional problems of planning and loading — but only, of course, if they could afford the freight charges.

Many, if not most, families (it is impossible to say just how large a portion) immigrated by covered wagon to avoid paying transportation costs. The journey was not easy. Overloading caused breakdowns, and valuable animals might die or wander off. But the difficulties of this move cannot compare with those experienced along the Overland Trail by earlier generations, who might have spent six months in transit. Farm families all along the way befriended the immigrants, filling their water barrels, sharing meals with them, offering overnight shelter, and inviting travelers to spend time in their homes. Ben and Pearl McIntyre, with their baby Mabel, moved from Nebraska to a homestead southwest of Haxtun in 1907. After traveling all day, they stopped at a farmhouse to see if they could water their horses and buy milk for the baby. One of the McIntyre children later recorded Ben and Pearl's memory of the encounter. "The lady had just baked bread and when Ben went after the milk she gave him a loaf of bread. As they finished eating supper the husband came down to the wagon and brought Ben and his family a nice dish of strawberries and cream." Nellie M. Snee also remarked on the "kind and friendly farmers" her parents met

Wes Plank homesteaded with his wife, Mary, near Fleming in 1908. In the spring of 1918, he posed next to his team, Buster and Bill, hitched to a covered wagon similar to those used by many other homesteaders. *Courtesy of William Plank, Sr., Fleming.*

when they traveled by wagon from Missouri in 1887. "They enjoyed each mile of their trip," she concluded, with perhaps some exaggeration.[17]

Some unknown fraction of homesteaders did not have to undertake a major cross-country move to their claim sites for the simple reason that they were already living nearby. Approximately two-thirds of homesteaders entering claims after 1900 gave Colorado addresses when they recorded their entries.[18] Most were local (Akron and Sterling, for example), but Denver, Colorado Springs, and Loveland addresses also appear in the land records. In part, these local entrants represented persons who had lived nearby for some period of time. Often they were the sons and daughters of earlier homesteaders. Many others were recent immigrants who had already registered with a local post office.

Among the first decisions facing prospective homesteaders was the location of a claim site. Clearly, those who intended to enlarge established family farms and ranches had limited choices. Other homesteaders searched for locations that satisfied emotional as well as practical needs. Settlers considered the proximity of cash-paying jobs and schools, and the suitability of the claim for the purpose intended — grazing or cultivation. But the nearness of family and friends also weighed heavily in their decisions. The land records contain numerous examples of a half dozen or more individuals with the same last name, presumably all members of one family, entering adjacent claims. Similar groupings of friends are more difficult to trace but probably occurred just as frequently. Missouri Valley, south and east of Akron, got its name from the concentration of Missourians who settled there.[19] Elsewhere ethnic enclaves developed, sometimes with the help of locators who settled together people with like national and cultural identities.[20]

Some would-be entrants made an independent search for just the right location; that is, one that looked like home. George Young, who emigrated from Illinois, found such a claim site in Washington County. Rejecting apparently desirable land along the Burlington route (although he had come out on a railroad pass provided by the company to prospective settlers), he finally settled on a quarter section near Arickaree. His daughter-in-law explained that "George was born and grew up on the Illinois prairies and the place he had decided to make his new home closely resembled those Illinois plains." One Ohio man spent the summer of 1883 traveling west in search of the perfect location. David Laybourn kept a record of his impressions in a small notebook. Of Illinois he wrote, "It is too flat." Nebraska fared no better: "Did not like the country," he noted. But Laybourn saved his most stinging comments for Iowa: "Worried beyond endurance with bugs. Horrors! Whew! Ugh!"[21]

David Laybourn finally settled his family on a homestead near Cope. According to his daughter, "There was a big lagoon on it and the [land] agent told him it was a lake and would have fish in it. Also the grass was so lush and green from the rains that year [1887] that he really thought he was locating in the garden spot of Colorado." Much to Laybourn's chagrin the water soon dried up, and the family ever after referred to this seasonal water hole as "Father's Lake." At least Laybourn's mistake remained a joke within the family. Another less fortunate neophyte became the laughing-stock of the entire community when his neighbors learned he had shipped out a stump puller and hauled it to his claim.[22]

If a few settlers held unrealistic expectations about farming on the plains, most of them, even in the early years, understood that Colorado's grasslands presented fundamentally different conditions from a prairie environment.[23] Immigrants from western Kansas and Nebraska already possessed what was essentially firsthand knowledge of Colorado's high plains. And they were familiar with one of the grassland's most noticeable features: the scarcity of trees.

In one respect, a treeless expanse made settlement easier because farmers did not have to clear their land before plowing. But the lack of trees also denied all but the most affluent the option of frame housing. Only settlers with ready cash could afford to buy lumber shipped out on the railroads. For newcomers like R. W. and Mary Plank, who as newlyweds came to Colorado with twenty-seven cents in cash, or like John Frese and his thirteen-year-old son, Willie, who arrived in 1914 with only a dime, buying lumber was out of the question. Some settlers cut timber at the "cedars," or "breaks," north of Limon and also in the canyons northwest of Sterling and in the vicinity of Deertrail. Further west, in the foothills of the mountains, they could find a virtually unlimited supply. But harvesting lumber exacted a heavy price in labor and often required the use of a wagon and team for many days.[24] Consequently, settlers used even this "free" lumber sparingly: for doors, for support timbers, for window and door frames, and occasionally — if the builders felt extravagant — for a plank floor. Otherwise, sod construction characterized settlement in north-eastern Colorado, just as it had on the plains of Kansas and Nebraska. (Indeed, long before white settlement, plains Indians had built sod houses.) Less often, homesteaders used adobe bricks or limestone as building materials. A few even built cement houses using blocks manu-factured by enterprising settlers who had shipped out special "cement block machines."[25]

Houses and their furnishings varied both in kind and in quality depending on the location and on the financial resources and skills of the settlers. These variations are important because they determined to a large extent the livability of dwellings, which in turn colored homesteaders' perceptions of their entire homesteading venture. Women, whose training and expectations directed them to a domestic role, placed a high value on attractive and comfortable homes. By closely examining homesteaders' houses, we can better appreciate both the challenges of housekeeping and the creativity women employed in making themselves and their families feel "at home" on the plains.

Settlers often learned the craft of sod house construction from their more experienced neighbors. Unfortunately, not all neighbors were adept teachers, nor did all newly arrived settlers prove themselves adept students. But skilled builders knew that creating a livable sod house began with the crucial job of cutting sods. The sod breaker hitched one or more draft animals to a plow with its edge sharpened to cut through the tough range

This cement shack built around 1890 on a site eleven miles east of Akron still stands today. A succession of newlywed couples lived here, giving rise to the name "Honeymoon Shack." *Courtesy of the Washington County Museum, Akron.*

grasses. Ruth Hall described how her husband and a neighbor struggled to cut sods for the Halls' first house. "Harry, ever the kind benefactor, came with his team of horses to help Orrin break that prairie sod. And 'breaking' is the proper word for the fight it was to drag a plow through those centuries-old tangles of buffalo grass roots which reached down toward China. The roots fought the plow every inch of the way and the horses strained and tugged to drag it along."[26]

Those grass roots presented a tough challenge to plows and horse-power. But without the roots' tangled mats, the sod bricks lacked sufficient internal structure to hold them together. The sods, in fact, crumbled if not cut in the spring after the rains had stimulated root growth. The bricks typically measured two to three feet long and one to two feet wide. Homesteaders laid them just like conventional bricks, assuring strength and stability by placing the vertical joints of adjacent sods in the middle of sods laid above and below.[27]

Another critical moment in sod house construction arrived when the builders decided how they would roof over the four sod walls. A few homesteaders had the good fortune to scavenge ready-made covers. A favorite resource was the lids from discarded railroad boxcars. But in the event they could not find such a treasure, homesteaders had to construct

Ruth and Orrin Hall with their daughter Vivien in front of the Halls' soddy. *Courtesy of Vivien Warren, Fleming.*

their roofs from scratch. A woman who homesteaded with her husband and children in 1907 described the steps for constructing a "good" sod roof — that is, one that did not leak. First, the builders laid boards on the tops of the sod walls. Next, they laid joists between facing walls and covered them over at right angles with more boards. To the top side of the roof planking they secured tar paper. Finally, they laid sods overall. A less substantial roof was sure to cause serious trouble, raining down muddy water or, worse, collapsing altogether. One inexperienced couple suffered the consequences when they simply "tacked heavy building paper on the cross-beams above for a ceiling." During a blizzard, snow drifted onto the roof. Mary Wright recalled, "Soon after the fire was started in the morning we heard drip, drip, drip, here and there in different parts of the room. We put pans and dishes around to catch that drip. Finally, the paper broke in places and down came piles of snow."[28]

Building a soddy was indeed an art. If improperly constructed and finished, a sod house could be a miserable place to live: lopsided, leaking, and infested with bedbugs, fleas, snakes, and rats, to name just a few of the more common vermin. One settler reported sitting up several nights in a row, shooting rats to keep them from biting his children. On the other

A sod house could last a long time. Photographed in the 1930s, this soddy was built in the early 1900s. *Courtesy of the Colorado Historical Society, Denver, F#5083.*

The same sod house in the 1960s, plastered and painted. *Courtesy of the Colorado Historical Society, Denver, F#5084.*

A substantial sod house built in 1909, sixteen miles south of Akron; the home of Mr. and Mrs. Wesley Cherry and family. *Courtesy of the Washington County Museum, Akron.*

hand, we have the testimony of a woman homesteader that a soddy could be "as nice a home as one could want."[29] Everything depended on the skills and know-how of the builders.

By using sods of equal thickness, homesteaders greatly enhanced the appearance and durability of sod houses. The sods could not be too wet lest the weight of water cause too much settling. Some moisture was desirable, however, and for that reason a good time for cutting sods was the end of May. By then the rains had stimulated root growth, but the ground was no longer waterlogged. Protected by a good roof, well-built sod walls could last many years.[30]

A basic level of living comfort depended on other construction details as well. If, for example, the builder located the entry door on any side but the east, it might drift shut during a blizzard. Along with an east-facing entry, many of the better sod houses also had wood floors. Wood planking made a house look more homey, and it reduced dust. But flooring was costly, and probably most sod houses had dirt floors. Women often hid a dirt floor by putting down straw and overlaying the whole with a rag carpet. If left uncovered, a dirt floor became as "hard as a brick" and required little care other than sprinkling to keep the dust down.[31]

Many homesteaders discovered belatedly that without plastered walls they could not keep wildlife from burrowing into their houses or dirt from

Members of the Ed Davis family, including their dog, in front of the family's dugout. *Courtesy of the Overland Trail Museum, Sterling.*

crumbling off exposed sods. Locally available materials provided the makings for plaster. Yet homesteaders often covered their walls with paper in the mistaken belief that layers of newspaper glued together with flour and water would provide an adequate substitute. Ruth and Orrin Hall used pink building paper, holding it in place with strips of lathing nailed to the sods. "This made the room much lighter and more inviting," but neither this nor any paper could stop the intrusion of bugs, snakes, and rodents.[32]

Homesteaders made plaster from a paste of clay and water. Many were fortunate in living near clay deposits containing "magnesia," a whitening compound that improved the interior appearance of a soddy considerably. The addition of a few geraniums in the windows and some furnishings created a bright and cheerful effect. One woman remembered a neighbor's soddy as a "wonderful place to visit . . . so clean and comfortable." Another remarked, "Anyone who has lived in this kind of house knows they can be fixed up to be very nice. . . . When finished up inside and out, you'd never know they were made of sod."[33]

The positive testimony of these women notwithstanding, the sod house suffered from what today we might label an "image problem." Homesteaders generally thought of the soddy as an improvement over a "dugout," a cavelike dwelling excavated out of the side of a hill or embankment. Many

The Calvin Cheairs' palatial frame house built of lumber freighted to Sterling in the 1870s. *Courtesy of the Colorado Historical Society, Denver, F#5882.*

would have reacted in the same manner as Clara Watson, who came to Washington County in 1915 and remembered being "a little disappointed at the thought of a sod house until after I saw a dugout." But Clara, like probably most other homesteaders, really preferred a frame house.[34]

Frame houses reminded settlers of their former homes. They represented orderly, prosperous, and civilized living. Wood construction, moreover, was expensive and symbolized a level of comfort and respectability to which nearly all aspired. In reality, few wood houses on the plains could inspire much envy, but the occasional substantial frame house served to enhance their symbolic power. The Cheairs family built one of the first such houses in the 1870s. For a while the family lived in a shack constructed of lumber hauled from Greeley, nearly a week's drive away. But the Cheairs had arrived with money, and they could afford something better. They soon built a new home that by homesteaders' standards was palatial: a one-and-a-half-story frame dwelling with two bedrooms upstairs, two downstairs, and a dining room and kitchen.[35]

Wood houses had serious drawbacks. Susceptible to fires, they also lacked the insulating qualities of sod, which kept soddies warm in the winter and cool in the summer. Some homesteaders added insulation by combining adobe with frame construction. The Cheairs lined the inside of their house with "adobe-mud brick for warmth." Another family used sod in a similar fashion, stacking it around their twelve-by-sixteen-foot frame shack "to make it warmer." The added insulation also had the advantage

The ruins of a homesteader's shack north of Sterling showing a combination of frame construction and sod insulation. The photograph dates from about 1930. *Courtesy of the Overland Trail Museum, Sterling.*

of providing ballast, for unless frame houses were large and well constructed on stable foundations, the wind might blow them away. William Little tried to compensate for the flimsy construction of the Littles' frame shack by nailing boards to the corners. "Each member of the family held on to a corner to anchor their home when the high winds came."[36]

Clearly, preference for wood over sod construction included an irrational component. We should recognize, however, that frame shacks did have advantages. Homesteaders could build them quickly, using skills with which they were often already familiar. During the summer months, shacks could provide adequate shelter for minimal effort. And homesteaders could transport shacks to new locations, or even recycle the lumber used for their construction in later houses.

Some settlers who did not have the money to build a frame house also lived in areas lacking sod. Homesteaders with claims in the "sandhills" of Washington County often found themselves in this predicament. One family arriving in 1913 solved their housing problem, at least temporarily, by erecting a frame of cement and lumber and covering it with tar paper. They constructed a barn out of bales of straw and thistles. Homesteaders in areas with clay deposits sometimes mixed straw and clay to make adobe bricks. Adobe provided insulating qualities similar to sod without its many potential problems. In areas around Fleming and Cope, settlers quarried

Hugh and Bettie Davis with their children, Lizzie and Avah, in front of their sod house near Merino in 1888–1889. The Davises used buffalo hides to cover their barn, visible to the right of the house in this photograph. *Courtesy of the Overland Trail Museum, Sterling.*

limestone from nearby outcroppings to build homes, barns, and other structures. Stone dwellings were substantial and attractive, particularly when their owners plastered and whitewashed the interior walls. The homesteaders who lived in these houses were proud of them.[37]

The job of construction usually belonged to men, but when the labor of males fell short of the need, wives pitched in and worked alongside their husbands. Neighbors commonly assembled for "sod bees," and while the men plowed and laid sods, children played and women prepared food and visited. When a single woman needed a house, she could usually call on family and friends for help. Otherwise, she might hire a man, or men, to construct a frame shack. Lois Ervin, a young schoolteacher who home-steaded in 1914, paid Mr. Plank $200 to build a fifteen-by-twenty-foot shack on her claim site.[38]

As a general rule, men also made any furniture in addition to what a family purchased or moved to the homestead. Furnishings were practical, spartan by modern standards, but adequate for homesteaders' needs. Typi-cally, they included a table, a "commode" or closet, cabinets (perhaps fashioned from orange crates or soap boxes), a few chairs or grocery boxes to sit on, a "topsy" or two-hole sheepherder's stove for heating and cooking, one or two kerosene lamps, and at least one wooden or iron bedstead. Some homesteaders had beds that folded away to conserve space when not in use. Straw ticks made "excellent" mattresses, according to one settler, although the filling crumbled and required replacement from time to time. With the addition of down- and feather-filled bed covers, homesteaders slept in warmth and comfort.[39]

Women assumed responsibility for such items as bedding, curtains, and kitchenware. One bride's list of cooking and serving pieces is representative: "an iron tea kettle, pots, skillets, bone-handled knives and forks, and a few dishes." China was a luxury that only a few women had the opportunity to enjoy. Instead, many women served meals on tin pie plates and used tin cans as cups. Women made curtains to conceal storage areas, and if a rug covered the floor, it too was likely to be women's handiwork. Neighboring women sometimes met at "sewing bees" to sew rags for the hostess. Woven into yard-wide strips, rag carpets brightened many settlers' homes.[40]

If somehow we could travel back in time and visit homesteaders' houses, we might be surprised to find an occasional piano or organ wedged into a soddy's cramped interior. In almost every case, its player was a woman.[41] As a centerpiece for family and neighborhood gatherings, a piano or organ served to reinforce a woman's social and domestic role. Whether a wife or a spinster living alone on her claim, a woman who could create music demonstrated a particularly feminine refinement by giving pleasure to her family and neighbors. But hauling a large object like a piano to a homestead required considerable effort and expense. Whereas a spinster might hire someone for the job, a wife usually depended on her husband for that service. Clearly, men enjoyed, as did women, gathering around for an evening's songfest. Yet the presence of a piano or an organ on a homestead represented more than shared entertainment. It stood as a symbol of middle-class ideals upholding domestic felicity and woman's central place within the home.

We could also conclude that these instruments served another symbolic function. As objects of more than middling value, they distinguished "respectable," middle-class homesteaders from those whose meager possessions suggested a laboring or working-class background. Indeed, we could draw the same conclusion from other luxuries among homesteaders' material possessions; for instance, china dishes, wood floors, or the Cheairs's two-story frame house.

In their writings, homesteaders never acknowledged what we would call "class distinctions" among themselves. Wealth measured by ownership of a piano, a substantial house, or any luxury may have inspired admiration or jealousy, but it did not bestow a guarantee of social superiority on certain homesteaders at the expense of their neighbors. Poorer settlers maintained a strong belief in their own upward mobility, what one woman homesteader called "sweet hope."[42] Under these circumstances, a wealthier neighbor did not loom as an object of class envy but as a role model for what others might attain. Poorer and wealthier settlers alike recognized their vulnerability to all sorts of misfortunes. At worst, a few bad years could leave everyone equally destitute. But even in good years, neighbors needed each other's help and company. They preferred to ignore real or potential class differences among themselves and to think of their communities as extended families. In the words of a homesteader characterizing her neighbors who settled near the town of Haxtun, "We were One Big Family."[43]

Homesteaders in northeastern Colorado found no great barriers to establishing bonds with their neighbors. Most of them came from similar backgrounds as white, American-born farmers who ranked neither among the most well-to-do nor among the poorest in their former communities. In their new role as self-employed landholding homesteaders, all qualified as members of the middle class. Most homesteaders, moreover, shared middle-class values (a topic I will pursue further in Chapter 4). In time, the sharing of work, meals, entertainments, religious services, births, deaths, and even children (as hired hands and domestic servants) erased most acknowledged distinctions between homesteaders. An early resident of Logan County probably spoke for the majority in his community when he wrote, "We were mostly all for one and one for all."[44]

Occasionally, local observers revealed tensions between settlers and the residents of towns. Anna Jane Sailor was thirteen years old in 1916 when her family moved from their homestead to a house in Fleming. She remembered the teasing she endured from her schoolmates. "I did not enjoy going to school in Fleming because the town kids made fun of kids coming in from the country." Mamie Northcott Couch lived with her family in Akron where her father worked as a banker. She hinted at the somewhat patronizing attitude of townspeople toward settlers in her account of an interview her mother conducted with a country girl for a job as a domestic. The girl "said she couldn't cook or sew or keep house and when mother asked her what she could do she said she could herd sheep. She was hired anyway and proved to be a good worker."[45]

The leading citizens of the larger towns, particularly Akron and Sterling, lived in ways that much more closely resembled upper-middle-class life in the urban Midwest and East than country life on Colorado's grasslands. Vivian Sutton Yeamans recounted the social activities her parents-in-law attended in nineteenth-century Akron:

These were the days of ice cream socials; "at homes," where each lady had her regular day of the week to "receive"; swank parties to which printed invitations were extended, such as the First Grand Ball of the Olivette Dancing Club, on December 11, 1888; . . . and the "Grand Ball and Banquet to be given under the auspices of the Akron Social Hour Club at the Palace Skating Rink, March 15, 1888." The ladies also vied with each other in raising flowers and lovely gardens. During that period the railroad made a practice of uncoupling the dining car and leaving it on a side track at Akron, rather than [taking] it into Denver. It was a social practice for the ladies of the town to have Tea there in the afternoon, taking advantage of the luxurious appointments of the diner.[46]

No doubt some homesteaders would have felt uncomfortable and unwelcome in the social circles Vivian Yeamans described. But we would be mistaken to assume that some great divide separated town from country. Settlers often moved to a nearby town to avoid spending the winter on a claim. They also stayed in town for extended periods working at cash-paying jobs or putting their children through high school. And if they did not participate in fancy dress balls or "at homes," neither did many townspeople. On the other hand, town leaders did not live in isolation. Mr. Yeamans himself had many dealings with homesteaders through his hardware and pump supply business. Organizations like the Women's Christian Temperance Union were active among both homesteaders and townspeople and drew members from all social classes.[47] Yes, class distinctions colored relationships in town *and* country, but those distinctions most often divided town elites from everybody else. Homesteaders' self-interest put a high premium on mutual assistance and upward economic mobility. Among themselves, they chose largely to ignore any links between social status and material wealth. Considering the relatively narrow range in the value of their housing, furnishings, and other possessions, homesteaders had little reason to respond otherwise.

Practical use rather than a desire to impress the neighbors guided the choices the majority of homesteaders made when they invested their time and resources. Most homesteads, for example, included a number of outbuildings to meet a variety of specific needs. Ranking high on most settlers' lists of essentials was a private "comfort station." In Ruth Hall's opinion, an outhouse "was necessary as on those prairies there were no tall corn fields to hide in and no bushes to squat behind." Her wood frame privy held up one end of the clothesline; the other end attached to a corner of her soddy. The line served double duty by tethering the privy in strong winds.[48]

The majority of homesteaders built a barn, though some settlers (usually European immigrants) simply divided their houses, reserving half for living space and turning the rest over to the stock. This arrangement required a high tolerance for odors, but for taking care of animals during bad weather its convenience overcame many objections. A henhouse, like a barn, numbered among the usual homestead landmarks because married women generally kept chickens to feed their families and to earn a little "egg money" on the side. Ollie Barden kept her hens in the piano box she had used to ship her things to Logan County. Later on the Bardens replaced the piano box with a more conventional henhouse "built of limestone rocks picked up on the prairie." Some homesteads also included a dugout cellar in which settlers stored food and ice and occasionally hid from violent storms. A few homesteaders, like blacksmiths and other artisans, added a small shop where they practiced a trade.[49]

The considerable ingenuity homesteaders displayed in building houses and other structures from the materials that lay at hand was also evident in their efforts to establish a reliable and varied food supply. Women, whose training for domestic duties included gardening, cooking, and seeing to the welfare of their families, had a special interest in food and its preparation. But to feed their families a diverse and occasionally even a sumptuous cuisine, women first had to adapt their gardening to the high plains environment and learn to overcome the often difficult circumstances of food preparation.

In the initial period of getting settled on the claim, before a garden or field crops started producing, few homesteaders enjoyed much variation in their diets. Missouri Propst, who emigrated from Alabama in 1874, wrote home shortly after arriving in Colorado of her cooking routine: "I have a fairly good cook stove and equipment, and we have no great variety to cook — buffalo meat and bread, bread and buffalo meat, pudding now and then to keep from forgetting how such things taste. Some times though I sigh for the 'Flesh Pots of Egypt.' "[50] Within a few years, wild buffalo had virtually disappeared, and later settlers harvested other game: jackrabbits, a few cottontail rabbits, prairie chickens, and an occasional antelope. One young woman homesteader killed a prairie dog, but in attempting to dress the meat, she found the flea-ridden carcass so unappetizing she threw it out. Others, according to a man whose father entered a claim in 1885, "had all the fresh meat we could eat" from livestock killed or crippled by the trains. This son of homesteaders claimed (no doubt with exaggeration) that the railroad men, of whom his father was one, spent "most of their time skinning long horn cattle."[51]

Missouri Propst immigrated to the South Platte valley from Alabama in 1874. She confessed that the monotonous diet of bread and buffalo meat made her "sigh for the 'Flesh Pots of Egypt.' " *Courtesy of the Overland Trail Museum, Sterling.*

Newly arrived settlers frequently had to buy or barter for staples in neighboring towns. In the 1870s "local" markets included such distant points as Greeley and Sidney, Nebraska. With the arrival of the railroads in the 1880s, many new trading centers appeared where settlers could more conveniently find such nonperishables as flour, cornmeal, oatmeal, rice, sugar, salt, coffee, and crackers. Stores also carried dried fruit, canned tomatoes, and canned corn, but these items rarely found a place in newcomers' budgets. After the turn of the century, pinto beans gained in popularity as a reliable crop. Some homesteaders lived almost entirely on a diet of beans, jackrabbits, and perhaps milk and eggs. Others ate more potatoes, sometimes digging them "on shares" (that is, for a share of the crop) near Greeley and in irrigated areas closer to home. One couple who homesteaded in 1910 ate potatoes and bread supplemented with rice, dried beans, and dried corn during their first winter on the claim. Their menu improved in the spring as egg and milk production increased.[52]

During the drought years of the nineties, homesteaders found little relief from a tedious and vitamin-poor diet. But in years of normal rainfall, the limited variety of food endured by newcomers gave way to an increasingly complex cuisine as crops matured, farm animals multiplied, and gardens and other kinds of farming endeavors came into production. Nate and Eva Andrews, who settled southwest of Akron, undertook one of the more ambitious homestead operations when they constructed a reservoir on their land and "kept it well supplied with fish." Other enterprising families established orchards. One Washington County homestead produced plums, pears, apricots, currants, cherries, and gooseberries; another grew cherries, plums, gooseberries, and mulberries. But these are uncommon examples. Few homesteaders dined on fish, and most settlers consumed little in the way of fruit other than the dried apricots, prunes, peaches, and apples they might buy in town. The only fresh fruits widely available were sand cherries and a kind of wild plum that grew in some areas.[53]

Families typically irrigated their gardens by hauling water from a nearby well or creek. These gardens yielded many kinds of produce, including potatoes (both white and sweet), tomatoes, lettuce, peas, beans, cabbage, turnips, cucumbers, sweet corn, popcorn, watermelons, muskmelons, pumpkins, squash, and even peanuts. Homesteaders stored or preserved much of their garden "stuff." They made sauerkraut out of cabbage and turnips; they pickled cucumbers, and dried and ground corn into meal for corn bread and cornmeal mush. But given the need to eat preserved food during much of the year, homesteaders particularly enjoyed their vegetables and melons fresh. Some women, impatient for their gardens to begin producing, delighted in gathering wild dandelions and lamb's-quarters when they "grew luscious and tempting in the spring."[54]

Corn remained the principal field crop until well into the 1910s and only gradually lost ground to wheat, oats, and barley. Homesteaders reserved a portion of most field grains for their own consumption, including barley, which they sometimes roasted and used as a coffee substitute. The remaining grain usually ended up as livestock feed. After 1900 wheat production soared with the introduction of dryland farming techniques. The railroads gave farmers ready access to distant markets, and wheat assumed importance as a cash crop. Homesteaders themselves began consuming more wheat flour, gradually replacing the corn bread in their diets with finer-grained wheat breads and cakes. Molasses syrup made from locally grown and processed sorghum cane sweetened these and other baked goods. Homesteaders spread the syrup on bread and pancakes and used it to make popcorn balls.[55]

Homesteaders continued to eat game, but as their farm animals increased in number, they began to butcher their domestic stock more regularly. Fried chicken remained the most popular main dish for a "company" meal. Homesteaders also prepared and smoked their own hams and bacon. Fresh beef, as well as dried, appeared regularly on some tables. Besides those homesteaders who benefited from the kills along the railroad tracks, some settlers formed informal cooperatives with the members taking turns contributing a steer and dividing the carcass equitably among themselves. In the absence of refrigeration, this arrangement allowed neighbors to enjoy fresh beef more frequently. A woman who participated in a cooperative thought "it really worked out nice and was so good to have fresh meat."[56]

Eggs, milk, and milk products made up an important part of some homesteaders' diets. A minority of settlers made cheese. More commonly they separated the milk, churned the cream into butter, and fed the skim to pigs and calves. For special occasions like the Fourth of July, a few homesteaders made ice cream, freezing the confection with ice bought in town or stored in their cellars during the winter. But the usual summer desserts were, according to Ruth Hall, "some kinds of cream pies most likely as we had lots of milk and eggs."[57]

Settlers could learn to eat well and live in modest comfort, but only if they had enough water for domestic use and a garden. And having sufficient water, more often than not, required major investments in labor or money or both. Homesteaders seemed to suffer from a version of Murphy's Law that virtually guaranteed some inconvenient distance would separate their houses from the water supply. Women, men, and children hauled water. If from town, they paid about forty cents a barrel. If from a neighbor's well, they paid about ten cents a barrel. Or they might have the water for free but accompanied by an obligation to reciprocate with some other favor. Many obtained their water supply from a not-too-distant creek. One family spent their Sundays collecting four barrels of water from a sand creek by digging six to ten feet down through the creek bed and dipping out the water with a pail. They carefully covered the filled barrels with cloths held on by barrel hoops to reduce splashing as the wagon bumped and swayed on the return trip. Under these conditions it comes as no surprise that well diggers did a booming business among homesteaders — as did water witches. Many settlers, in fact, attributed a successful well to

After a year of hauling water from a neighbor's well, the Planks developed their own water supply and located the house and barn nearby. The windmill pumped water into a cistern covered by the well house. The cream separator was kept in the well house during the summer months to take advantage of the cooler temperatures. *Courtesy of William Plank, Sr., Fleming.*

A water wagon served as a platform on which the Price children posed for their picture in 1905. *Courtesy of the Washington County Museum, Akron.*

the uncanny ability of a witch to locate water through the twitchings of a forked stick.[58]

Water obtained at so great an expenditure of effort was precious. And women, who required water for many household chores, used and reused it sparingly. One housewife saved her baby's bath water to wash clothes. She used the dirty wash water to scrub the floor and carefully poured any remaining water around the family's only tree. Understandably, another woman cried when her clothesline broke and the wet laundry fell to the ground. Not only did she have to rewash the clothes but first she had to haul more water.[59]

Taking a bath, like washing clothes, required planning and effort. Homesteaders carried water by the bucket from a cistern or storage barrels near the house to a container on the stove. A washtub set up near the stove doubled as the bathtub. Men sometimes had the option of going to a town barbershop where, for twenty-five cents, they could find bathing facilities provided for patrons. But women might have to wait many years before taking a bath in a "real tub." Ruth Hall related her own experience. "My first bath taken in a real bath tub was in our very own home built on the homestead many years later — in the house we built [in 1918] after the soddy. This was the first modern house, with a bath, hot and cold running water, which was built out in that neighborhood of homesteaders." In the eight years since Ruth had joined Orrin on the claim, the Halls had achieved much: a substantial frame house; but more than that — good quality well water pumped by a windmill and piped into their home. "Running water!" Ruth exclaimed. "No one who had not carried water for years can really appreciate what that means to a housewife."[60]

An easier problem to solve than the scarcity of water was the lack of conventional fuels. From the earliest days of westering on the plains, immigrants had learned to find substitutes for wood. Colorado homesteaders were only following a long-standing tradition by exploiting the most readily available of those substitutes, buffalo or cow "chips." Harvesting "prairie coal" typically employed all but the youngest members of a family. But according to Zella Wrape Payne, "Sometimes a group of people would gather chips together, making *almost* [Payne's emphasis] a 'social event' of it."[61]

Informal rules governed chip gathering, and homesteaders and ranchers alike considered certain areas their rightful collecting grounds. Such conventions, and the natural scattering of fuel as cattle wandered the plains, led some homesteaders to seek ingenious solutions to their gathering problems. Walter Greenwood had used all the chips near his shack when he saw cowboys driving a herd of cattle in his direction. He ran to get his camera, and as the drovers drew near, he asked their permission to take some photographs. Between taking pictures and engaging the cowboys in conversation, he prolonged their stay about an hour — long enough to have his winter fuel supply deposited within easy collecting range. The cowboys never knew that Greenwood had no film in his camera.[62]

Cow chips were an inefficient fuel. They burned quickly — two large washtubs-full lasted only through one winter's evening with a few chips remaining to start up a fire the next day. Cow chips also left a large residue of ash, creating the never-ending job of "carrying out the ashes." Greenwood himself partially solved the problem by harvesting the hard-packed droppings left behind by sheep camps. Cut in five-inch slabs, they burned hotter than cow chips. A few settlers burned animal fuels more efficiently by using "trash burners." A daughter of a family homesteading at the turn of the century remembered that "in the morning, a big iron pot with two handles was lifted off a frame and carried outside where trash [corn cobs, manure, and other waste] from the barn yard was packed tight into this big pot. A well packed pot would burn 24 hours and gave lots of heat."[63]

Apart from the practical problems connected with burning cow chips, some homesteaders — usually, but not always, women — found the very idea of handling and burning them objectionable. A particularly fastidious middle-aged woman from Iowa never touched one without first putting on gloves. A younger couple from Missouri shared her disgust. They were "horrified and speechless" when they discovered that a neighbor was burning cow chips. Out of necessity they soon learned to do likewise, but they hid the chips out of sight in a cave near their house. One day their young daughter retrieved a "huge" specimen to show some visitors, who were greatly entertained when her parents "nearly collapsed with embarassment [sic]." Regaining their composure, the visitors assured the couple that they also burned cow chips. "After that, we breathed easier," the wife wrote, expressing relief that she and her husband no longer had to fear their neighbors' disapproval.[64]

Most people, regardless of age or gender, quickly grew accustomed to using "prairie coal" and had little feeling of revulsion toward it. True, gathering chips presented occasional hazards. Rattlesnakes sometimes curled up underneath them, presumably to take advantage of the warmth generated by bacteria in the dung. But cow chips were available and free for the taking, and consequently they remained an important fuel until the end of World War I. During the years of combat, their use even increased among homesteaders as the government diverted coal and oil supplies to the war effort.[65]

Whenever possible, homesteaders used less troublesome fuels. The more affluent bought coal or kerosene in town. Others scavenged coal that had dropped along the railroad tracks or dug their own from natural deposits near Deertrail and at the "breaks" near Limon — the same areas where they gathered wood. Settlers also burned old railroad ties and corn cobs retrieved from the pigpen, using corn stalks as kindling. Inevitably, stores of fuel ran low, and when this happened during a blizzard, homesteaders simply went to bed.[66]

Nearly every winter, at least one life-threatening storm swept across the plains. The big spring blizzards of 1888 and 1913 produced fifteen-foot drifts during several days of wind and snow. Trapped in houses and barns, some people and stock came close to suffocating. A story survives from the 1913 blizzard of a neighbor digging out a woman who lived alone in a shack on her claim. The neighbor found her safe in a clothes closet, where she had huddled to escape the snow that filled the rest of her house. Many settlers told of horses and cattle trampling down snow as it sifted into a shed until the animals' backs pressed against the roof.[67]

Far greater dangers awaited luckless settlers and livestock stranded without shelter during a storm. Cattle, like people, could quickly become disoriented and die of exposure. Horses, on the other hand, saved many a settler's life by their ability to "home" when given a free rein. For a person on foot, even the short trip from the house to the barn could spell disaster, and few homesteaders ventured out without the security of a tether. Some homesteaders avoided this risk by simply bringing their stock into the family dwelling for the storm's duration. It was the suddenness of plains blizzards, catching humans and animals exposed and unprepared, that made them so dangerous. After the turn of the century, as more settlers acquired barometers to warn of approaching bad weather, the hazards diminished to some extent.[68]

Summertime had its own complement of violent weather in the form of tornadoes and hailstorms. Both could devastate individual farms, but they usually affected limited areas. When crops and buildings escaped damage from a hailstorm, many homesteaders counted themselves doubly fortunate and collected the hailstones to make ice cream. But even the victims could find some solace in a shared dish of ice cream. Fosta and Shelby Bricker and their neighbors lost crops and cattle in a "terrific" hailstorm south of Akron. Looking back on that day, Fosta recalled that

> for a few hours the farmers were completely stunned. Too stunned to know what to do or where to turn. But these were strong, sturdy people. And instead of sitting down and feeling sorry for themselves, they got all of the neighbors together and all their ice cream freezers and made ice cream. So by getting together and sharing their plight with their friends and neighbors, their burden did not seem so hard to bear.[69]

Some homesteaders complained of the constant wind. Ruth Burtis's daughter remembered her mother's lament, "Oh the wind — won't the wind stop blowing?" In Edna Sullivan Camp's opinion, "Nowhere in the continent were the winds so persistent": cold in winter and "like blasts from a fiery furnace" in summer. Eventually, most homesteaders got used to it; even Edna Camp convinced herself that at times the wind merely "caressed the land."[70] Perhaps she and other homesteaders underwent a change of heart when their families first installed a windmill. A steady breeze, after all, provided the energy for a wind-driven pump. And although homesteaders might still have to haul their water from the well, at least they did not have to operate a hand pump or a bucket and windlass to get the water out of the ground.

The wind never seemed more menacing than when whipping up a "prairie" fire. Long before people lived on the grasslands, lightning strikes had regularly set fire to large areas of the plains. With the coming of the railroads and permanent settlement, sparks from locomotives and the actions of careless people increased the frequency of these grass fires and created havoc for settlers in their path. Homesteaders plowed strips of bare earth around their houses and outbuildings to act as fire guards, but they could not exclude burning tumbleweed and flying embers. Sod houses provided a degree of protection from fire that wooden ones could not. Still, the sight of distant smoke put fear into everyone's heart. Neighbors turned out en masse to fight a fire, contributing plows, shovels, barrels of water, and gunny sacks used soaking wet to smother the flames. Men worked the fire lines; women donned overalls and ferried barrels of water with teams and wagons. Women also prepared food for the fire fighters. Such episodes caused great hardships when homesteaders lost crops and winter feed for their animals. Until the next growing season replenished their food stores, farmers had to buy the necessary supplies. Long separations disrupted families when husbands and fathers left home in search of cash-paying jobs, while wives and children shouldered heavier work loads on the claim.[71]

Rattlesnakes, like fires, inspired fear among homesteaders. One settler remarked, "We were in constant dread of rattle snakes when we were working or the children out playing." Women, in particular, commented on their experiences with "rattlers" and indicated their initial fright, and later their pride, in learning to deal with them. Some said they always carried a weapon, often a handle from an old hoe or a rake. If they came upon a snake and were unarmed, they marked the spot with a bonnet or apron while they ran to fetch a tool. Women bragged to each other about the size and number of snakes they had dispatched. One even sent a "sizable cardboard box" filled with rattles back to Missouri to impress her parents. "When they [her parents] opened the box and saw the contents they were amazed and decided we were living in a zoo!"[72]

Many settlers also feared coyotes because of their apparent habit of stalking people across the plains. Parents cautioned children to get home from school before dark and sometimes armed them with sticks. Only one settler reported an attack. She claimed that "late one afternoon a drove of coyotes attacked a sheepherder. He was forced to climb a windmill and the poor fellow had to stay there all night." Most homesteaders had no clear evidence on which to base their fears, other than occasional raids on sheep and poultry. Coyotes, like wolves, suffered then as they do now from a long-standing public relations problem. Homesteaders, moreover, may have confused the two species. And though modern animal behaviorists have debunked the reputation of either animal as an indiscriminate killer, homesteaders had only rumor and myth to guide them. For some home-steaders, those who perhaps felt most keenly their isolation from neighbors, the coyotes' nightly howling conjured up terrifying images of savagery and death.[73]

A more likely danger came not from any predator but from the half-wild long-horned cattle that "would attack anyone on foot." Women more often than men recorded bad experiences with range stock. Perhaps men chose to remain silent about their mishaps; or perhaps women's long skirts flapping in the wind aroused the longhorns to belligerence. Jessie Hassig Challis recorded a story of her mother's — a "real thriller," according to Jessie.

> Before there was even a barbed-wire fence around the house, Mother was chased into the house by a wild long horned Texas steer. She ran into the house closing the door behind her. The baby, my brother Frank, was having his nap and Mother was afraid he would awaken and cry. The steer stood with his front feet on the large white rock that was the door step, and Mother was afraid any noise inside would cause the animal to crash thru the door. Father came home and chased the steer away.

As stockgrowers replaced their scrub animals and gradually fenced the range after the turn of the century, reported attacks declined. But for many years some women never went anywhere on foot without carrying a stick and a pan or some other noisemaker to scare away threatening cattle.[74]

Despite the perils of bad weather and venomous or otherwise danger-ous animals, living on the plains had its rewards. Several settlers remarked on the initial absence of flies. A man who homesteaded in 1910 wrote, "We had no flies on the homestead for over a year, but after more settlers came, we had plenty."[75] Other homesteaders commented on the beauty of the landscape, especially in early summer when the wildflowers bloomed. Still, an appreciation for the grassland was an acquired taste. Men as well as women often expressed initial repulsion for what they saw. Ezra Alishouse, who was seventeen when he moved with his family from Indiana to Colorado in 1910, recalled his first impression of their homestead and how barren it looked without any trees. "It was a place that you felt like you wanted to run away from." Nancy Johnson, who arrived with her husband in 1886, related that "many people who homesteaded at that time have told me that they had a dreary time, that there was no place to go and nothing to see." Nancy Johnson, however, disagreed. "I did not find it so. It seemed to me that the long vistas of green prairie were beautiful, and I never tired driving over it to the distant hills that seemed to recede and fade away as we advanced. . . . There were flowers, also, that I used to puzzle over and birds and ponds of water, blue as indigo, and it seemed a beautiful and attractive land to me."[76]

June was the month when Colorado's plains came into full bloom, providing not only a spectacle of color to winter-weary settlers but also the occasion for an annual celebration of youth. Girls and boys gathered baskets of flowers to decorate the schoolhouse and church (often the same building) on the last day of school and on a special Children's Day sponsored by local congregations. The children could choose from many different kinds of blossoms: yucca, wild poppies, black-eyed Susans, blue-bells, violets, wild geraniums, buttercups, moonflowers, sweet peas, and, regrettably, locoweed, a plant poisonous to stock. Some areas specialized in a particular species. Parts of the sandhills glowed "a solid pink" as the wild phlox came into bloom. The pink and yellow blossoms of the prickly pear transfigured Cactus Valley in Washington County, giving the area its name. These yearly displays of nature's beauty and the festivities they inspired remained among the fondest memories of the children who called the grasslands "home."[77]

Children's Day, like other events, drew settlers from miles around. Homesteaders shared a strong desire to socialize, and they did not allow the scattered pattern of land settlement to deter them. Traveling by horseback and all sorts of horse-drawn vehicles — from carts and buck-boards, lumber wagons and spring wagons, to buggies and winter sleighs — settlers overcame the isolation of far-flung homesteads. Some even bought bicycles, peddling as much as seventy miles round-trip from a job in town to visit the family claim on weekends. Many others traveled on foot, for even if they owned a horse, they might wish to spare a valuable animal for essential farm work.[78]

Homesteaders and their children routinely walked many miles to visit friends, to attend school and church, and to buy and sell. Lengthy journeys might place travelers away from home at sundown, but they could usually count on receiving a hospitable reception and food and lodging, even from strangers. One man's experience in 1914 illustrates attitudes and events common to homesteaders in northeastern Colorado from the earliest days of settlement. George Bauer hiked twenty-five miles to buy a team of horses. As he prepared to return, he learned that a grass fire blocked his way. The horse trader, fearing that Bauer might lose his way or fall down an abandoned well, insisted that he stay overnight. The following day, the trader accompanied Bauer part of the way home.[79]

By custom, travelers could also help themselves to food and lodging at homes where the owners were absent. Well-behaved visitors, however, observed a cardinal rule. As one old-timer expressed it, "Be sure to do the dishes and everything was all right. Dishes left dirty and you were in trouble." Such hospitality assured populations of bedbugs and lice at one time or another in nearly every household. But most settlers stoically accepted this fact of pioneer life.[80]

Other acts of mutual aid also bound the community together. Settlers gave help freely and expected help from others. They exchanged labor by helping each other build houses, harvest crops, and preserve food. They assisted each other in caring for the sick, in burying the dead, and in childbirth. When a tornado or a fire destroyed a homestead, neighbors helped rebuild. If a family of newcomers needed food, neighbors provided it. On those occasions when claim jumpers tried to seize homesteads, the community defended its members, sometimes forcing interlopers to leave under the threat of bodily harm.[81] Neighbors joined together to build schools and churches, and they organized dances, suppers, debates, and other entertainments. These activities ultimately served homesteaders' self-interests, given the generally accepted moral obligation to reciprocate for services received. As Chet Kincheloe put it, "We were all on our own and would help each other but if we ran into a dead beat and his family they were soon weeded out for all of us had to carry his own load." Such sentiments notwithstanding, homesteaders expressed a real and generous concern for others, a concern symbolized in the common practice of placing a lamp in the window at night and during storms, "in case some lonely wanderer had got lost."[82]

A woman, who as a girl in 1911 settled on a Washington County claim, summarized her family's homesteading experience this way: "We lived pretty well." Perhaps her parents might have told a different story; possibly time had edited her memory and she remembered only her family's happier moments. Still, this woman's reminiscence presents a point of view seconded in the stories of other settlers who earned the rewards that homesteading could offer: a land patent, modest prosperity, and a sense of pride in achievement.

One who finally experienced those rewards was Ruth Hall. Despite her initial reluctance to join Orrin on the homestead, she gradually gained the satisfaction of knowing that her gamble had paid off. For Ruth, her day of vindication came eight years after she began life as a homesteader, when the Halls moved from their soddy into a modern frame house. Ruth was later to recall the emotions that overcame her on that occasion. "I was so terribly proud of what Orrin and I had accomplished in those eight years on the homestead."[83]

4

At Work and Play

In 1908 Mary Baetge and R. Wesley Plank began their married life on a homestead northwest of Fleming in Logan County. Like the marriages of most homesteaders, theirs was a business partnership as well as a personal commitment between husband and wife. Their children, two sons and a daughter, remembered Mary and Wesley as hard workers. "[Our father's] theory was anything earned by the sweat of your brow was the only way to get ahead. . . . Our mother could keep up with a lot of men when it came time to haul hay, milk cows, build fence and any other homestead job that needed to be done." But the Plank children learned more from their parents than a work ethic; they also learned how to behave toward one another. "Our parents taught us — Honesty is the best policy — Each member of a family is equal — and No rule is better than the Golden Rule."[1]

The Plank children did not explain what their parents meant by "equal." Nor did they elaborate on their mother's feelings about keeping up with men as she engaged in heavy labor around the farm. But what the Plank children did say raises questions about homesteaders' attitudes toward gender, work, and the twin issues of deference and control. What kinds of work did men, women, and children do around the homestead? What jobs did these men, women, and children perform in the community? Did gender define and set limits on work roles? And a final question: What effect did homesteading have on the distribution of decision-making powers between the sexes and between adults and children?

In every historic period, religious leaders, physicians, writers of pre-scriptive literature, and other defenders of the social order have advised women to defer to men. In the nineteenth century, however, the economic conditions underlying female submission underwent a marked change. Whereas men and women had once shared workplaces and cooperated in the performance of many tasks, beginning in the 1820s social arbiters began to talk about the work worlds of women and men as two separate spheres. Women ideally occupied themselves with the moral and practical issues relating to the nurturance of children and the management of the home. To men belonged the duties of providing material support for their families and directing public affairs. As in earlier times, women more than men assumed responsibility for maintaining harmonious relations between the sexes, for in the event of conflict, women were to obey the directives of husbands or fathers.[2]

The notion of separate, gender-defined spheres originated among the urban middle classes in the industrializing Northeast. When workers (mostly men) left home to take wage-earning jobs in the new factories, women gained control of the domestic environment. The separate-spheres ideal arose out of this division between men's and women's work worlds and gave legitimacy to a situation created by the emergence of industrialism. Gradually, this ideal spread to other regions and other classes, eventually becoming the accepted standard by which most Americans measured proper gender relations.

From the available evidence, we know that farm families were slow to adopt the separate-spheres ideal. John Faragher's study of mid-nineteenth-century midwestern migrants on the Overland Trail showed that these agrarians organized themselves along the lines of the preindustrial patriarchy; that is, men dominated women in most areas of their lives.[3] But with the spread of low-cost printing techniques during the latter half of the century, farmers of the middle and lower-middle classes (the owners and renters of medium to small-sized farms) began to receive an intense education in the separate-spheres ideal. Popular magazines, books, and newspapers with a wide circulation through much of rural America carried countless articles and advice columns stressing women's domestic responsibilities as mothers of children and helpmates to husbands. New England–based churches, women's clubs, and reformers repeated the refrain, citing women's central role in the home as essential to health and virtue. The Creator, after all, had made women less sexually passionate than men and, hence, their moral superiors. Thus the very order of society depended on women's restraining influence over men during courtship and later within the family circle.[4]

Understanding the appeal of this message to farm and urban women alike requires little imagination. Women of that era had few choices in life, but through their allotted domestic sphere, they could practice a measure of autonomy and receive the plaudits of ministers, editors, writers, and other social commentators for their virtue and moral leadership. Still, the

separate-spheres ideal encountered a major stumbling block in its acceptance by farm families. For how could rural women confine themselves to
a domestic role when the farm economy might require their labor in the
fields or elsewhere as the need arose? The solution to this dilemma appeared
in farm women's focus on the "helpmate" role. By performing "male" tasks
in the capacity of their husbands' (or fathers') helpers, women could work
outside the domestic sphere and still maintain the integrity of the ideal. In
this manner, rural families assimilated an urban-based model for gender
relations that otherwise clashed with the labor needs of the farm.

Homesteaders in northeastern Colorado, like farmers in other parts
of the nation, heard the gender prescriptions of reformers and the popular
press. Many, if not most, homesteaders were already familiar with the
separate-spheres ideal because of their previous residence in the Midwest
and other localities heavily influenced by New England culture. Homesteaders, moreover, had many contacts with townspeople in Akron, Sterling, and other communities where local architecture, church affiliations,
lodges, clubs, and reading materials all suggested a strong link with eastern
social forms. Some of the same bearers of New England culture in the towns
(for example, the Presbyterian church and the Women's Christian Temperance Union) also organized within communities of homesteaders. Many
settlers, moreover, subscribed to their hometown newspapers and to magazines whose editorial policies promoted and reinforced the separate-spheres
ideal. In addition to the usual farm journals, the *Saturday Evening Post*,
Cosmopolitan, *Harper's Magazine*, and *Redbook* numbered among the peri-
odicals homesteaders read. No doubt many copies received the same
treatment as each issue of *Youths' Companion* that arrived at the Lewis
homestead: "It was read and re-read, and passed on to other families."[5]

Homesteaders' familiarity with the separate-spheres ideal seems clear.
Yet homesteading created extraordinary pressures against a sharp division
of gender roles. Even more than other farmers, homesteaders suffered from
a labor shortage that drew women, and sometimes men, into work outside
their allotted spheres. This same labor shortage created a pattern of child
rearing in which both girls and boys performed work around the homestead
at an early age and often did the same jobs. What is more, children of both
sexes also experienced a great deal of freedom because adults were too busy
to give them close supervision. But perhaps the most important breach in
the separate-spheres ideal originated in the extension of federal land rights
to unmarried women. In granting unmarried women the opportunity to
become landowners and entrepreneurs in their own names, lawmakers

unwittingly subverted the model for gender relations that confined women to the domestic sphere.

The degree of subversion varied with women's inclinations and circumstances. A few women homesteaders sidestepped gender roles by entering claims, singly or in groups of two or three, without family nearby. Freer from the shadow of parental interference than those who claimed homesteads to expand family holdings, these women briefly created a new niche for themselves as independent businesswomen and farmers. But such women were rare and left little trace of their presence. Ernest Lewis mentioned one of them in his reminiscence — "a Miss Annie Turner [who in 1893] took up a claim about a mile west" of his parents' Washington County homestead.

> She had no tools, no money, just determination. It is said that she schooped [sic] a little dug-out shelter from the side of a hill with a tablespoon and a saucer. She was a small, rather frail woman, but she stayed and proved up on her claim, carrying all her water from our well, about a mile away. Once, after a severe snowstorm, Dad and [a neighbor] fought their way through the drifts to see how she fared. They found only a few inches of stovepipe sticking through the snow. If they hadn't come to dig her out, she would almost surely have perished. After she proved up on her claim she left, married and moved to Corpus Christi, Texas.[6]

When Annie Turner married, she presumably entered into a domestic role. No doubt domesticity held many attractions after the hardships of homesteading alone. Still, we might well wonder if Annie Turner's years of independence on her homestead did not affect her relationship with her husband and her attitudes about gender roles. If she had any income from her property, did she control it, and if so, how did she use it? In Annie Turner's case, we simply do not know. Nonetheless, a remarkable story remains, despite Ernest's dubious reference to the tablespoon and saucer. Yes, Annie Turner's neighbors helped her. But unlike most homesteaders, she proved up on her claim without sustained family encouragement and assistance.

Lois Ervin also proved up a homestead, but she left a clearer record of her attitudes and choices. As soon as Lois patented her claim, sometime around 1918, she sold the land to a rancher for sixteen hundred dollars and bought a quarter section adjoining her parents' farm. In 1920 Lois married. Five years later she sold her quarter section for four thousand dollars. More than a decade after this sale, Lois invested her money in a van for her son's moving company. Each of these transactions over a period of twenty years occurred because Lois — not her parents and not her husband — made the decision to buy or sell. Yet on the occasions when Lois invested her money, she used her resources to benefit her family. In the first instance, she enlarged her parents' farm. In the second, she established her son in a business of his own.

Lois Ervin's example would have reassured lawmakers who might have had second thoughts about granting single women federal land rights. Lois did savor the opportunity to make her own economic choices, and she felt a personal pride as a landowner and as a person of means. "I think I thought I was rich," she confided. But when she invested, she did not challenge domesticity or gender roles by using her money "selfishly" on enterprises benefiting herself above her family. In other words, even though homesteading had changed Lois and how she felt about her power and status as a woman, those changes worked more subtly than radically to shape relationships between Lois and the other people in her life.[7]

Similarly, homesteading encouraged subtle rather than extreme alterations in gender roles for settlers generally. And, indeed, some jobs remained strongly associated with one sex or the other. Women, for example, nearly always had the job of dispensing hospitality by feeding and bedding down visitors to the homestead. Most women accepted this chore without complaint and even enjoyed it because of the opportunity to socialize. Vera Stewart Bartlett recalled that "unexpected company was always welcome." Seeing someone approach, "Mother would hurry and catch a fryer, wring its neck, soon having it ready for the skillet." Louise Annable's hospitality extended also to nearby families. "She cooked and carried many a hot meal to lonely neighbors." But some women, expecially those on well-traveled routes, grew tired of acting as community cooks and hotel keepers. After a seemingly endless stream of uninvited guests, Madge Scott Parker finally succeeded in discouraging most of them by posting a sign advertising Meals 25¢.[8]

Women united in providing other services in the community freely and gladly. During childbirth, friends and relatives gave their emotional support and skills as midwives to the expectant mother. Sometimes a woman came days beforehand to help prepare for the birth, and often a neighbor girl stayed with the family to help out for weeks afterward. Occasionally, women had their husbands or a male physician in attendance, but such births were exceptional. Doctors were scarce, and women often preferred the comfort of sharing their confinements with close women friends and relatives. Important, too, were financial considerations.

Mrs. Colburn, who practiced midwifery near Crook, never charged her patients. " 'Be a neighbor' was her motto," according to her granddaughter, Marion Flock Brecht.[9]

Women also tended their communities' sick and injured. Mrs. Colburn practiced midwifery in addition to treating cowboys and others who had broken bones or fallen ill. "She would bring them home and keep them until [their] bones were healed. She set many a broken arm or leg, and treated any sickness — all free, no charge." Women often shared the task of helping a stricken neighbor. When a widow and mother of nine children contracted blood poisoning after stepping on a nail, one neighbor came every day to bathe her foot; another moved in and stayed up nights with her until she recovered.[10] Yet nursing was by no means an exclusively feminine role. Men also served in this capacity, usually — though not always — taking care of other men.

Many men sat up nights with sick or dying neighbors. And like some women, certain men gained reputations for their special medical skills. Martin Skiles, in the words of his daughter, "would sit up with sick people [and] was also called to doctor sick horses and cows."[11] During the 1918 flu epidemic, the need for nurses was so great that all able-bodied persons found themselves in high demand as household after household became incapacitated from the spread of the illness. Ben and Pearl McIntyre together took care of a family for two weeks. When the McIntyres fell ill, their neighbor, a man, cared for them. Percy Crosby, who also nursed flu victims, described the need for his services: "I was 17 years old at this time, and my mother and I were about the only persons within an area of several miles who were not sick. We put in our entire time nursing in the homes of the less fortunate ones. We did not work at the same place as there were too many homes in which nearly all of the family were ill."[12]

Just as men might assume the role of nurse and care giver, women occasionally undertook "male" duties when someone died. Sarah McDonald "quite often conducted funeral services of neighbors" because the community of homesteaders around Fleming lacked a resident minister. Another woman "made coffins . . . buried people, and did everything that could be done, other than preaching the sermon." In the usual course of events following a death, the neighbors (either women or men, depending usually on the gender of the deceased) "laid out and dressed the body." Homesteaders could buy coffins at an early date in Akron and Sterling, but because of the expense, they often did the carpentry themselves. Men built coffins and women lined them with cloth. Mabel Hayes Rudder described her parents' roles in the final illness and death of a neighbor: "His horse fell on

A community gathering sometime after the turn of the century at the White School. The schoolhouse was one of the more imposing sod structures in Washington County. *Courtesy of the Washington County Museum, Akron.*

him and broke his leg. Father and other neighbors sat up with him and did all they could but 'mortification set in' and no one could save his life. Father made his coffin at the workbench by our barn. Mamma tacked in a lining of black calico with a little white flower pattern."[13]

Death did not always unite the community. One unfortunate family had to bury, at night and without assistance, their three children lost to diphtheria. The neighbors stayed away, fearing that they or their children might catch the disease.[14] But when infection did not threaten, deaths even more than births brought homesteaders together. Women and men shared the rituals of preparing the body for burial, while adults and children of all ages marked the occasion with funeral services.

The shared responsibilities of women and men in nursing their neighbors and burying the dead extended to the establishment of schools and churches. Homesteaders typically erected a schoolhouse first, using the building also for church services and neighborhood socials. But the interval between settlement and construction of a school varied considerably, reflecting settlers' different needs and resources. One Washington County community populated largely by Danish bachelors lacked a school for at least ten years after their arrival in the mid-1880s. Yet even in areas settled by families with school-age children, insufficient tax revenues sometimes prevented a district from hiring a teacher.

Homesteaders did not have to pay taxes on their claims until they received a patent, and many avoided taxes for up to seven years by putting off their final proof as long as legally possible. Faced with inadequate revenues, a group of families living near Fleming at the turn of the century assessed themselves $6 a month to establish a school for their children. But most homesteaders could not afford to give their children a privately funded education. Instead, they relied on tax money, which generally provided no more than the minimum needed to operate a school for three months. Some parents tried to make up for short sessions by sending their children to more than one school when the terms occurred at different times of the year.[15]

In neighborhoods without schools, many mothers and fathers tutored their children. Some parents sent their children away for their schooling. Maude and Jim Munday arranged to have their eight-year-old daughter, Grace, stay with another family who lived near the school. Still other parents moved with their school-age sons and daughters. Nellie Snee said of her own and her siblings' education, "When we were ready for school, Dad [and Mother] moved to town." This family never resumed farming, but the Williams family, who went back to Missouri for three years to secure an older son's high school education, did return to their Washington County homestead. Country schools offered only an eighth grade educa- tion, and the minority of teenagers from farms who went to high school had to move to town. Many parents rented a house where their children lived together on their own while attending school. Homesteaders referred to these unsupervised living arrangements as "batching."[16]

After the turn of the century, when the homesteading population (and tax revenues) increased, homesteaders found building schools and hiring teachers somewhat easier. Sometimes settlers pooled their money and bought land for a school. One family, "terribly worried" about their children's education, followed the example of settlers in other districts and donated land. Neighbors worked together to construct a building or refur- bish an abandoned house, donating whatever books and materials they had to offer.[17]

The effort and resources needed to establish a school represented a considerable investment, yet it was one that most homesteaders with children were unwilling to forgo. In one district where a fire destroyed their newly built schoolhouse, parents promptly started construction on a replacement. In this and other actions, parents expressed an unspoken conviction that a civilized and ordered society rested on the three Rs and the discipline of the hickory stick. James Plant recorded incidents from his childhood that illustrate just how highly his parents and uncle valued the schooling of their children.

> School was an important matter to our parents in those days. A child had to show definite proof of illness, such as measles spots, mumps, or the like [to stay home from school]. I remember after going a few days my first year I decided I didn't like it and wouldn't go any more. Mother accompanied me a short way with a hair brush and after that I liked it real good. On another occasion, I believe sister Murliene and [two cousins] had joined us by then, Dad and Uncle Henry shielded us with a lap robe by walking ahead of us and spreading the robe by holding the corners, *during a howling blizzard* [emphasis added].[18]

Religious observance occupied a place of importance similar to education in the lives of many homesteaders. For a number of reasons, however, the construction of churches lagged behind the construction of schools. Again, the presence of families played a determining role. Those same Danish bachelors who lacked an interest in schools held no church services either. The availability of schoolhouses or settlers' homes to double as places of worship was also an important practical consideration. And in a few cases, homesteaders' differing denominational loyalties inhibited them from working together to build a church.[19]

The divisive effects of denominational differences did not last for long. Congregations of homesteaders often had a notably ecumenical makeup. Members of various Protestant sects, and Catholics too, joined together for church and Sunday school. These gatherings served as a kind of glue in the process of community building, uniting many people from diverse religious backgrounds. Even where congregations did exist along denominational lines (most commonly in towns), they often shared resources. In Akron the Presbyterians and Methodists raised money for a church used by both congregations. In Otis the Congregationalists helped the Presbyterians build a church. The men shingled the roof while the women prepared dinner. As one woman remembered, "There was a building of friendship that was never broken." Such shared experiences allowed churchgoers who relocated to transfer their memberships with hardly a qualm. The convenience of attending the nearest church or Sunday school outweighed loyalties to any particular denomination.[20]

A Sunday school gathering at LeRoy in 1885. *Courtesy of the Overland Trail Museum, Sterling.*

Because most congregations of homesteaders could not afford to support their own minister, they took turns with other congregations hosting a circuit preacher. During the minister's absences (the majority of Sundays), religious services centered on classes taught by both women and men. Women typically organized these Sunday schools, but men willingly participated, often walking many miles with their families to attend meetings.[21] The Sundays when a preacher officiated qualified as special occasions. Families on the circuit provided bed and board and generally considered themselves honored by the minister's presence in their homes. But too long a stay with one family could wear out the welcome, for clergymen had a reputation for evading chores around the farm. Children, however, had their own reasons for enjoying the preacher's visit. As the son of one homesteading couple recalled, "We always had the best dinners then."[22]

Whether or not a minister was present, Sunday offered a welcome break from the week's routine. No matter how lonely, dull, or difficult the other six days might be, homesteaders looked forward to Sunday as a time for resting from some kinds of work, for sharing religious feelings, and for visiting with other families. In an era predating competition from automobiles and the ready access they gave to towns and other centers of entertainment, religion provided one of the few settings for regular and frequent socializing. During the middle of the growing season with its temporary lull in farm chores, some families might spend a week together, occasionally even a month, attending revival services. A woman homesteader in Washington County described her family's attendance at a series of summer "camp meetings" this way: "A very enjoyable week was spent camping, with preaching, singing, visiting, and plenty of food." Some congregations also organized ice-cream socials and Fourth of July celebrations; a few opened their church buildings for performances of concerts and plays.[23]

Of all the religious holidays during the year, none inspired more festivities than Christmas. Families sometimes celebrated singly or together with a special supper, featuring such delicacies as oyster stew. But the main social event was a communitywide party held in connection with the school, the Sunday school, the church, and other local institutions. Around 1890 one group of families celebrated in the Lindon town bank and hotel dining room. Unlike most settlers who made do with a Christmas tree of ash or cottonwood, or even a simple framework draped with a sheet, these families had a real evergreen brought from the "cedars" north of Limon. Women decorated the tree with popcorn, colored paper chains, and candles and sewed cheesecloth stockings in which "everyone received a treat." The participants shared dinner in the dining room and enjoyed the evening's entertainments: a man dressed as Santa Claus and a communal songfest that included such local favorites as "Papa's Pants Fit Johnnie Now" and "Put My Little Shoes Away."[24] Other Christmases in other places varied in the details, but the essential feature of these celebrations remained the same: Although women, men, and children had their own parts to play, they celebrated together in a way that increased an easy familiarity with each other and softened the barriers of gender and age.

A relaxed friendliness also characterized homesteaders' other social gatherings. Dances provided the obvious opportunity for young adults to become acquainted with each other. But they also brought together parents, grandparents, and children in an atmosphere of fun and sociability. Because settlers often came from many miles distant over tracks invisible in the dark to any but the most practiced eye, dances typically lasted all night. With the soddy or shack cleared of furniture and the children bedded down in out-of-the-way corners, adults swung their partners to one or more musicians' renditions of "Turkey in the Straw," "Irish Washerwoman," and other tunes. At midnight the hosts served coffee along with cakes and sandwiches supplied by the guests. The partying continued until dawn, when the revelers breakfasted before the drive home.[25]

An Old Settlers picnic at Cope Grove sometime around the turn of the century. *Courtesy of the Washington County Museum, Akron.*

During the summer months, two events diverted homesteaders from their usual routines. The Fourth of July provided the occasion for picnics accompanied by patriotic orations, songs, and readings of the Declaration of Independence. Much of the day's real interest, however, centered on games and foot and pony races. Mary Clark Peterson noted the "excitement and hilarity" inspired by the greased pole competition. "A pole of about six inches in diameter and twelve or fifteen feet long would be liberally greased and set firmly in the ground. Some money would be placed on the top of the pole and the winner took all. Sometimes a small pig was greased and turned loose for the youngsters to catch."[26]

In August annual Old Settlers picnics drew families from miles around to Cope Grove, an old tree claim north of Akron. Pitching their tents in the shade of the grove, settlers gathered for two or three days of visiting, dancing, baseball games, horse races, and other amusements.

Over the years, these gatherings became increasingly elaborate, adding stock shows, rodeos, and fairs with merry-go-rounds, concession stands, and special entertainments for children. Many homesteaders heard their first phonograph recordings and saw their first moving pictures in booths or tents set up at these picnics. Eventually, the Old Settlers festivities at

Cope Grove evolved into the modern-day Washington County Fair and Rodeo.[27]

Few events could match the excitement of the Fourth of July or Old Settlers Day, but homesteaders' many smaller social occasions also fostered comfortable and informal relationships between men and women, and between adults and children. Homesteaders sometimes held box suppers to raise money for such community projects as funding a school. Mabel Plummer Drew recalled her father's many invitations to serve as auctioneer for these functions. "When the various districts had built schoolhouses, some started having box suppers, and Joe was often asked to, and did, auctioneer the selling of the boxes. These were social gatherings for both old and young. They raised money for the schools, and Joe enjoyed every minute of it." Some of the most popular amusements contained undercurrents of self-improvement. Spell downs and semimonthly or monthly "literaries," where homesteaders debated and recited, regularly brought together most of the community. Still, the usual intent of settlers' get-togethers — singing bees; baseball games; card and game parties; fishing, swimming, and berry picking expeditions — was the sharing of informal fellowship and good times.[28]

Women and men assumed complementary roles in neighborhood entertainments. Women usually initiated these events and almost always prepared the food. The community expected men to appreciate women's handiwork, sometimes with cash payments, as in the case of box suppers where homesteaders raised money for some project. But bachelors as well as single women and married couples also entertained their neighbors. Ray McFarlin, according to his son, regularly took his turn putting on the "*weekly* [emphasis added] community dance. All the furniture was set outside [Ray's sixteen-by-thirty-two-foot frame house] to give floor space for dancing."[29]

The participation of women, men, and children in homesteaders' gatherings was sometimes contrary to the practice observed at similar events in towns. Take the examples of the Akron ladies' Fortnightly Club meetings and homesteaders' literary nights. Both groups shared a commitment to cultural uplift and good citizenship through lectures, discussion, and debate. But only the homesteaders' literaries provided occasions for individuals of all ages and both sexes to take turns performing recitations, skits, and musical pieces before their neighbors. Formal debating at literaries was a male preserve, but it was an activity that could prove hazardous to masculine prestige. Glen Durrell described a debate in which his father participated with three other men: "Resolved: The Pen Is Mightier Than the Sword."

> Dad was one of the speakers and Earl Richardson was his partner. They got together at night at our house to prepare for the event. Most of Dad's efforts, as I recall, were spent, not at gathering material but at keeping Earl convinced that he could do it. The fact that grown men could be afraid to get up and speak before a group of their friends made quite an impression on me.[30]

The leveling effect between the generations, apparent in the above reminiscence, grew out of homesteaders' shared social experiences. A similar leveling also characterized relations between the sexes. In this more egalitarian social climate, women felt less compelled to create a circle of intimate female friendships to the possible exclusion of other emotionally close relationships. Women did, of course, seek out each other's company. Older women sometimes made a particular effort to ease a newcomer's isolation with visits and small presents. Mary Wright, who homesteaded as a bride in 1887 near Otis, remembered seeing the Presbyterian minister's wife approaching her soddy in a buggy. At first she did not recognize her visitor, but at last she realized, "It was *Mother Lower!* and she had her sewing machine tied on the back of her buggy. *That Dear Woman!* [Wright's emphases]. How sweet and kind she was to show me how to make little clothes for our first babe. . . . What a blessing Mother Lower's visit was to me."[31] Women also organized clubs, with names like the Merrie Minglers Sewing Club and the Sunshine Club, to provide more opportunities for sociability. But when these groups met, the husbands frequently tagged along to spend their time visiting with each other, playing cards or checkers, or throwing horseshoes.[32]

Geography contributed to this extensive mingling of the sexes. In the years of heavy in-migration after the turn of the century, when some areas sprouted a house on nearly every half or quarter section, settlers had to travel only short distances to see their neighbors. But even short trips became risky at night or in bad weather without good roads and readily visible landmarks. Longer journeys to faraway homesteads increased the dangers in proportion to the distance traveled. Consequently, for reasons of safety and convenience, settlers included all ages and both sexes in their gatherings.[33]

Beginning in 1893, political developments may also have encouraged more mixing of the sexes. In that year Colorado's male voters granted full suffrage to women. And in both Logan and Washington counties the measure passed by nearly two to one, a considerably greater margin of victory than it received statewide. The strength of the favorable vote implies that many women already shared decision-making powers with men. Moreover, some women homesteaders worked in behalf of their own enfranchisement, suggesting a self-image that conflicted with legal constraints. One of those women workers was the same Mary Wright who rhapsodized over her meeting with Mother Lower. She and another woman "spent several days, driving from house to house, to get signatures for the cause."[34]

For some women, attainment of suffrage and subsequent opportunities to hold public office inspired unconventional behavior. The 1895 election slate included several women who astonished their neighbors by campaigning in vests, ties, red suspenders, and culottes — the last in order to straddle a horse "clothespin" style. This was a time when proper women, including those living on homesteads, wore "long skirted riding habits" and rode horses sidesaddle.[35]

Few women so daringly flouted conventions in dress and behavior as did these women candidates. Still, the voters chose two of them, Nannie Gunn and Georgia Sanders, to fill the offices of county clerk and deputy county clerk. Both Nannie Gunn and Georgia Sanders belonged to well-known families who had settled in the South Platte valley in the early 1870s. Perhaps the voters' long acquaintance with these two women allowed them to dismiss as "good fun" any misgivings they had about Nannie's and Georgia's "mannish" behavior. But we may also speculate that the majority of voters did not have misgivings about Nannie's and Georgia's actions and approved their move into the public (and male) world of government and politics.

The sharing of responsibilities by men and women in organizing community projects and entertainments helped create the conditions that led to homesteaders' approval for women's voting rights and their election to public office. Similarly, shared work and responsibilities within families allowed women, and men too, more opportunities to experiment with gender roles. Custom still assigned many homestead tasks on the basis of gender, but on those numerous occasions when labor shortages arose, men and women performed unfamiliar jobs.

Stella May Stewart told a story about one of those occasions when necessity compelled her mother to do a "man's" job. Recently widowed and living with six-year-old Stella and a neighbor girl who had come to stay and help out, Anna Stewart butchered a pig. "Mrs. Stewart had a young pig which she wanted to butcher and decided she could do it as well as anyone, so she attempted to do so by cutting its throat, but found it a bigger task than she had anticipated, but nothing daunted her, so while they both [Stella and the neighbor girl] held the pig down, she cut off its head."[36] If that pig had been much larger, Anna might have lacked the muscle power to kill it. The strength required to catch and kill a pig generally made butchering a man's job; women handled the fine preparation, grinding meat for sausage and "frying down" lard for later use in making soap. In fact, butchering was such a big job that families often helped each other, turning this strenuous undertaking into a social occasion.[37]

Many of the really hard jobs around the homestead, like butchering, employed men, women, and children in different stages of the operation. At harvest time, many families pooled their labor to gather in each other's grain crops. For several days in succession, women fed the threshers (all men) three meals a day beginning with breakfast before dawn. Children performed odd jobs, including the important one of hauling water for drinking and washing up.[38]

Families also cooperated in the difficult task of digging wells. Men worked alone below ground, and women emptied buckets of dirt pulled up by horsepower. A few women homesteaders, however, managed this strenuous and dangerous job without assistance from men. The three Mosser sisters, who in 1910 homesteaded adjoining claims in Logan County, dug a well to a depth of forty-six feet. Lowered in a bucket by her two sisters, the smallest Mosser burrowed her way into the earth while her sisters raised the loose dirt to the surface.[39]

Many jobs around the homestead that required less muscle power — hauling water, milking, and gathering cow chips — carried no particular gender assignment. In a given family, either the husband or wife might perform these tasks, often shifting the responsibility to the children as they grew older.[40] Churning cream to make butter, on the other hand, was a job controlled by women though often performed by children. Butter, along with eggs from the chickens women raised, occupied an important place in the domestic economy. The sale of these commodities sometimes supplied the only cash income a family had. Women sold their butter locally or simply traded it for groceries and other items. One woman made a contract with a railroad man, who bought her butter and sold it to his friends in Denver. Women earned from ten to thirty cents a pound for as much as fifty to one hundred pounds of butter produced every week. For comparison, at a time when butter brought twelve cents per pound (in the late 1880s and early 1890s), eggs sold for five cents a dozen and corn for seven cents a bushel.[41]

Women's other work within homesteading families included the traditional tasks of keeping house, cooking, canning (meat, fruit, and vegetables), sewing, washing, and ironing. They also tended young children and usually kept a garden. Toward the end of the nineteenth century, however, automation began to change the nature of some jobs. For homesteading women, one of the most important purchases was a sewing machine. Women commonly made all the family's clothing, excluding men's heavy suits and coats. As one matron observed, "Only women who have struggled along sewing by hand can realize what a sewing machine meant to me."[42]

The hand-operated washing machine lightened what was perhaps the most arduous of all women's work — doing the family laundry. With a mechanism that amounted to little more than a paddle and handle for manually agitating the wash, the machine's principal laborsaving feature was that children could readily operate it and thereby relieve their mothers of the backbreaking job of scrubbing clothes on a washboard. Otherwise, wash day scarcely changed over many decades. Women heated water carried in from the well or cistern in a boiler on the stove. They transferred this hot water to the washing machine or to washtubs where they cleaned the laundry with soap of their own making. White items often received a second wash in boiling water softened with lye. Women used a broom handle to transfer the boiling hot garments to fresh, cold rinse water before wringing out the wash by hand and hanging it on the line to dry. The entire washing process took all day and required women's attention at most stages. It also involved a considerable amount of hard physical work. Despite the help given by daughters, who might participate in all phases of the operation, or by sons who hauled water or operated the washer, wash day was one of the busiest in a woman's week.[43]

Men had no day in their weekly routine to compare with women's wash day. On the whole, their labor was more seasonal, with intense periods of activity during planting and harvest. Through the rest of the year, their work had less variation than women's, centering largely on the care of stock and occasional heavy jobs having to do with construction and repairs.[44]

An important though understated aspect of men's work was their role in parenting. In many families, children of both sexes started doing fieldwork and cross-country errands at an early age — usually by their ninth or tenth year. Their chores included helping with the planting, hoeing, and harvesting; herding cattle; hauling feed, fuel, and water; trading at local

"Mowing with horses." The women wore large-brimmed hats to protect their complexions from the sun. *Courtesy of the Washington County Museum, Akron.*

stores; and taking crops to market. Children often performed these tasks under the supervision of their fathers.[45] This arrangement involved men intimately in the training of their older offspring, and it implies an unusually strong paternal influence on daughters.

The close association with fathers caused daughters to internalize, to some extent, male role models. Moreover, the competition that naturally arose between brothers and sisters performing the same "masculine" jobs enhanced this internalization.[46] In some families, girls as well as boys continued to perform additional farm duties as they grew into young adulthood. During harvest the Gray sisters drove the header barge team of horses while the men loaded, stacked, and unloaded. Margaret Berry took turns with her father as they drove the team and wagon to Flagler (a forty-mile round-trip) in order to sell grain and buy coal and groceries. And Maud Huston, according to her brother Harry, "was a real good cow hand; could ride as far and fast as any of the boys."[47]

Girls assumed some jobs out of necessity when, for example, they had no brothers old enough to do the work. For this reason, the Middlecoff sisters cut and shucked corn with their father; and the Nelson girls drove the family's cattle the twenty-five miles to the Sterling winter feedlot. Necessity also played a part in Eva Morris's assumption of the farming when her father was absent. In her case, however, a family member left a uniquely clear statement illuminating Eva's attitude toward men's and women's work. "Farming and working with animals was her main love — housework was for girls, not for Eva." Her distaste for traditional female occupations affected even her choice of transportation. "Because it was too confining and domesticated, she wouldn't ride to church in the buggy, she would ride her horse instead."[48]

In a few households, rigid divisions between men's and women's work prevailed, even in circumstances of great need. The Hooker boys ordinarily helped their father haul feed and corn. But when the sons attended school, the elder Hooker performed these tasks by himself, and with some difficulty, without any assistance from his daughters or his wife.[49] The Hookers more than most other homesteaders equated respectability with a strict adherence to the separate-spheres ideal. In other homesteading families, the need for workers and the preferences of some individuals outweighed customary rules assigning particular jobs to one sex or the other.

In general, homesteading expanded the work roles of both women and men, but not to the same degree. Women more often than men stepped out of their sphere and as "helpmates" assisted their husbands with the fieldwork — or as one daughter wrote of her mother, "did whatever was needed." Mary Frances Barnhouse "worked right along with the men, helping with the farming, raising the stock as well as cooking, sewing and keeping house." Similarly, Rena Lee Shedd "though . . . frail and never in the best of health worked right along with [her husband] Charlie." Rena, moreover, developed an unusual talent for a woman: She became a skilled carpenter. When "she needed a chicken coop, a screen door, or something else, [Rena] went right ahead and built it." Yet many married women did men's work only in cases of special need, when, for example, a young couple put in their first crops, or a husband was absent or ill, or the labor of sons and daughters was insufficient to run a homestead.[50]

From her study of white settlers on the Great Plains, historian Christine Stansell concluded that men exploited women's labor. In her view, men compelled women to labor in the fields, thus simultaneously robbing women of their domestic sphere and working their wives and daughters to exhaustion as farmhands.[51] Stansell's work prompts the question, did men within the homesteading families on Colorado's grasslands exploit women's labor when wives and daughters worked at jobs traditionally performed by men? Clearly, some women and girls (Rena Lee Shedd and Eva Morris, for example) did not object to performing "male" tasks or even preferred working at men's jobs. But what about those women who left no record of their choices? In the absence of an unequivocal answer,

Mary Plank preparing to mow hay in 1918. Mary always wore a dress, even when working in the fields. She said that "if she had to work like a man, she wanted to look like a lady." *Courtesy of William Plank, Sr., Fleming.*

we can approach the issue of exploitation obliquely by looking at instances where men did jobs ordinarily assigned to women.

Men and boys performed nontraditional work more reluctantly than women and girls. The boys in one family helped their sisters sew carpet rags only as a punishment. Homesteaders' records, moreover, show many more girls and women transcending gender-defined work roles than boys and men. Not only did males actually do less nontraditional work than females but men failed to mention the "female" tasks they performed. Clark Woodis never recorded in his diary that he washed dishes and cleaned house. We only know he performed these chores because of the notations in his wife's diary kept during the same period.[52]

Clark's motivation for performing domestic tasks was the same governing many women who labored in the fields — necessity. Ruth Woodis suffered from a heart condition that ended her life in her early forties. Similarly, necessity compelled Russell Fulford to take over the family cooking when a prolonged illness incapacitated Mrs. Fulford. Yet some men also helped their wives when the need to do so was far from dire. Orrin Hall ironed Ruth Hall's clothes (including the artificial bosom of starched ruffles worn under her "full chested shirt waist") during the period when she taught school — a job that provided their household with much-needed cash income.[53] The evidence remains inconclusive, but the fact that some men, as well as women, filled jobs traditionally performed by the opposite sex argues against a pattern of men coercing women to work at jobs that women found too arduous or somehow threatening to an ideal of "proper" womanhood. The needs of the homestead involved all family members in a daily round of chores, and as long as women saw men engaged in vital work and even helping on the domestic front when needed, women probably did not feel abused.

Vital work on homesteads included earning cash income. Everyone, except the smallest children, contributed to the family's cash resources, though in ways that ordinarily varied by age and gender. Married women, as we have seen, earned money from marketing their surplus production of butter and eggs. Some women also marketed their garden vegetables or other domestic products, including bread, sausages, and cheese. One woman, with the help of her daughter, ran a millinery store in a room of the family home. More commonly, women took in boarders (often teachers or railroad workers), charging them at the rate of ten dollars per month for their food, accommodation, and such additional amenities as washing, ironing, and mending. Women also washed, ironed, and sewed for local bachelors, worked as dressmakers for their neighbors, and served as postmistresses. Wives usually earned cash from jobs performed in the home environment. But a few wives, even some with small children, did work that took them away from home during the day — primarily teaching school and helping with domestic chores in the homes of their neighbors or of families in town. Even fewer worked away from home for weeks at a time. In one case, a wife and mother took a teaching job at some distance from the homestead because of the family's pressing financial problems. Another woman worked in town one winter as a seamstress, while her teenage daughter performed her domestic work on the farm.[54]

Although daughters' domestic work might free their mothers to take cash-paying jobs, daughters, too, earned wages. Some found employment in the hotels of nearby towns; a few even owned and operated restaurants. Others worked as domestics in private homes. Salaries for housework were low — about two dollars a week in the 1890s. Teaching jobs, because they paid three or four times as much, were considerably more desirable. Many wage-earning daughters lived with their families and contributed to the support of their families, although the portion of income they kept for their own use is unclear.[55]

Another class of daughters — those who claimed homesteads to expand family holdings — exercised varying degrees of control over money they earned. A portion of any wages they earned went to pay the expenses of proving up. In a few cases, the remainder went to the families; in other cases, it did not. Elva Bowles supported herself with money earned from teaching school and a one-third share of the income from her land, farmed by her brother-in-law. Lois Ervin, recalling her experience as a homesteading daughter, said the money she earned from teaching was hers to use as she wished. Amy Dickensen Worthley, on the other hand, said she and her siblings pooled their earnings to pay for their college educations. She added, however, that she thought this practice was unusual. In fact, few homesteaders attended college, and most families did not plan for the expenses that higher education entailed.[56]

Male children in homesteading families began earning cash at an earlier age than their sisters. One eight-year-old had a summer job herding sheep at a salary of $7 per month. When school was not in session, older boys worked as farmhands for wages of $1 to $2 a week. Some hunted jackrabbits and other animals with their fathers and brothers, selling the hides and carcasses. The income of young boys went to the family. But young unmarried men, like young women, kept some or all of the money they earned. Many young males taught school because the salaries were relatively high: $25 to $40 a month in the period around the turn of the century. In contrast, ranch hands earned about $15 a month. The affluence of the school district, the time period, and sometimes the number of students affected the pay of the teacher, but a woman teacher could expect to receive the same salary as a man. Young men, however, made up only a small percentage of teachers, in part because males, both young unmarried sons and older men, had many more kinds of work available to them than did females.[57]

An early observer of agricultural settlements in Nebraska claimed that women could acquire homesteads more easily than men because of the good wages they could earn doing domestic work. Men, he said, had few opportunities to earn cash, and consequently they had to "endure great privation" to prove up their claims.[58] This situation certainly did not prevail in the subsequent settlement of Colorado. Colorado's economy of the late nineteenth and early twentieth centuries generated jobs in agriculture and the processing of agricultural products, in railroading, in construction, and in what we would call "service industries." Moreover, railroad connections allowed homesteaders to take temporary jobs hundreds of miles from home. Male settlers, therefore, found employment in a nearly endless variety of jobs, even if we discount those who owned businesses in town and homesteaded as a sideline. Men did not necessarily earn more money, for women's work was sometimes steadier, but men did hire out at more kinds of occupations. Many jobs, such as those in railroading, construction, and mining, carried a male gender bias. Husbands were also freer to leave home because wives' domestic role and the presence of children prevented most women from working far from the homestead.

Many men held weekday jobs in town as sugar factory workers, grain elevator assistants, brick factory operatives, barbers, and cooks. Men also worked as mail carriers (jobs that a few women also held), threshers, road workers, railroad workers, cheese makers, ranch and farmhands, sod breakers, carpenters, well diggers, well pipeline installers, stone masons, cement block makers, fire guard plowmen, cattle skinners, gopher exterminators, sheep shearers, house plasterers, tree claim plowers and planters, and buffalo bone collectors (they sold the bones to the agents of eastern fertilizer companies).[59] Some men traveled hundreds of miles, for months at a time, working the harvests in Kansas or Nebraska. One man found employment as a lumberman in the gold camps of Cripple Creek and Victor; another as a dynamiter in the Black Hills mines; still another as a delivery man for a Denver lumber company. One husband spent a winter in Iowa pursuing his carpentry trade.[60] Taken together, these absences had a significant impact on women and children, increasing their work load and responsibilities, and thereby their importance, when fathers and husbands were away at distant jobs.

The contributions of women and children to the family economy earned them a voice in decisions affecting family resources. Parents recognized their older children's increasing autonomy by allowing them to keep a larger proportion of their earnings as they matured. Parents also presented their children with livestock. One father gave each of his sons and daughters a heifer calf. His daughter Jessie Hassig Challis wrote: "These [heifers] grew up and had calves and that way each of us had something of our own. If a cow or steer was sold, part of the money would go into another calf or two, and we could buy a coat or pair of shoes and have money for our own school supplies. Later on, when we went away to school, we had our own money for tuition and books." A similar arrangement in the Young family provided each of twelve children with a filly. "Each child was given a mare colt when he was small and all the offspring was his own, so each child had a little start when he or she left home. Also Mr. and Mrs. Young gave each child a milk cow when he or she was married."[61] Of course, parents benefited from the financial self-sufficiency of children, but parental generosity also indicates a willingness to confer some decision-making power in order to prepare children for full independence as young adults.

Homesteading couples generally shared family resources and decisions about their use. This sharing of responsibilities flies in the face of claims that women had little or no control over farm income. Observers who make these claims say that men invested surplus capital in additional land and machinery rather than in laborsaving devices for domestic chores or in improvements to homes.[62] Conceivably, additional land and equipment could increase farm income and ultimately benefit women. But let us assume that if farm families rarely or never invested in domestic improvements, women would indeed have had no voice in family expenditures. Among the American-born families of Colorado's grasslands, many husbands did spend time and money for the convenience and ease of their wives. One of the first cars in Washington County was the Model T Ford Abe Ingraham bought for his wife. She suffered from "dropsy" (edema) and could no longer ride in a buggy to town for visiting and trading. Ernest Royle connected Anna Royle's washing machine to the windmill so that the up and down motion of the pump could run the washer. Later (around 1917) he installed a gasoline motor to free wash day from the vagaries of the wind.[63]

More revealing than husbands' courtesies to wives are instances when women themselves influenced or determined how couples made decisions about sizable investments. Mrs. Dickensen received an inheritance that she used to buy land next to the Dickensens' farm in Nebraska. When the family moved to Logan County, the sale of her land helped buy the new farm. But Mrs. Dickensen was distressed at losing title to her own real estate, so her husband made her a co-owner of the Colorado property. When Ollie and Willis Barden moved to their homestead in 1903, they lived in a "half dug out." Three years later they moved into a three-room frame house. Meanwhile, Willis used a walking plow that someone had given him for breaking sod. No doubt Willis enjoyed the new house, but would he have chosen it over a team of horses and a new plow if he had not needed to consider Ollie's preference? In 1917 Orrin and Ruth Hall had a bumper wheat crop. They invested their profits in a four-bedroom frame house with indoor plumbing. Ruth eagerly anticipated "all this luxury after eight years in the little sod house." But Orrin was in no hurry to move, thinking their new quarters should "cure for a while." Ruth strongly disagreed, and she got her way. "The wildlife could have the soddy. I was getting out. So we moved into our new house in April 1918."[64]

Wives' power to command resources and direct expenditures appeared in other circumstances as well. When Mary and Samuel Wright decided to buy new furniture, one of their purchases was a sewing machine. Mary Hayes also bought a sewing machine, as well as lace curtains, with money she earned from taking in boarders. Jessie Hassig Challis had title to her own cattle and her own brand. And Jessie still owned her brand long after her husband sold his.[65]

The stories of these women suggest that wives exercised considerable influence within homesteading families. Men did not dictate how families used resources, nor did they control the actions of their wives. Men and women generally had different roles to play, but the cooperation between the sexes enforced by the needs of settlement expanded women's power to negotiate and to see their judgments prevail. Inevitably, the strength of women's position affected the power dynamics of the whole family. When Mary and Wesley Plank taught their children that "each member of a family is equal," they were, in part, acknowledging Mary's decision-making powers.[66] Recognition of Mary's authority does not mean, of course, that equality actually existed in the Plank family or in any other homesteading family. But the fact that it appeared even as an ideal holds significance.

Not all women homesteaders welcomed the chance to work as partners with their husbands. The move to Colorado had caused too many painful feelings associated with changing work roles and disrupted relationships for these women to adjust. Usually, those who felt the most distress were "set in their ways" — women of middle age and older, or women accustomed to an urban environment. One woman who was in her forties when her family arrived in Colorado in 1887 from Jewel County, Kansas, never adapted to the "lonely, barren prairie." A rumored Indian scare left her "terribly frightened," and before her death in 1891 "she made her family promise not to bury her on the prairie but in the cemetery at Sterling."[67]

Another woman had trouble "moving out of the city into the wilderness" after living in Plattsmouth, Nebraska, where her husband was a railroad worker. Only in her twenties in 1908 when the family moved into their homestead soddy, she "shed a few tears" as she "set to work making the place look like home." Resistance to the changes brought about by removal to the plains of Colorado was not, however, an attitude found exclusively among women. Among the early settlers in the South Platte valley were the Armour family and Maggie Armour's brothers, sisters, and

Mary and Wes Plank in the early 1920s on the homestead they had built together. *Courtesy of William Plank, Sr., Fleming.*

parents. Maggie's husband, believing the area unsuitable for raising children, decided to return home. The urgings of his wife finally convinced him to rejoin the family some years later.[68]

Loneliness affected many women who settled the grasslands. Yet lonely women did not necessarily lead lives that were physically isolated from other people. In fact, most women were in daily contact with family members. Meetings with neighbors occurred once a week or more, and women as well as men made regular trips to town. Clara Watson looked forward to harvest because "we women were so lonely much of the time that it was fun to help each other cook for the 'threshers.' " But Clara also described the frequent "good times" the families in the neighborhood shared: dances and weekly get-togethers when "we would all gather at one home for Sunday dinner."[69]

With regular opportunities to socialize, why were Clara Watson and others like her lonely? The explanation probably lies in women's development of close personal ties to other women whose friendships formed much of the meaningful fabric of their former lives. These rich emotional relationships, with their associations of place and time, had no easy substitutes. New relationships of similar intensity were necessarily slow to develop. In the meantime, it may be that the emotional vacuum women felt encouraged a closer rapport with men and that the growing closeness with men further delayed the development of intimate friendships among women. The lowering of culturally prescribed barriers between the sexes, together with the labor shortage, can explain the expanding work roles of homesteading women and men.

Most women had mixed emotions about homesteading. A Mrs. Kennedy, who left Missouri in 1906 with her husband and three children, recalled her own feelings. "I was very sad, but happy too. The prospects of having a home of our own made me very happy, but to leave my home and parents that I had never been away from in my life, and going so far that I was sure I could never get back, made me sad." Ruth Hall admitted that had she been able to foresee the hardships on the day she arrived in Colorado to become a homesteader's bride, she "wouldn't have decided for him, the sod house, or the rugged prairie." But looking back from the vantage point of later years, she decided, "I wasn't sorry that I stayed."[70]

Unreserved enthusiasm for homesteading almost always indicated youth. Jessie Nolan was fifteen when her family moved to Washington County from Boone, Iowa. Jessie reported that she and the other children were "jubilant" about the move, although their mother felt many misgivings over her husband's decision to close his blacksmith shop and take up a homestead. Ollie Barden was a young bride in 1902 when she and her husband settled near Haxtun. Ollie later reminisced that "we lived and were happy, had good neighbors and we were One Big Family."[71]

Young, single women often viewed homesteading as an exciting and romantic adventure. Excerpts from Mary Anderson's autograph album illustrate this point. In 1886 Mary and a friend, Bee Randolph, homesteaded adjoining quarter sections and shared a shack built over the property line. Mary's wedding the following year caused some feelings of melancholy for Bee, who composed these lines.

> Dear Mame — Here we are in our little preemption home for the last time together, at least for some year [*sic*] to come. But I hope sometime we may visit it again. We cannot be happier than we have been here, although we may have wealth, and other great pleasures. Can you not almost remember every day from the first, what has happened? Our laughing, singing, playing, working, our company, etc.

Mary's sister Ruth added her own musings. "Dear Mame — I will never forget our ride behind 'Old George,' when the ground looked like a mist, Joe and his grindorgan, nor Ida and Will, nor the kerosene barrel that served as a well, nor the rattle snakes all around us, nor Mame, either."[72]

These young women found adventure in homesteading for several reasons. One was the excitement of shared experiences with friends of both sexes. Another was the possibility of danger — from rattlesnakes, for example. But the essential attraction was the independence proving up a claim offered. Self-determination was not an option generally available to women, and homesteading held out that possibility. The homestead laws had extended claim rights to single women in order to encourage settlement by families and thereby encourage social and political stability on the nation's hinterlands. The laws, however, also had an unanticipated result: They fostered a class of independent, landowning young women.

Women ultimately accounted for nearly 18 percent of the homestead entrants in northeastern Colorado. At 18 percent, their participation in homestead entry rights involved the vast majority of eligible women.[73] The elevated status and autonomy of this numerous group in the local female population served both as an inspiration and as an example to other women and girls in the community. The labor shortage and the relative isolation of the family unit, which forced its members to greater reliance on each other, played a part in raising women's and girls' expectations by diminishing cultural divisions between males and females. The possibility of acquiring land gave a solid economic base to those expectations. As a young schoolteacher, Lucy Bigler Wilson had observed that "everybody lived on the free land, and I thought 'Why can't I have some, too?' "[74] Other young women asked themselves the same question. And although wives generally could not themselves enter claims, they could share in the self-esteem that unprecedented opportunities for landownership offered their daughters and other members of their sex.

As women and men saw themselves and their children engaged in more and more tasks novel to their gender, and especially as they saw women claiming land and participating in the economic privileges of landownership, power relationships between the sexes moved in the direction of negotiation and compromise. For some women, it is true, the possibility of enhanced freedom and elevated economic status was not worth the hardships and the disruption of gender roles that proving up a claim imposed. But for those of a more resilient disposition, homesteading had much to offer.

5

I Thought It All Foolishness

Among the stories of women who homesteaded on Colorado's grasslands, one stands out. Not only is this story unusually complete, but it holds a rare immediacy, coming to us as it does through letters and financial statements instead of through the usual route of reminiscence.[1] I found out about Alice Newberry almost by accident when I was working as a volunteer, processing manuscript collections at the Colorado History Museum. One day the library received a new acquisition of family letters, including some written by a woman who had homesteaded in eastern Colorado. As I undertook the painstaking task of reading and sorting the collection, I began to realize that here was a unique "find." True, Alice Newberry did not write voluminously about her homesteading experiences. But her letters, taken together with her business papers, told a remarkably detailed story — one that spanned half a century and revealed the important financial and emotional role farm ownership had played in her life.

Alice Newberry was nearly twenty-five years old in 1903 when she filed on a homestead in Kit Carson County. She had lived in the area most of her life and had been eligible to enter a claim for nearly four years. Writing in 1907 from her "burrow" to her mother in Illinois, Alice explained one reason she delayed filing on a homestead. "When I took the claim I thought it all foolishness, and only did so because Mr. Wellman [an old family friend] insisted that I use my right while I had a chance to get good land near town."[2] Such was the inauspicious manner in which Alice began a lifelong relationship with her land. If she once doubted the wisdom of homesteading, the experience of landownership was to change her mind.

Like many women who claimed land, Alice Newberry earned her living as a schoolteacher. She had, in fact, taught school since the tender age of fourteen when the failure of her parents' marriage forced her to find work. The elder Newberrys were themselves homesteaders, and when the family broke up, Mrs. Newberry returned to Illinois with the other children. Alice remained behind — not to live with her father, from whom she was estranged, but to earn money to ease her mother's financial burdens. Illinois law stipulated a minimum age for teachers of seventeen. In contrast, Kit Carson County required only that prospective teachers pass a qualifying examination. A good student, Alice successfully cleared this hurdle and promptly secured a position in the Seibert school at a salary of thirty dollars a month.[3]

This first job was difficult. Grover Blake, one of Alice's four scholars (all Blakes), recalled years later how "terribly homesick" his teacher was. Alice had gone to live with the Blake family when the Seibert school offered the teaching position. Grover remembered that Miss Newberry "would lie on the floor and cry it out."[4]

Despite her loneliness, Alice persevered. Indeed, she had few alternatives. Through the 1890s, Alice taught in several Kit Carson County schools and earned enough money to support herself and send money to her mother. During this period, she also worked to prepare herself to graduate from high school, for she was determined to move to Illinois and complete her secondary education. With help from home, Alice periodically rejoined her mother in order to complete her coursework, and in 1901 she finally received her diploma.[5]

Why Alice returned to Kit Carson County after her graduation remains something of a mystery. By 1901 she was twenty-two years old going on twenty-three, well past the minimum age for teaching in Illinois. By her own testimony, she had no desire to homestead. She probably chose the course that seemed to present the fewest obstacles: to take up the threads of her life again in a community she knew intimately, where she was sure to find employment.

For a time Alice drifted. She conscientiously performed her teaching duties, but long-term goals eluded her. She lacked both the commitment and the material resources to act decisively on the options that were open to her. Marriage was one possibility, despite the discouraging example set by her parents. Getting a university education to further her teaching career was another. A third course also offered itself: to claim government land. Alice's decision to homestead was initially a delaying tactic that allowed her to postpone the need to make other choices. Meanwhile, during the years of proving up her claim, she tested the alternatives of marriage and career and shaped her life's direction.

Alice's unenthusiastic, even reluctant, attitude toward homesteading soon gave way to ambivalence. Although she dreaded having to deal with the snakes and centipedes that invaded her dugout,[6] she was also quick to appreciate her claim's potential sale value and the added status land-ownership conveyed. Writing from her claim in 1907 to "Mama," Alice referred to these advantages explicitly and implicitly. A neighbor had just sold an "unimproved quarter with nothing on it but buffalo grass . . . for $2,400." Alice's land was farther from town, but she noted that "I have sixty acres [that I have had] broken. There are a hundred acres of bottom land, the rest is slightly rolling." She declared that she would not take so little for her claim and, further, that to admit any willingness to sell was risky.

> I was talking with a newcomer the other day. He said "Miss Newberry, you have a fine piece of land, but I mustn't tell you that for when you prove up I want to buy it." I told him I wouldn't sell. You know if you make any negotiations toward selling and anyone wants to take the matter up against you [by going to the government land office and contesting the claim as a land speculation], he can make you lose your right to the quarter. . . . I always tell people that I mean to live here always and be buried here.[7]

As Alice's pride in ownership grew, so too did her appreciation of independence. Like so many single schoolteachers who boarded and roomed with local families, Alice chafed under the forced intimacy such arrangements compelled. The government's requirement for entrants to live on their claims freed her from this burdensome living pattern. Repeatedly, Alice remarked in her letter how she enjoyed living on the claim. "I have never felt so rested to go back to school," she wrote to her brother Eldon after spending Christmas on the claim. Again she was happy to return to her land for the summer of 1907. "I am glad I have a place of my own to go to. I can feel a little more independent." And a year later, back on the claim, she was still writing in these terms. "It has been such a carefree life the last month with nothing weightier to worry about than wonder if my baking will be as nice as it ought."[8]

Alice's "carefree" independence rested in large part on her ability to pay for her living expenses and for the improvements required to patent a claim. Her teacher's salary not only covered her bills, it also provided ready cash that gave Alice a decided edge over some of her neighbors. Her advantage became evident in the spring of 1909 when the Rock Island Railroad delivered less than half the seed ordered by Kit Carson County growers. Alice paid cash for twenty-five bushels of seed and had them hauled to her claim. The Rock Island's regulations required buyers to transport their own seed, and some farmers, applying a literal interpretation to the rules, complained when Alice hired a hauler. The railroad, however, supported her action, saying she had "paid for hers" and had not asked to receive the seed on credit.[9]

Clearly, Alice's independence achieved through the combined enter-prises of schoolteaching and homesteading gave her material advantages and personal satisfaction. But repeated bouts of loneliness cast a shadow over these rewards. One especially difficult period occurred following an Easter celebration with her neighbors. Back in the dugout, she wrote a letter to Mama, consoling herself with the thought that her own "little room" was "comfy." Reflecting further, she concluded that her membership in the Women's Christian Temperance Union had enriched her life. Although she did not feel she had accomplished much in her jobs as WCTU district secretary, county superintendent of medical work, and superintendent of legislation, she decided "the work has helped me in many ways. I've met bright, interesting women" and engaged in useful occupations.[10] Still, these compensations did not answer Alice's need for a lifelong commitment.

Marriage was a solution she considered with increasing interest. Alice's homestead provided her with an opportunity to experiment with the homemaking side of matrimony during the period when a hired man put in the first crop. The arrangement required her to board "Henry," whom she described as a "respectable married man . . . good, mild, meek, patient." Yet for all that, Henry was a "bother." After nearly a month of feeding Henry, Alice's enthusiasm for matrimony waned. "I have decided not to marry. Three warm meals a day, three-hundred-sixty-five days in the year for the term of my natural life is more than I can face. I have decided to study up a little and try to fit myself for a higher calling." Poor Henry. As a stand-in for a future husband and a symbol of married life in general, he possessed decidedly fewer attractions than the Latin grammar Alice asked her mother to send. But in truth, Alice's strong words masked a lack of resolve. A few weeks after expressing these sentiments, she admitted in a letter to Mama that she would marry if "I could find anybody who would have me."[11]

As Alice grew older and prospects for marriage faded, she contem-plated bringing her mother out from Illinois to live with her permanently on the claim. At one point she sent home plans for a cement block house, twenty-six-feet square, "exclusive of the piazza across the front," for Mama's consideration. Alice admitted that she did not have the $2,000 the house would cost and that she would "have to earn and save money faster than I ever have, if it is built in our lifetime." She knew her scheme might appear fanciful, and she feared her mother would not take her seriously. "Now laugh at me and call me visionary," she wrote. Still, she encouraged her mother to have faith in the earning potential of the homestead. "Just wait till all this land on the flat produces three crops of alfalfa a year, at fifteen dollars a ton."[12]

Alice, in fact, never built her cement block house. In June 1909 she received the patent to her land, and by the fall of that year she was teaching in Denver and making plans to enter the university. Alice realized her impulse to create a real home where she and her mother could live, not on her Kit Carson County claim but on an urban lot. Here she lived until she died, a teacher until she retired and a lifelong spinster.

Alice's defection to the big city did not mean that she severed her ties to the claim. On the contrary, her land continued to play an important role in her life. Indeed, without the money the farm produced, Alice might have lacked the means to build her Denver house. In 1911, when Alice had to budget every penny, her farm paid $17.57, or about one-quarter of the annual $72 of interest due on her $1,200 house loan. Of the $34 Alice received from the farmer who grew and marketed her crops, she paid $11.83 in taxes, $1.20 for recording her land patent, and $3.40 as a tithe to her sister Florence who worked as a missionary in Africa. The rest went toward the payment on her Denver home.[13]

Over the years, income from the claim, in addition to her teaching salary, gave Alice a narrow measure of financial security. Her finances were always meager, but she still managed to pay off the mortgage on her house, and in times of need she provided family members with small gifts and loans. Her help was especially crucial during the 1930s when the Great Depression brought her brother Eldon and sister Edna to the brink of financial ruin.[14]

As Alice entered retirement, her own need for income from the farm increased. In 1938 she revealed to her sister that her pension amounted to only fifty dollars per month. Beginning in 1939, an annuity paid her an additional twenty dollars each month. But not until 1952 did she receive any increase in her pension. Meanwhile, the currency inflation generated by World War II pushed the value of the dollar sharply downward. A letter Alice wrote in August 1953 to her brother and sister-in-law testifies to the importance of her farm income. She reported that her share of the wheat crop totaled 313 bushels. With the market price at only $1.94 a bushel, Alice felt she would anger the local farmers if she sold her wheat before the price reached $2.07 a bushel. With storage costs set at seven cents a bushel, Alice looked forward to receiving in excess of $600 (before taxes) from her

Alice Newberry in her classroom not long after her arrival in Denver. *Courtesy of the Colorado Historical Society, Denver, mss #1202, ff 274.*

farm for the year. At that time, her probable gross income from other sources (her monthly pension of $100, her $20-per-month annuity check, and a small oil lease payment) amounted to $1,440. In other words, close to 30 percent of her income for the year came from her Kit Carson County homestead.[15]

Almost as important to Alice as the money her homestead produced were the psychological benefits she derived from owning land. The most enduring of these was the knowledge that her claim was always available as an ultimate haven in the event she lost her Denver home. For a brief period following her receipt of a patent, Alice had considered selling her land. But sometime around 1911 she made the decision to hold on to the homestead. Especially as she got older, she wrote about her attachment to the claim as a potential home. "I keep it, thinking of it as a cheap place to live if I want ever to sell here and go there. Sometimes I think I do, but I think too of all the conveniences here, and do not! But it is always a last resource." In another letter she elaborated on the drawbacks of moving to the farm: the need for a modest house and the "big expense" it would entail; the isolation of living without telephone service, five and one-half miles from town and medical care. Still, she added, if it were not for the "rattlers, I'd like the claim."[16]

Although the farm had many shortcomings as a homesite, it gave Alice an outlet for expressing her considerable managerial leanings. In a letter written early in 1938 to the farmer who worked her claim, she lectured him on her desire to let the ground lie fallow that summer. Citing an article in *Country Gentleman* about the causes of wind erosion and her own experience as an amateur botanist and longtime resident of Kit Carson County, Alice emphatically stated her wish to "let it [the land] alone." She reminded him that only 60 of her 160 acres were "broken up," and she regretted having even that much tilled. "You will remember that I refused to let you break out more."[17] Alice took her responsibilities as a good steward of the land seriously. And even in 1938 when she faced retirement and a greatly reduced income, she chose to do what she considered scientifically correct rather than what appeared expedient for her material gain. In following her convictions, she not only expressed confidence in her superior knowledge of land management but also demonstrated that she could impose her own will.

The extent to which Alice's land contributed to her sense of security and defined her self-importance remains difficult to measure. Still, additional evidence suggests that the claim provided these advantages, and more. We can only guess at the excitement and anticipation Alice felt when she heard the news of oil discoveries in Kit Carson County. But Alice's sister Edna unmistakably referred to Alice's dreams of riches and enhanced status in a letter written in 1938. Edna asked, "Do you mean the bank was unusually courteous because you had land down in that eastern Colorado oil boom territory?"[18] Alice, in fact, was never to receive any remuneration from the development of oil on her land. But the possibility was there — the source, no doubt, of many happy musings.

In April 1954, as she approached her seventy-sixth birthday, Alice died. In accordance with her will, the claim passed to her four nieces and nephews. In the words of one of them, Ethyl Yergen, the land has never produced "significant" income, just "sufficient to pay taxes." Nonetheless, Alice's heirs kept alive their aunt's dreams for eventual oil development, a possibility that clung to life because of negotiations for lease agreements.[19] Certainly, if Alice could have seen the way her family continued to value her land, she would have been pleased. It had, after all, meant much to Alice — in her struggles to support herself and in many other ways as well.

6

Homesteading in Perspective

Looking back across long vistas of time and technological development, we who live in the late twentieth century may have difficulty
understanding the appeal homesteading held for the tens of thousands of
claimants who settled on Colorado's grasslands. Making a living from a
homestead was never easy, and when crop failures and a multitude of other
misfortunes reduced farmers to the barest levels of subsistence, life could
be brutally hard. Even prospering homesteads, judged by modern standards,
offered little more than modest security in exchange for the unending toil
required to keep them operating.

The contrast between today's standards of leisure and the hard labor
performed by wives and mothers in their daily round of chores on the claim
has strongly affected our perceptions of homesteading women. Moved by
mixed feelings of admiration and pity for these unsung "heroines," we may
even feel some outrage over the "selfishness" of husbands who seemed to
have condemned women to such difficult and apparently unrewarding
lives. But judgments based on our own experience are anachronistic. By
the standards of their own day, women on eastern Colorado homesteads
lived reasonably well. Furthermore, most of them occupied an influential
and respected position in their families. Perhaps nowhere in American
society of that period did women achieve a truer partnership within
marriage than did many of these women homesteaders.

For spinsters, homesteading offered an opportunity rarely available to
women of that day: the possibility of owning land. Significant numbers of
single women took advantage of their homestead rights, succeeding at a
rate equivalent to that of men. Homesteaders' narratives confirm that
female patentees received compensation for the sale of their claims, even
when they originally entered them to increase family holdings. The patenting of land by single women, moreover, encouraged rising expectations

among other females in the community. In an environment where women enjoyed some of the same economic choices as men, the prevailing labor shortage coupled with an easy companionship between the sexes stimulated the development of novel behavior patterns among women and girls.

If women alone had set aside cultural prescriptions by performing tasks and duties outside their domestic sphere, we might accuse husbands and fathers of placing excessive and callous demands on women's labor. But men also departed from rigid, gender-determined role patterns, albeit to a lesser extent. Consequently, relations between the sexes underwent modifications analogous to the blurring of class distinctions that sometimes occurred among western men.[1] Homesteading encouraged women to enlarge the scope of their activities in their communities, and it stimulated the expansion of women's responsibilities and decision-making powers within families.

To say that homesteading promoted greater equity between the sexes is not to claim that settlement affected men and women equally or in an identical manner. Although both single men and single women could patent government land, married women, unlike married men, were not generally eligible to enter claims. Deserted or separated wives could enter claims, as could those wives designated as heads of households because of their husbands' mental or physical disabilities.[2] But the wives in this study of Colorado homesteaders benefited indirectly from land acquisition.

Women, moreover, suffered more acutely from some of the hardships connected with new settlement. Their intimate friendships with others of their gender made the separations produced by the migration especially wrenching. Their training for the domestic sphere rendered the primitive housing and the difficulties of food preparation substantially more burdensome to women than to men. Nonetheless, the period during which women experienced acute loneliness and deprivation was generally short-lived. New friendships gradually formed, and in the meantime, the extensive contacts and mutual reliance between male and female homesteaders suggest that both sexes partially compensated for their loss of old friendships by forming closer bonds with each other.

In time also, the level of material comfort rose, so that within a few years the homesteaders' standard of living was not substantially inferior to that of Americans living in many older, established farm communities. Homesteaders' soddies, though much maligned in the descriptive literature of the plains as primitive and vermin-infested dwellings, could, in fact, be comfortable homes. However, settlers who failed to learn the techniques of sod construction or who lacked an understanding of its advantages and shortcomings did indeed suffer from leaky roofs and invasions of snakes, rats, centipedes, and other pests. Like homesteaders who lived in houses made of wood, stone, adobe, or concrete blocks, soddy dwellers found that the skills of the homebuilder were all-important in determining the quality of domestic life. Many homesteaders, too, learned to produce a varied as well as a reliable food supply. And in contrast to the masculine job of construction, food production and preparation were tasks over which women had more direct control in their capacities as gardeners, poultry and dairy farmers, and cooks.

On the whole, the conditions of homesteading on Colorado's grass-lands do not create a picture of exploited and oppressed womanhood. Living standards, expanding work and community roles, relations between the sexes, economic opportunity, and even such stark demographic indica-tors as life spans support the conclusion that the benefits to women outweighed the penalties. True, the land records show that nearly half of all entrants did not patent the land they claimed. But the records do not reveal how many of these apparent "failures" made a profit by selling their relinquishments to other claimants. Those claimants who really did fail (that is, they abandoned their claims or suffered a net loss to their assets) left no evidence that homesteading failures affected women more adversely than men. Some women, it is true, did suffer disproportionate psychological distress from transplantation to a homestead, but they were usually older or temperamentally ill-equipped to cope with change. Certainly, their story is important, but it should not obscure the real advantages other women realized through the process of settlement and patenting government land.

Many studies of western settlement have found that women lost much more than they gained as they left behind familiar places and supportive female friends only to find their domestic work devalued amid the labor needs of their new surroundings. These studies, however, focus on the migration experience or they look at times and places in the West's history that offered women few opportunities either to make decisions for them-selves or to pursue the kinds of entrepreneurship available to homesteaders. Women of the early and mid-nineteenth century, of course, could not claim homesteads in most of the West because Congress did not pass the first homestead act until 1862.[3] Antebellum farm families, moreover, typically lived within the patterns of rigid patriarchy characteristic of preindustrial and colonial families.

Patriarchal family patterns began to change in the urban Northeast in the 1820s as males left home to go to work in the new factories and a new social construct for ideal gender relations emerged. The older patriarchal order assigned men authority over women in all areas of life, whereas the new separate-spheres ideal promoted a division of men's and women's work into distinct, and "equal," public and domestic spheres. Women gained obvious advantages from the concept of separate spheres because it allowed them a measure of autonomy over their domestic work. But women's dominion over domesticity remained primarily an eastern, urban model until the growth of popular journalism in the 1860s hastened the spread of city values to the countryside. By the time homesteaders began to settle northeastern Colorado, women's elevated status within the limits of their domestic sphere had become a widespread ideal throughout much of American society. Agrarian women embraced the ideal, but they developed a flexible view of women's work in order to meet the labor needs of the farm. They saw no contradiction in performing "men's" field labor as their husbands' "helpmates," while maintaining philosophical agreement with the separate-spheres ideal.

In the closing years of the nineteenth century, eastern upper-middle-class reformers, like farm women, evolved a flexible definition of domesticity — one that transcended a purely homebound existence. Under the influence of these reformers, women began expanding their domestic sphere by turning their attention to those societal conditions affecting homes and families.[4] Women soon discovered that just about everything from street cleaning to international affairs affected the welfare of their domestic circle, and they began entering areas of public life in which they had never before participated. Women justified their actions by citing their roles as mothers of children and protectors of family health and morals. These "new" women received attention in the popular press, creating a more activist image for women. Through churches and clubs like the Women's Christian Temperance Union, reform-minded women set an example of self-direction and self-esteem that reached others of their sex all over the nation, including those who settled Colorado's grasslands.

The passage of time, which signaled changes in the ways many farm women viewed themselves and their roles, did not affect all farm women uniformly. Different locales harbored distinct family types that sometimes resisted change, producing geographically distinct family styles. American colonial historian Philip Greven found evidence for such differences when he identified within the preindustrial patriarchy three separate family patterns based on the relative power exercised by the eldest male. In the most rigidly hierarchical families, Greven found that only the father's obedience to God limited his power. Because these strongly patriarchal families felt threatened by even the modest power sharing that occurred within more democratically organized colonial families, they tended to cluster together to shield themselves from the liberalizing influences of other kinds of families.

As industrialization spread in the nineteenth century, the family variations existing in the preindustrial period became even more complex with the development of companionate family patterns arising out of the separate-spheres ideal.[6] Certainly, nineteenth-century companionate families were also patriarchal, but their greater limits on male authority were sufficient to set them apart from earlier forms. Further, although the shift over time has generally moved away from hierarchical and toward more companionate families, the contrasting styles have continued to coexist. Consequently, racially and ethnically similar women may have experienced agricultural settlement in different ways because of variations in the distribution of power within their families. What was true for one population does not necessarily apply to another of the same race, ethnicity, and nationality, because family organization with its consequences for women varied significantly across the American West.

Evidence for variations in western families comes from sources scattered over time and place. Helen Carpenter, who traveled as a bride on the Overland Trail in 1857, wrote in her diary, "Some women have very little help [from men] about the camp." She singled out "Missourians" for the bad treatment they accorded their wives. "I am lucky in having a Yankee for a husband, so am well waited on."[7] Abigail Scott Duniway, whose family were among the Kentucky pioneers who settled Tazewell County, Illinois, in the 1820s and 1830s, made similar observations. Soon after the Kentuckians arrived, Yankee merchants and land agents looking for new markets and investment opportunities took up homes on neighboring land. Many areas of friction arose between the two groups — not the least of which was their contrasting family styles. Southern men were lazy and their wives overworked, according to Yankee perceptions. Duniway herself reflected the prejudices of the Kentuckians in her resentment of the superior airs assumed by Yankee women. But she admired and envied the way New England women dominated the domestic, artistic, and spiritual aspects of family life and the deference their men gave them.[8]

Some of the more striking examples of variations in farm women's experiences emerge from stories of European immigrants. Accounts from the Canadian West often paint a grim picture of female exploitation and oppression among that country's large population of foreign-born homesteading families. Yet literary and historical sources from Nebraska and

Colorado suggest other scenarios. Novelist Willa Cather wrote of strong immigrant women on Nebraska farms.[9] Although she portrayed many instances of heavy-handed patriarchal authority, two of her most enduring protagonists were women who overcame male domination through the medium of landownership and farming. By hard work, innovation, and shrewd management, Alexandra Bergson and Antonia Shimerda achieved security and fulfillment on the land they loved.

We might dismiss Cather's portrayals as merely fiction if it were not for women like Mary Hradecky, the daughter of Moravian immigrants who homesteaded near Fleming, Colorado. Like Cather's heroines, Mary worked hard and took advantage of the opportunities around her. She earned some of her money working in Sterling and Iliff as a domestic, a job few daughters of American-born parents were willing to take. (Those daughters were much more likely to qualify for teaching positions, which carried more prestige and paid considerably higher salaries.) By the time Mary was in her early thirties (about 1910), she had acquired a homestead adjoining her parents' land, twenty to thirty head of cattle, and three to four hundred dollars in cash. Mary had accumulated an impressive estate above "what she gave those at home for clothing and groceries."[10]

Mary Hradecky undoubtedly found encouragement to pursue her own interests in the Yankee notions of female worth circulating among many of her homesteading neighbors. Still, the contrast between her experience and that of so many daughters of European-born homesteaders in the Canadian West underlines the important influence of economic forces on power dynamics within families. Canadian spinsters, unlike their U.S. counterparts, could not homestead in their own right. The government declared that it did not want to foster a class of independent young women.[11] Patriarchal authority in the Canadian provinces, therefore, escaped some of the undermining economic pressures that operated on U.S. homesteading families.

A study of women homesteaders in Mormon Utah further illuminates the tension between patriarchal culture and women's ability to patent government land. Jill Thorley Warnick looked at the percentage of entrants who were women, their success rates (as compared with men), and the identifying characteristics of the women who entered claims (their age, marital status, and family connections). Before 1900 about 10 to 13 percent of Utah's land entrants were women, approximately the same percentage as in northeastern Colorado. After 1900 the percentage of Utah's women land entrants did not materially change. In Colorado, on the other hand, the percentage jumped to about 18. Warnick's demographic profile of women land entrants in Utah reveals another contrast with women home-steaders in northeastern Colorado. Her subjects were much more likely to be older, married (including plural wives whose marriages the federal government did not recognize), and heads of households. Only 28 to 37 percent of her sample of women claimants were young and single.[12] In northeastern Colorado, young spinsters accounted for about 78 percent of the women claimants. Utah's male and female claimants had lower patent rates than their Colorado counterparts, but (as was the case in Colorado) men and women patented land at about an equal rate. In both Utah and Colorado, similar patent rates for men and women reflect the presence of families and groups of friends who helped each other prove up.

How do we explain the differences between Utah and Colorado women homesteaders, namely, the unequal percentages of women home-stead entrants after 1900 and the differing ages at which most women entered claims? To grasp the meaning of the contrasts, we must first recognize the many paradoxes in the laws and social dictates governing Utah women's lives. For example, European immigration to Utah, as well as Mormon religious beliefs, reinforced patriarchal authority.[13] Yet many of Utah's American-born homesteaders were the heirs of New England culture, as were homesteaders on Colorado's grasslands.

Populations in both regions inherited from their Puritan forebears the ideal of family harmony, which had significant benefits for women. And both groups assimilated elements of the separate-spheres ideal giving women power within their domestic sphere.

Nineteenth-century Utah women enjoyed legal rights denied to most other American women. Divorce was relatively easy to obtain. Utah women could vote. The territorial legislature granted woman suffrage in its constitution of 1870, and Mormon women also voted in church elections. Moreover, until the federal government stepped in, the territorial legisla-ture did not recognize the rule of common law under which wives had no legal identity separate from their husbands. Utah's Married Person's Prop-erty Act, which operated from 1872 to 1887, established a system of community property giving women equal rights to assets acquired during marriage.[14]

Mormon lawmakers intended none of these legal privileges to enhance women's rights as individuals. Granting women the right to divorce served the cause of harmony within the Mormon community. Like the Puritans before them, Mormons had tried to isolate themselves from an ungodly world in order to create an earthly Zion as an example for all the world to see and emulate. The Mormon community's enforced "togetherness" coupled with the need to maintain an orderly and harmonious public image tended to direct angry feelings inward toward the private side of life and heightened the potential for discord within families. As a tool of last resort for resolving dissension, Mormons, like the Puritans, tolerated divorce because they recognized that divorce could reduce open conflict in families.[15]

The Puritans had also allowed woman suffrage within the church, and Mormons, too, granted women ecclesiastical suffrage to help bind women's loyalties to Mormonism. But Mormons expanded woman suffrage to elections for public officeholders, thus guarding Zion from outsiders by potentially multiplying the Mormon vote. Similarly, the territory's community property laws protected Zion and its polygamous hierarchy by eliminating wives' claims under common law to widows' "thirds." According to common law, a man had to preserve from sale or transfer a third (or "dower") portion of his property for the use of his widow as long as she lived.[16] In this manner, the common law attempted to prevent a widow from becoming a public charge on the community. But the common law's protection of widows' thirds did not serve the interests of polygamous males. In theory, a polygamous man could have *all* of his property secured from sale to satisfy dower rights. The supersession of the common law by community property rights prevented such a scenario from becoming reality.

Mormon women recognized their elevated legal standing relative to most other American women. Many Mormon women, in fact, regarded their legal status as a shining example to the women's rights movement and regarded themselves as equals with men in the "education and growth of knowledge on all progressive matters."[17] Nonetheless, neither women's legal rights nor women's self-esteem posed any substantial challenge to the Mormon patriarchy. Mormon women, like Mormon men, believed themselves threatened by a hostile gentile world. Polygamous marriages placed Mormon women beyond the pale of respectable non-Mormon society. Even after the church no longer advocated polygamy, its shadow darkened outsiders' perceptions of Mormons' sexual relations. Probably most important, Mormon women had a religious commitment to Mormonism, and this attachment, in combination with the real benefits women enjoyed under the law, provided the internal glue for sustaining their loyalty to the Mormon community and its leaders. External threats served to further strengthen that loyalty.

The unique cultural and legal climate in Utah limited women's pursuit of homesteading opportunities. Neither the Mormon community nor women themselves expected "proper" Mormon women to speculate in land for their personal benefit. In contrast, Colorado's women homesteaders learned to speculate in government land as enthusiastically (and as selfishly) as men. Indeed, women's participation in the prevailing land fever after 1900 can explain the sharp rise during those years in the percentage of women land entrants. Economic opportunity coupled with the development of relatively egalitarian family styles in homesteading communities on Colorado's grasslands permitted increasing numbers of women to reach for self-determination through land speculation and ownership. As these women worked to prove up their claims, they gained a sense of their own empowerment, creating an example that became a common and accepted model for their communities.

In Utah no such evolution in attitudes occurred. Consequently, the percentages of women entrants did not increase over time. In the absence of the kind of land fever that hit the South Platte valley, Utah women did not internalize a communitywide land hunger. But more important, Mormons believed that women had a religious calling as wives and mothers that left essentially no room for dreams of personal gain. Therefore, the entrepreneurial aspect of homesteading had far less appeal than it had in Colorado, where family and religious influences posed few, if any, objections to the economic opportunities individual women found through homesteading.

Many Colorado women homesteaded to increase family land holdings, but in general these women as individuals profited from the eventual sale or lease of their lands. Utah women, on the other hand, homesteaded almost exclusively for the benefit of their families. They either added their land to a family farming operation or, in the case of many polygamous wives, they farmed their claims to support themselves and their children. The fact that women land entrants in Utah were much less likely to be young and single, and much more likely than their Colorado counterparts to be older and married or heads of households, is a reflection of women's differing goals in the two homesteading regions.[18] Mormon women held unusually strong religious and group loyalties. And these ties diverted them from achieving the same kinds and levels of economic advantage acquired by other women who filed for land under the federal homestead laws.

In Texas, as in Utah, the story of women homesteaders diverges from the pattern set in other western states, albeit for different reasons. Texas retained control over its public lands under the terms Congress accepted for Texas's statehood. Consequently, Texas wrote its own homestead laws. Beginning in 1870, constitutional and statutory law in Texas denied single women the right to claim land. By 1898 homesteading opportunities effectively ceased in Texas because unclaimed land was no longer available. These two conditions — the denial of homestead rights to single women and the early termination of homesteading opportunities — limited women's access to landownership. Of the land claims entered in Texas between 1870 and 1898, women held only about 4 percent.[19]

Outside of Texas and Utah, in non-Mormon areas of the American West where federal land laws prevailed, women established land entry patterns similar to those set by Colorado's female claimants. In South Dakota, where extensive European immigration occurred, we might expect that strong patriarchal traditions would have curtailed homestead entries made by women. But neither patriarchy nor the unusually harsh natural environment discouraged women from claiming and patenting land. Paula Nelson studied South Dakota women land claimants, many of them American-born, and concluded that most were speculators hoping to make money off their claims. Nearly 82 percent of the women in her sample were spinsters, most of them probably young. Nelson reported that many women worked at cash-paying jobs while they proved up, sometimes doing nontraditional kinds of work such as delivering mail or hauling freight. The majority of these women homesteaders succeeded in patenting their claims and gained in the process both self-esteem and the respect of their neighbors.[20]

In Wyoming, women homesteaders also followed the Colorado pattern. According to an analysis by Paula Bauman, women demonstrated a strong interest in claiming land as a means of capital accumulation. Over time, the proportion of women claimants increased as more women came to appreciate the advantages of landownership.[21]

But even more revealing for our purposes are land record data gathered by Elaine Lindgren, who studied Scandinavian, German-Russian, and other homesteaders in North Dakota. The percentages of women land recipients she found in the period before 1900 were low, on average 7.4 percent of the total number of patentees. Lindgren observed that after the turn of the century, the average percentages of women land recipients doubled and even tripled.[22] These findings have particular significance because Lindgren's subjects lived in communities with strong ethnic traditions and presumably followed a stronger patriarchal tradition than most American-born homesteaders. Here were populations whose original internal family hierarchies probably had much in common with those in Mormon families. But these North Dakota settlers, feeling relatively unthreatened by outside influences, did not have the same kind of fierce group loyalties, nor did they exercise the same degree of internal discipline.

A Kansas dust storm similar to ones that blanketed eastern Colorado during the 1930s. *Courtesy of L. Scotty Odell, Akron, Colorado.*

Economic considerations more than the practice of religion influenced family and individual decisions. In consequence, North Dakota's ethnic Scandinavian and German-Russian women took advantage of their right to acquire government land in ever-growing numbers, just like their assimilated American counterparts.

The Utah case aside, entrepreneurial opportunity under the federal homestead laws had an enormous impact in the agricultural West, expanding women's public roles as well as their private influence. The oppressive conditions endured by some pioneer women probably reflect the absence of such opportunity. Studies that look only at the migration phase, for example, necessarily exclude women's economic and speculative activities during settlement.[23] They focus instead on a part of the pioneering process likely to have inflicted the greatest physical and psychological pain. Homesteading, however, provided women with business opportunities that the migration could not. Homesteading was unique both in allowing single women to acquire government land on the same terms as men and in generating relatively large numbers of women entrepreneurs whose example created rising expectations among others of their sex.

The virtual end of homesteading by 1920 in eastern Colorado, coupled with a deepening agricultural depression, removed many of the economic opportunities formerly available to farm women. The federal government offered homesteads until President Franklin Roosevelt withdrew the remaining public domain from entry in 1935; but as early as the end of World War I, much of the remaining patentable land was unsuitable for farming. Moreover, during the war, expanding markets for meat and grain encouraged cultivation and grazing on marginal lands, so that after the armistice farmers faced the consequences of overproduction and a damaged natural environment. As markets disappeared, the plains region entered a dry cycle made worse by extensive plowing during better times. Unprotected top soil blew away by the ton, leaving much of the drylands in utter ruin during the dust bowl years of the 1930s. These disasters coincided with the worst economic depression the nation had ever experienced, lasting from the stock market crash in 1929 until World War II.

During the 1920s and 1930s, many families lost their land and had to seek employment in the city. The Kennedys, who settled in Logan County in 1905, were among the many dislocated families. Through homesteading and purchase they had acquired a farm for which a prospective buyer offered them $48,000 at the beginning of World War I. This deal collapsed because the purchaser failed to produce the down payment. By 1923 the Kennedys had lost their land and were farming as tenants. In 1934 they moved to Denver, having been unable even to feed their chickens with what they grew.[24]

In an environment where such stories were commonplace, most people considered themselves lucky just to find a place to live and put food on the table. Personal ambition under these circumstances seemed selfish and out of place. For farm women particularly, the declining position of agriculture was a calamity. They suffered, as did men, from the loss of income and, in some cases, from the desperate poverty these years brought. But in addition, they lost the momentum toward expanding options that homesteading, and prosperity, had created.

The helpmate role wives once used to increase their responsibilities and influence within families and communities would now be more limiting. In the absence of economic opportunity, women's place narrowed to supporting, with their labor and encouragement, the primary position of their husbands. Fred Zysset, Jr., recalled how his young bride helped him after their marriage in 1934. "Bertha . . . was a good example of a real pioneer woman. She never complained. She pitched in. She helped milk, chopped wood and picked up cow chips."[25] We cannot be sure why Bertha "never complained," but one possible explanation lies in her realization of limited options. Long gone were those better times when women as well as men strove for modest prosperity through homesteading.

The softening of gender-based prescriptive behavior experienced by homesteaders did not become a model for Bertha and other women — largely because homesteaders remained unconscious of the changes in gender relationships they had experienced. Regardless of how frequently the work roles of homesteading men and women overlapped or how completely men and women shared decision-making powers, homesteaders adhered in spirit, if not in fact, to the concept of separate spheres. Like other westerners, including the authors of western romances and histories, homesteaders followed an internal script ordering gender relations. Women as well as men found sufficient comfort in long-standing rules defining their proper roles that they were able to overlook the substantial gaps separating "ideal" from actual behavior. When economic hardship removed the self-determination promised by landownership and expanding work roles, homesteaders sought stability in their personal relationships. They re-affirmed the order they sought in a renewed loyalty to the behavioral formulas underlying the separate-spheres ideal.

But a decline in opportunity was not the only reason for this return to older, more hierarchical behavior patterns. At the beginning of the twentieth century, progressive reformers began to focus on rural life as the model that could save the urban United States from corruption and political turmoil. High immigration rates and expanding big business seemed to threaten the nation's stability and its ideals grounded in the Jeffersonian myth of the Virtuous Farmer. In an organized effort that acquired an identity as the country life movement, progressives worked to pass legislation designed to improve rural conditions. After all, any blemishes that obscured the rural ideal would impede reformers' efforts to convert city dwellers to agrarian values. Many progressives, for example, believed that farm wives suffered from overwork. The solution, according to these reformers, was the division of tasks among family members along gender lines. Such a division, they assumed, would improve the lives of farm wives and at the same time increase the operating efficiency of family farms.[26]

The establishment in 1913 of the Bureau of Home Economics within the Department of Agriculture and the funding of county agents by the Smith-Lever Act of 1914 marked the reformers' success at enlisting the government to implement their program. An official description of the 1914 law, under the heading "How Farm Women May Get Help Under the

Smith-Lever Act," outlined the methods used to educate farm women and girls to their separate work roles.

> The funds appropriated under the extension act . . . are given to the State agricultural colleges to enable them to employ men and women as county agents and experts who will move about among the farming people, demonstrate good methods of agriculture and home economics, cooperate with them in studying their farm and home problems, and assist them in the adoption of better methods on their farms or in their homes. . . .
>
> In the Northern and Western States the principal work has thus far been done by home economics experts connected with the agriculture colleges, but a beginning of the canning club work for girls has been made. The number of home economics experts who are doing work among the farm women is being rapidly increased. It is hoped that before long, there will be women agents in every county in the United States.

Home demonstration clubs were, in fact, active in northeastern Colorado, spreading the message of efficiency through gender-defined work roles.[27] By training women for certain farm jobs while leaving others to men, club organizers wanted to promote the kind of cooperative division of labor that they imagined occurred on the assembly lines of manufacturing plants. Efficient production, so the reformers theorized, would lead to increased family income and less labor for farm women. But limited work roles also subordinated women's work to the "real" work performed on farms by men.

As one historian has pointed out, the progressives who wanted to narrow the scope of farm wives' labor were not "simply reinforcing a subordinate and separate status for women."[28] Reformers believed that with a reduced work load, farm women would have more leisure time. And presumably women would put their leisure time to good use. They would rest and prepare for their many domestic duties. They would involve themselves in their children's activities and schoolwork. They would decorate their homes. They would engage in volunteer activities in their communities. Farm wives' "leisure" time would, in other words, not only benefit the women themselves but also their families and their neighbors.

However well intentioned their goals, progressive reformers nonetheless began a process of limiting options among women on homesteads that the loss of economic opportunity subsequently reinforced. Indeed, the generation born during the waning years of homesteading may have actually received a more thorough schooling in the ideals of their grandparents than did the children of those grandparents. Growing up with little hope of ever owning their own land, some granddaughters betrayed an acceptance of gender-based hierarchies when they wrote of homesteading mothers or aunts in phrases reminiscent of their grandparents' time. "[She was] another pioneer devoted to rearing a family and graciously helping others"; and, "[She was her husband's] constant companion . . . who gave him encouragement or sympathy as needed and was always at his side."[29]

Those same homesteading mothers and aunts might have described their marriages in more egalitarian terms. Ruth Hall, who homesteaded with her husband Orrin, declared how proud she was of "what Orrin *and I* [emphasis added] had accomplished . . . on the homestead."[30] She did not say that she was proud of what Orrin had accomplished with her help. In Ruth's opinion, Orrin and she were equal partners who had helped each other achieve a common goal. The next generation, however, did not adopt the same democracy in gender relations that Ruth and Orrin had practiced. Greatly reduced economic opportunities reordered women's priorities, focusing women's energies on family needs to the exclusion of personal dreams.

Urban women as well as farm women suffered many losses during the Great Depression of the 1930s. But the economic hardships (which for many farmers began at the end of World War I) lasted longer and, in general, had more serious consequences for the nation's rural population. Measured by the acquisition of such amenities as telephone service and electric power, the standard of living on farms between the world wars became markedly worse than that of city dwellers. By 1935 farm electric utilities lagged so far behind city services that President Roosevelt created the Rural Electrification Administration to bring electric power to country homes. Five years later, electricity extended to only about one-quarter of northeastern Colorado farms, and telephone service reached only slightly more than one-third.[31]

The popular image of farmers suffered deep and lasting damage as a result of the wide gap between city and country standards of living. Urbanites' sense of their own superiority has a long history in the United States, but during this period the derision of rural inhabitants reached new levels as jokes about dumb country "hicks" and promiscuous farmers' daughters multiplied.[32] Country people, women no less than men, responded with greatly intensified fear and distrust toward city residents. Even today these feelings can affect women, adding trauma to a decision to leave the farm to take a job or attend school in town.

The poverty generating these deep-seated prejudices proved to be less enduring than the attitudes it created. With a renewed cycle of good weather and an increased demand for farm products during World War II, prosperity returned to Colorado's grasslands. But the conditions of land-ownership and of farming differed from those the homesteaders experienced, leaving women with little opportunity for a direct entrepreneurial role. Land prices remained low — lower even than they were in 1930 — but free homesteads were only a memory. Agriculture itself was developing into a big business, requiring larger holdings than in the past. The average farm in 1940 covered nearly twice the acreage of the average-sized farm in 1925, and the trend toward larger and larger farms continued in subsequent years.[33]

Mechanization and the competition to increase production and income encouraged farmers to buy more land and put additional acres under cultivation. Bigger farms and new equipment, of course, required ever-greater capital investment by farm families. And women were much less likely than men to command the necessary resources to start a farming venture. Furthermore, the operation of tractors and other farm machinery had remained until World War II an essentially masculine skill. During the height of U.S. participation as a combatant, a government-sponsored campaign encouraged women to take over all aspects of farming, including operating heavy equipment. But the official message, reinforced by advertising and other shapers of public opinion, always reminded women that their total involvement in men's work was temporary, that their real job was running the home.[34] Farm women did little to challenge this message, and the expanding agricultural economy with its rising costs for land and equipment gave few encouragements to women who otherwise might have stepped out of their helpmate role in the pursuit of farm ownership.

The helpmate ideal has a venerable history. The Old Testament author of Proverbs (31:10–31) asked, "Who can find a virtuous woman, for her price is far above rubies" and then proceeded to describe her in terms of the helpmate ideal. So when economic and social pressures during the 1940s focused farm women's energies on helping husbands, those pressures resonated with religious teachings long familiar to women raised in the Judeo-Christian tradition. That many farm women continue to define themselves as helpmates reflects the enduring strength of the ideal and the perpetuation of economic conditions that place farm ownership beyond the reach of the great majority of farm women. A Colorado woman rancher interviewed by Teresa Jordan in the summer of 1979 expressed a common view of a wife's proper relationship with her husband when she described her marriage of twenty-three years. "I like to see the man hold the reins. But a woman has to be able to take them in a runaway. There is so much responsibility to a ranch, and I think a woman has to be keenly in the harness with her husband to make it successful. They work together. I'm not the head of the family. I'm just the helpmate."[35]

The revitalization of feminism, which had begun in the 1960s, offered little competition to this ranch woman's view of gender relationships. Feminists addressed a primarily urban audience concerned with equity in wages and access to professional training. They had little to say that agrarian women found relevant. Nonetheless, changes in farm women's lives were beginning to move in directions that many feminists would have found encouraging. Starting in the sixties and continuing to the present day, the steadily rising costs of agricultural production have promoted women to become involved in the operations and decisions that keep family farms running.

Rising costs for land, labor, and equipment continue to reduce the chances that individual women can acquire farms. Census data, in fact, suggest that in recent years the ratio of women to men owning or operating farms in Logan and Washington counties is significantly smaller than it was during the homesteading era of the early twentieth century.[36] On the other hand, expensive labor and the large size of individual farms have been compelling reasons for women to assume a working partnership in running an agricultural enterprise. Not all farm women, of course, wish to participate directly in a farming operation, and many contribute indirectly by earning wages in nearby towns. But the wives and daughters who prefer outdoor work have found that the high costs of farm labor have provided husbands and fathers with the incentive to welcome women's participation. The Reverend Gertrude Horn, who has served congregations over a large section of eastern Colorado, observed in 1982 that "women now, many of them, get out and run a tractor as much as their husband does." Whether women do farm work or hold outside jobs, she added, their employment outside the home "has made men . . . more used to fending for themselves [around the house]."[37]

Where women participate full-time in the operation of family farms and ranches or make substantial financial contributions toward those enterprises, they expect a commensurate voice in business and family decisions. And significant numbers of men do, in fact, respect these women as full partners. Still, many women display a curious inconsistency in their self-image by persisting in describing themselves as the lesser half of the partnership. A common opinion expressed by a young rural woman sums up this paradox: "I don't believe in women's lib, but I think I should have [the] same pay as somebody for the same job."[38]

Mildred Starlin preparing to drive one of many truckloads of wheat to the Akron grain elevators during the 1992 harvest. *Courtesy of the Washington County Museum, Akron.*

The source of this contradiction lies in farm women's deeply held apprehensions directed toward the feminist movement. Many rural wives see feminism as a threat to their marriages. They perceive it as alienating males either through a confrontational stance on issues or through its defense of that seemingly ultimate rejection of men, lesbianism. Farm women worry that if they appear to oppose men, they will jeopardize the economic security and companionship they hope to find in marriage. More simply put, rural women often equate "women's lib" with divorce.

Divorce for farm women signifies much more than the breakup of a marriage. Just as surely as foreclosure, divorce can end a familiar and loved way of life tied to the land, to animals, and to natural forces. And chances of re-establishing a farm partnership are slim. A failed marriage probably means that a woman must find employment in town, and she may be fearful of the urban environment and the people who inhabit it. Despite a standard of living on the plains that is no longer a cause for embarrassment, and despite the education and business acumen that farmers and ranchers must possess to run a successful operation today, agrarians of both sexes often see themselves as lacking the skills and sophistication to cope with city life.[39]

For women actively involved in agriculture, there is still another and more subtle fear. As ranch or farmhands, they perform "masculine" jobs.

Lucinda Starlin standing next to the combine she operates. *Courtesy of the Washington County Museum, Akron.*

Proud of their strength and endurance, they are sometimes ill at ease with the larger culture's prevailing definitions of "feminine" dress, appearance, and behavior. As long as their homes and families are secure, these agrarian women do not have to confront ambivalent feelings about their gender. But placed in a town setting around "feminine" members of their sex, they may question their femininity as somehow inadequate. In an interview with Teresa Jordan, a Wyoming ranch woman alluded to such feelings when she confided:

> I've always been terribly strong. Too strong, really. I never tried to be, but I was. In high school I had muscles like a man. . . . The guys would even comment on it. . . .
>
> A very embarrassing thing happened to me a couple weeks ago. . . . A girl attacked me in front of the bar. Just like that, she came up and clawed my face. I'd never been in a girl fight; I detest them. But when she attacked me I flung her to the ground, doubled up my fist, and beat her head. . . . There I was, on the ground, face to face with her, and suddenly it all came to me. I

Range land near Akron. The house and outbuildings in the distance appear little larger than dots on the landscape. *Photo by author.*

was shocked, really horrified. I'm still horrified. I hate to set foot in [town] yet because they are all talking about it. . . . I am really, really embarrassed.[40]

Another ranch woman described a less confrontational, and presumably more common, encounter with town women.

[A woman friend] and I try to go to Las Vegas together every year. And here sit all these ladies with their really long painted fingernails. . . . Our fingernails are all short and broke, and there's a little stain here, a little grease there. But it doesn't bother us. And nobody there even notices. That's not what they're looking at. They're looking at our friendly appearance or whatever.[41]

Rural women may continue to believe that differences in life-style and values separate them from urban women. Such feelings have some justification given that town women generally have available to them a greater variety of jobs — jobs that may offer more independence from husbands and families than farm wives typically find. But in recent years,

A relic of a bygone era, a sod building stands like a sentinel in a plowed field near Akron. *Photo by author.*

increasing numbers of women from farms and cities have come to recognize their common problems. The attention given to practical legal issues by the women's movement has gained a larger audience among agricultural women. For example, inheritance tax laws that discount wives' contributions to the farm economy have treated farm widows unfairly, and they know it.[42] These and other instances of second-class status accorded women under the law frustrate farm wives who are fully aware of their essential roles in family farming operations.

Frustrations, however, remain subdued given the recent depression in agriculture that has focused women's energies on saving the family farm. In the press of financial worries, women have not had the stamina to fight the law's gender-based double standard. But even in good times, farm women tend to suppress feelings of indignation over their second-class legal status. Wives do not want to risk whatever economic security they have, and they know that the realities of farming bind them to their husbands as long as they wish to remain on the land. Many farm women, moreover, appreciate the functional partnership grounded in shared work and mutual reliance that they and their husbands have created. Undeniably, some women have to contend with the whole spectrum of male chauvinism, including the extreme of abuse. But the demonstrated competence of women involved in running farms and ranches has earned many of them equal or nearly equal standing in the eyes of their male co-workers.

Still, individual farm women of today rarely have the opportunity to own land or to speculate with profits from farm income or land sales. To the extent that they share decisions about the management and disposition of farmland, they participate in the capitalist economy of the family farm. But as partners in a farming operation, they lack the freedom to make unilateral decisions about land use and capital investment that the mostly single women who entered homestead claims exercised. Married women living on homesteads claimed by their husbands engaged in a degree of power sharing with their husbands that is similar to what modern farm women experience. Both homesteading wives and farm wives of the present day have demonstrated that egalitarian partnerships between the sexes are possible, and perhaps even probable, when economic advantages accrue from shared work and decision making. But neither married women homesteaders nor most contemporary farm women have experienced the range of economic choices that were available to many women homestead entrants.

The fundamental advantage enjoyed by women entrants was their ownership of a land claim or patent. To be sure, a land claim was not technically the same as landownership. Yet claimants as well as patentees could sell their homesteads, and they had the same freedom as owners to make decisions about land use and to manage their property as they wished. In the history of agriculture, and indeed through much of U.S. history, opportunities for women to exercise control over economic decisions have rarely arisen. But historic precedent gave way to change when federal homestead laws operating in the late nineteenth and early twentieth centuries opened up new possibilities for capital accumulation and investment to thousands of women whose chances of inheriting land were virtually nil.

Given the small fraction of the population engaged in agriculture today and the vastly better career opportunities open to women in the cities, the achievements of women who homesteaded on Colorado's eastern plains may seem irrelevant to contemporary Americans. But women homesteaders left a legacy that can still teach us valuable lessons. For one, they demonstrated that women and men can work as partners in the pursuit of common goals. They showed, too, that flexibility toward gender roles allows women and men greater freedom to become acquainted with each other as *persons* outside the context of male and female stereotypes. But for those who place a high value on the availability of choices, the most important legacy left by these women homesteaders may be a basic lesson in economics; namely, that the ability to plan and direct the course of one's life requires some control over capital and the means of producing it. From the homesteading wives who set aside part of their egg and butter income to buy a sewing machine or a pair of window curtains to the women who developed or sold their own claims to finance a separate household or start a new business, women homesteaders demonstrated the connection between the ability to control resources and the freedom to make choices.

Notes

Introduction

1. Lois Ervin, tape recorded interview with author, Sterling, Colo., June 7, 1980.
2. Roy Robbins, *Our Landed Heritage: The Public Domain, 1776–1936* (Gloucester, Mass.: Peter Smith, 1960), 91.
3. The Oregon Donation Land Act, passed by Congress in 1850, granted 320 acres to male settlers who arrived in Oregon before 1850 and an additional 320 acres to their wives.
4. Beverly J. Stoeltje, "A Helpmate for Man Indeed: The Image of the Frontier Woman," *Journal of American Folklore* 88 (January–March 1975): 25–41; Annette Bennington McElhiney, "The Image of the Pioneer Woman in the American Novel" (Ph.D. diss., University of Denver, 1978), chaps. 2 and 3.
5. Jack E. Eblen, "An Analysis of Nineteenth Century Frontier Populations," *Demography* 2 (1965): 399–413.
6. Annette Kolodny, *The Lay of the Land: Metaphor as Experience and History in American Life and Letters* (Chapel Hill: University of North Carolina Press, 1975), 7–9, 133–134; Howard R. Lamar, "Rites of Passage: Young Men and Their Families in the Overland Trail Experience, 1843–1869," in *Soul-Butter and Hog Wash and Other Essays on the American West*, Charles Redd Monographs in Western History, no. 8 (Provo, Utah: Brigham Young University Press, 1978), cited in Lillian Schlissel, *Women's Diaries of the Westward Journey* (New York: Schocken Books, 1982), 14.
7. On women's civilizing role in western fiction, see McElhiney, "Pioneer Woman," part 1. On women's civilizing role according to historian Dee Brown, see his *The Gentle Tamers: Women of the Old Wild West* (New York: Bantam Pathfinder Editions, 1974).
8. Barbara Welter, "The Cult of True Womanhood, 1820–1860," *American Quarterly* 18 (Summer 1966): 151–174; Glenda Riley, *Inventing the American Woman: A Perspective on Women's History* (Arlington Heights, Ill.: Harlan Davidson, 1987), 237.
9. O. E. Rolvaag, *Giants in the Earth: A Saga of the Prairie* (New York: Harper and Brothers Publishers, 1927).
10. Sheryll Patterson-Black, "Women Homesteaders on the Great Plains Frontier," *Frontiers* 1 (Summer 1976): 68.
11. Elinore Pruitt Stewart, *Letters of a Woman Homesteader* (Lincoln: University of Nebraska Press, 1961), letter dated January 23, 1913.
12. Charley O'Kieffe, *Western Story: The Recollections of Charley O'Kieffe, 1884–1898* (Lincoln: University of Nebraska Press, 1960), 7.
13. Christine Stansell, "Women on the Great Plains, 1865–1890," *Women's Studies* 4 (1976): 96.

14. Kathryn Kish Sklar, *Catherine Beecher: A Study in American Domesticity* (New York: W. W. Norton and Company, 1976); Welter, "True Womanhood."

15. Everett Dick, *The Sod-House Frontier, 1854–1890: A Social History of the Northern Plains From the Creation of Kansas and Nebraska to the Admission of the Dakotas* (Lincoln: University of Nebraska Press, 1979), 233–235.

16. Walter Prescott Webb, *The Great Plains: A Study in Institutions and Environment* (Boston: Ginn and Company, 1931), 505–506; Rolvaag, *Giants in the Earth*.

17. Einar Haugen, *Ole Edvart Rolvaag* (Boston: Twayne Publishers, 1983), 1–8.

18. Rolvaag, *Giants in the Earth*, 318.

19. Ibid., 349.

20. Brown, *Gentle Tamers*, 269.

21. Hamlin Garland, *A Son of the Middle Border* (New York: Macmillan Company, 1938), 416.

22. Ibid., 62–63, 243–244, 367–369, 440.

23. Daryl Jones, *The Dime Novel Western* (Bowling Green, Ohio: Bowling Green University Popular Press, 1978), 61–75, 106–109; Don Russell, "Foreword," in *The Life of Hon. William F. Cody Known as Buffalo Bill* (Lincoln: University of Nebraska Press, 1978), v–viii.

24. Mari Sandoz, *Old Jules* (New York: Hastings House Publishers, 1935).

25. Mari Sandoz, *Slogum House* (Boston: Little, Brown and Company, 1937).

26. Ibid., 10.

27. Mari Sandoz, *Sandhill Sundays and Other Recollections* (Lincoln: University of Nebraska Press, 1970), 115.

28. Willa Cather, *O Pioneers!* (Boston: Houghton Mifflin Company, 1913), 65.

29. Willa Cather, *My Antonia* (Boston: Houghton Mifflin Company, 1918), 353.

30. Willa Cather, *O Pioneers!*, 308.

31. Stansell, "Women on the Great Plains," 96.

32. John Mack Faragher, *Women and Men on the Overland Trail* (New Haven, Conn.: Yale University Press, 1979).

33. Julie Roy Jeffrey, *Frontier Women: The Trans-Mississippi West, 1840–1880* (New York: Hill and Wang, 1979), 72–73.

34. Glenda Riley, *The Female Frontier: A Comparative View of Women on the Prairie and Plains* (Lawrence, Kans.: University Press of Kansas, 1988), 4.

35. Sandra L. Myres, *Westering Women and the Frontier Experience, 1800–1915* (Albuquerque: University of New Mexico Press, 1982), 269–270.

36. Ibid., 9–10, 238, 269–270.

37. Ibid., 269–270.

38. Schlissel, *Women's Diaries*, 83–84.

39. Paula Petrik, *No Step Backward: Women and Family on the Rocky Mountain Mining Frontier, Helena, Montana, 1865–1900* (Helena: Montana Historical Society Press, 1987).

40. Sarah Deutsch, *No Separate Refuge: Culture, Class, and Gender on an Anglo-Hispanic Frontier in the American Southwest, 1880–1940* (New York: Oxford University Press, 1987).

41. Riley, *The Female Frontier*; Jeffrey, *Frontier Women*; Schlissel, *Women's Diaries*; and Stansell, "Women on the Great Plains."

42. Carl Degler, *At Odds: Women and the Family in America From the Revolution to the Present* (New York: Oxford University Press, 1980); Eli Zaretsky, *Capitalism, the Family and Personal Life* (New York: Harper Colophon Books, 1976); Joan Kelly, "The Doubled Vision of Feminist Theory: A Postscript to the Women and Power Conference," *Feminist Studies* 5 (Spring 1979): 216–217. Zaretsky and Kelly, both Marxist-feminists, offered some hope for the resolution of this conflict. Degler, however, found the clash between women's individual needs and family needs to be an eternal "given."

43. Emma Burke Conklin, *A Brief History of Logan County, Colorado, With Reminiscences by Pioneers* (Denver: Welch-Haffner Printing Company, 1928), 61.

44. Bureau of the Census, *Thirteenth Census of the United States, Taken in the Year 1910: Abstract of the Census With Supplement for Colorado* (Washington, D.C., 1913), 600, 604; Bureau of the Census, *Fourteenth Census of the United States, Taken in the Year 1920*, vol. 2, *Population, 1920* (Washington, D.C., 1922), 1331; Bureau of the Census, *Fourteenth Census, Taken in 1920*, vol. 3, *Population*, 139, 144, 146, 149; and Census Office, *Compendium of the Eleventh Census: 1890*, part 1 (Washington, D.C., 1894), 10, 478.

45. Norton Juster, *So Sweet to Labor: Rural Women in America, 1865–1895* (New York: Viking Press, 1979).

46. I did not include in my analysis those veterans of the Civil War and their widows who claimed soldiers' homesteads.

47. Don E. Fehrenbacher, ed., *History and American Society: Essays of David M. Potter* (New York: Oxford University Press, 1973), 283–284.

Chapter 1

1. For a discussion of the West as garden and desert, see Henry Nash Smith, *Virgin Land: The American West as Symbol and Myth* (Cambridge: Harvard University Press, 1978), 174–183.

2. Nell Brown Propst, *Forgotten People: A History of the South Platte Trail* (Boulder, Colo.: Pruett Publishing Company, 1979), 43–125; Dale Wells, *The Logan County Ledger* (Logan County Historical Society, 1976), 3–11; and Robert Athearn, *The Coloradans* (Albuquerque: University of New Mexico Press, 1976), 74. See also Stan Hoig, *The Sand Creek Massacre* (Norman: University of Oklahoma Press, 1961).

3. Propst, *Forgotten People*, 58–59, 62, 110; Dean Krakel, *South Platte Country: A History of Old Weld County, Colorado, 1739–1900* (Laramie: The Powder River Publishers, 1954), 191–194; and Wells, *Logan County Ledger*, 11–13.

4. Propst, *Forgotten People*, 127–128; and Emma Burke Conklin, *A Brief History of Logan County, Colorado, With Reminiscences by Pioneers* (Denver: Welch-Haffner Printing Company, 1928),61–66, 76.

5. Conklin, *Logan County*, 62, 74, 78, 86; and Wells, *Logan County Ledger*, 18.

6. Conklin, *Logan County*, 78, 143, 145, 154, 156; Propst, *Forgotten People*, 138, 148–149; and Wells, *Logan County Ledger*, 17.

7. Conklin, *Logan County*, 145; and Wells, *Logan County Ledger*, 25.

8. Conklin, *Logan County*, 145–146.

9. Ibid., 78–80, 86–87; and Propst, *Forgotten People*, 136.

10. Propst, *Forgotten People*, 134–136.

11. Conklin, *Logan County*, 334.

12. Propst, *Forgotten People*, 134–136, 146–167.

13. Missouri Propst, letter of May 28, 1876, to her mother, Mrs. Powell, quoted in Conklin, *Logan County*, 155–156.

14. Conklin, *Logan County*, 81, 150; and Propst, *Forgotten People*, 136–137.

15. Conklin, *Logan County*, 148; and Propst, *Forgotten People*, 136–137.

16. Conklin, *Logan County*, 150–151; and Propst, *Forgotten People*, 148–149.

17. Conklin, *Logan County*, 151.

18. Margaret C. Detamore, interview with M. Armour, Civil Works Administration, *Interviews Collected During 1933–34 for the State Historical Society of Colorado: Logan and Phillips Counties*, Document 15, Pamphlet 341, Colorado Historical Society (hereafter cited as CWA, Doc, Pam, CHS).

19. Robert Athearn, *Union Pacific Country* (Chicago: Rand McNally and Company, 1971), 184; and Athearn, *Coloradans*, 140. See also Wells, *Logan County Ledger*, 25–26; and Steven Mehls, "The New Empire of the Rockies: A History of Northeastern Colorado" (draft prepared for the Bureau of Land Management, Colorado State Office, 1981), Chap. 5, 17–19.

20. Wells, *Logan County Ledger*, 28, 33–34; and Conklin, *Logan County*, 90, 146, 165–167, 169, 171–172.

21. Conklin, *Logan County*, 161; Athearn, *Coloradans*, 167; and Millard Fillmore Vance, "Pioneering at Akron, Colorado," *Colorado Magazine*, September 1931, 175, 177.

22. S. S. Worley, interview with M. Armour, CWA, Doc 27, Pam 341, CHS; Washington County Museum Association, *The Pioneer Book of Washington County, Colorado* (Denver: Big Mountain Press, 1959), 83 (hereafter cited as PBWC); Athearn, *Union Pacific Country*, 196; and Vance, "Pioneering," 175.

23. PBWC, 199, 377; and Mehls, "New Empire," Chap. 5, 17–19.

24. Washington County Museum Association, *The Pioneer Book II of Washington County, Colorado* (Fort Morgan, Colo.: Print Shop, n.d.; Aurora, Colo.: Rocky Mountain Press, n.d.), 622 (hereafter cited as PBWC II); PBWC, 61–62, 236, 238.

25. James C. Malin, *The Grassland of North America: Prolegomena to Its History* (Ann Arbor: Edwards Brothers, 1956), 317.

26. Census Office, *Report on Agriculture by Irrigation in the Western Part of the United States at the Eleventh Census, 1890* (Washington, D.C.: GPO, 1894), 120.

27. Roy Robbins, *Our Landed Heritage: The Public Domain, 1776–1936* (Gloucester, Mass.: Peter Smith, 1960), 89–91, 206–207, 218–220; and Sheryll Patterson-Black, "Women Homesteaders on the Great Plains Frontier," *Frontiers* 1 (Summer 1976): 67–68.

28. PBWC, 54, 62, 77, 84, 258.

29. Ibid., 90–91, 140, 259–260, 331; and Census Office, *Report on the Statistics of Agriculture in the United States at the Eleventh Census, 1890* (Washington, D.C., 1895), 359, 407, 503.

30. Census Office, *Report on the Statistics of Agriculture, 1890*, 120. On the doctrine of prior appropriation, see Walter Prescott Webb, *The Great Plains: A Study in Institutions and Environment* (Boston: Ginn and Company, 1931), 431–452.

31. Ernest Staples Osgood, *The Day of the Cattleman* (Chicago: University of Chicago Press, 1929), 194–215.

32. Ibid.; Mehls, "New Empire," Chap. 4, 4–6.

33. Farmers in Nebraska could not afford fencing either. The problems cattlemen had with fences were largely of their own making. Osgood, *Day of the Cattleman*, 190–193, 242; Propst, *Forgotten People*, 166; PBWC, 41, 62, 174–175.

34. PBWC, 41, 61, 323, 345–346.

35. Ibid., 76, 90, 200; Propst, *Forgotten People*, 159.

36. Mehls, "New Empire," Chap. 4, 19.

37. Propst, *Forgotten People*, 158, 165; and Clifford P. Westermeier, "The Legal Status of the Colorado Cattleman, 1867–1887," *Colorado Magazine*, May 1948, 111, 117.

38. Krakel, *South Platte Country*, 183–184, 187.

39. Propst, *Forgotten People*, 171.

40. Colorado State Planning Division, *Colorado, 1959–1961: Year Book of the State of Colorado*, ed. Salma A. Waters (n.p., n.d.), 420. Between 1914 and 1960, the Akron station reported an average annual rainfall of 17.48 inches; between 1931 and 1960 the Sterling station reported an average rainfall of 14.10 inches. Propst, *Forgotten People*, 176.

41. PBWC, 179, 219–220, 354–355; and Wells, *Logan County Ledger*, 42.

42. PBWC, 354; Mehls, "*New Empire*," Chap. 9, 1–8. Of 248 Logan County farm owners in 1889, 29.44 percent irrigated; only 0.28 percent of 356 farm owners in Washington County irrigated. Census Office, *Report on Agriculture by Irrigation, 1890*, 100–101.

43. PBWC, 65, 84; Detamore interview; Propst, *Forgotten People*, 176–177. In Logan County the tenancy rate reached 11.6 percent in 1900, up from 2.4 percent in 1890. In Washington County the tenancy rate in 1900 was 7.5 percent, about double the 1890 rate of 3.7 percent. Census Office, *Report on the Statistics of Agriculture, 1890*, 126–127; and Bureau of the Census, *Thirteenth Census of the United States, Taken in the Year 1910: Abstract With Supplement for Colorado* (Washington, D.C.: GPO, 1913), 639, 641.

44. PBWC, 211, 219, 364; Mehls, "New Empire," Chap. 9, 3.

45. Washington County's population in 1890 numbered 2,301; in 1900, 1,241. Logan County's population rose slightly during the same period, from 3,070 to 3,292. The gain reflects the growth of Sterling, where the population increased from 540 to 998. Elsewhere in Logan County, the population declined. Census Office, *Twelfth Census of the United States, Taken in the Year 1900: Population*, part 1 (Washington, D.C.: GPO, 1901), 12, 85. Logan County's sheep population in 1890 numbered 15,603; cattle, 11,710. By 1900 the number of sheep had increased to 30,021; cattle to 55,089. During the same period, Washington County sheep counts rose from 5,003 to 18,635; cattle counts rose from 3,677 to 24,628. In 1890 stockgrowers ran more sheep than cattle in both counties. Census Office, *Report on the Statistics of Agriculture, 1890*, 240, 279; and

Census Office, *Twelfth Census of the United States, Taken in the Year 1900: Agriculture*, part 1 (Washington, D.C.: GPO, 1902), 422–423. See also *PBWC*, 260; Mehls, "New Empire," Chap. 9, 1–3.

46. *PBWC*, 220.

47. Wells, *Logan County Ledger*, 43–44; Propst, *Forgotten People*, 172.

48. Alvin T. Steinel, *History of Agriculture in Colorado* (Fort Collins, Colo.: The State Agriculture College, 1926), 260–261.

49. Ibid., 245–252.

50. Ibid., 271–274, 276–277; and Mehls, "New Empire," Chap. 10, 18.

51. Steinel, *Agriculture in Colorado*, 269, 277. Propst, *Forgotten People*, 131; and Webb, *The Great Plains*, 334–348.

52. Propst, *Forgotten People*, 131. In the 1860s farmers near Littleton planted the first sugar beets in Colorado. Kenneth Rock, " 'Unsere Leute': The Germans From Russia in Colorado," *Colorado Magazine*, Spring 1977, 162. Steinel, *Agriculture in Colorado*, 295, 299.

53. The number of acres in Logan County planted in sugar beets rose from 5,352 to 19,539 in the period between 1909 and 1919. During the same decade, sugar beet cultivation in Washington County expanded from 584 to 1,780 acres. Bureau of the Census, *Thirteenth Census Taken in 1910: Abstract With Supplement for Colorado*, 645, 647; Colorado State Board of Immigration, *Year Book of the State of Colorado, 1921* (Denver: Welch-Haffner Printing Company, n.d.), 55. Dena Sabin Markoff, "The Beet Sugar Industry in Microcosm: The National Sugar Manufacturing Company, 1899 to 1967" (Ph.D. diss., University of Colorado, 1980), 1–30; William L. Hayes, interview with M. Armour, CWA, Doc 2, Pam 341, CHS; Mehls, "New Empire," Chap. 10, 12–18; and Wells, *Logan County Ledger*, 73–76.

54. *PBWC*, 135.

55. Propst, *Forgotten People*, 186, 197–198; and Wells, *Logan County Ledger*, 74, 76.

56. Steinel, *Agriculture in Colorado*, 299–308.

57. Timothy J. Kloberdanz identified all 1,174 Russians in the 1920 federal census of Logan County as German-Russians. See his "People Without a Country: The Russian Germans of Logan County, Colorado," in Wells, *Logan County Ledger*, 233.

58. Ibid., 225–247; and Rock, " 'Unsere Leute,' " 155–183. For an in-depth study of German-Russians in America, see Richard Sallet, *Russian-German Settlements in the United States*, trans. LaVern J. Rippley and Armand Bauer (Fargo: North Dakota Institute for Regional Studies, 1974). The German-Russians acquired the Russian part of their identity when their forebears accepted the invitation of their countrywoman Czarina Catherine II to settle in her adoptive country. A number of conditions induced the emigration from Russia, including famine, drought, over-population, and pressures to assimilate. Beginning in the 1870s, immigrants began arriving in the United States. A larger migration occurred after the turn of the century, following the Russo-Japanese War of 1905 and appeals for workers from the U.S. sugar beet industry. Most of the German-Russians who immigrated to the Sterling area were Roman Catholics from the Volga region.

59. Sallet, *Russian-German Settlements*, 51, cited in Rock, " 'Unsere Leute,' " 176.

60. Robert G. Dunbar, "History of Agriculture," in *Colorado and Its People*, vol. 2, ed. LeRoy R. Hafen (New York: Lewis Historical Publishing Company, 1948), 141, cited in Rock, " 'Unsere Leute,' " 165.

61. Ibid. See also Bureau of the Census, *Thirteenth Census Taken in 1910: Abstract With Supplement for Colorado*, 600, 604; Bureau of the Census, *Fourteenth Census of the United States, Taken in the Year 1920*, vol. 3, *Population* (Washington, D.C.: GPO, 1922),139, 149; and Nell Brown Propst, "The New Americans: A History of the Ethnic Groups Who Settled Logan County: The Mexicans," in Wells, *Logan County Ledger*, 217–223.

62. Mehls, "New Empire," Chap. 10, 19.

63. Propst, *Forgotten People*, 186–187, 193.

64. Ibid., 199–200; *PBWC II*, 111.

65. *PBWC*, 61.

66. Robbins, *Our Landed Heritage*, 296–298.

67. Ibid., 362–363, 387; Mary Wilma M. Hargreaves, *Dry Farming in the Northern Great Plains: 1900–1925* (Cambridge: Harvard University Press, 1957), 337–363; Colorado State Board of Immigration, *Year Book of the State of Colorado, 1918* (Denver: Brock-Haffner Press, n.d.), 189; and Colorado State Board of Immigration, *Year Book of the State of Colorado, 1920* (Denver: Welch-Haffner Printing Company, n.d.), 167.

68. Robbins, *Our Landed Heritage*, 296, 298.

69. Propst, *Forgotten People*, 183.

70. *PBWC II*, 63, 146–147, 205, 343.

71. R. E. Arnett, "Ranching in Northeastern Colorado in the Early Eighties," *Colorado Magazine*, November 1943, 211; Wells, *Logan County Ledger*, 44; and Fleming Historical Society, *Memories of Our Pioneers* (Iowa Falls, Iowa: General Publishing and Binding, 1971), 89.

72. By 1920 renters operated about one-third of the farms in Logan County; in Washington County, about one-fifth. The average value of farmland per acre in Logan County at the turn of the century was $7.79. That figure rose to $19.25 in 1910 and to $44.34 in 1920. In Washington County the average price per acre rose from $2.54 in 1900 to $10.25 in 1910 and to $26.88 in 1920. Bureau of the Census, *Thirteenth Census Taken in 1910: Abstract With Supplement for Colorado*, 633, 635, 639, 641; Bureau of the Census, *Fourteenth Census Taken in 1920*, vol. 6, part 3, *Agriculture*, 181, 183; Census Office, *Report on the Statistics of Agriculture, 1890*, 126–127; and *Year Book of the State of Colorado, 1921*, 72–73, 76.

73. Wells, *Logan County Ledger*, 57–58, 86; and Conklin, *Logan County*, 113–115.

74. *Year Book of the State of Colorado, 1921*, 108; Wells, *Logan County Ledger*, 91; and *PBWC II*, 40, 87, 194, 255.

75. *Year Book of the State of Colorado, 1920*, 225; *Year Book of the State of Colorado, 1921*, 120; Wells, *Logan County Ledger*, 54–55, 83–84; and *PBWC II*, 204.

76. *Year Book of the State of Colorado, 1918*, 143, 189.

77. *PBWC II*, 37, 106.

78. By 1919, 338 tractors operated in Washington County; 225 in Logan County. *Year Book of the State of Colorado, 1921*, 68; and *PBWC II*, 32–33, 56, 197, 291.

79. Inez S. Corsberg, *Remembering 1916: Some Recollections of a One-Room School Teacher* (Sterling, Colo.: Royal Printing Company, 1969), 9; and Rock, " 'Unsere Leute,' " 179.

80. Mehls, "New Empire," Chap. 10, 25.

81. In 1920 the population density averaged 4.4 persons per square mile in Washington County. In Logan County the population density averaged 10.1 persons per square mile.

Rural areas in Logan County averaged 6.6 persons per square mile. Bureau of the Census, *Fourteenth Census Taken in 1920*, vol. 1, *Population*, 96–97, 152.

Chapter 2

1. Washington County Museum Association, *The Pioneer Book of Washington County* (Denver: Big Mountain Press, 1959), 157 (hereafter cited as PBWC).

2. I used the following published collections of family histories: PBWC; Washington County Museum Association, *The Pioneer Book II of Washington County, Colorado* (Fort Morgan, Colo.: Print Shop, n.d.; Aurora, Colo.: Rocky Mountain Press, n.d.) (hereafter cited as PBWC II; Crook Historical Society, *No Fuss and Feathers — Crook: A History of the Crook Community*, ed. Dorothea Safford and Helen Taylor (Fort Collins, Colo.: Economy Printing, 1977) (hereafter cited as CHS, *No Fuss and Feathers*); and Fleming Historical Society, *Memories of Our Pioneers* (Iowa Falls, Iowa: General Publishing and Binding, 1971) (hereafter cited as FHS, *Memories*). Tract books of the land office records are available on microfilm from the Bureau of Land Management. The American-born subjects of this study include persons with foreign-born parents. Data in the family histories are often inadequate to make distinctions between first- and second-generation Americans. In tabulating these and other data, I have divided them (where the sample size was sufficiently large) into two periods — before and after 1900 — so that I could make comparisons over time.

3. James C. Malin, *The Grassland of North America: Prolegomena to Its History* (Ann Arbor: Edwards Brothers, 1956), 288.

4. John Ise in Howard Ruede, *Sod-House Days: Letters from a Kansas Homesteader, 1877–1878*, ed. John Ise (New York: Cooper Square Publishers, 1966), 40, n. 9.

5. The government issued approximately 41 percent of all federal land patents in the period between 1868 and 1897, and 59 percent of the patents between 1898 and 1917. Everett Dick, *The Lure of the Land: A Social History of the Public Lands From the Articles of Confederation to the New Deal* (Lincoln: University of Nebraska Press, 1970), 303; Louise E. Peffer, *The Closing of the Public Domain* (Stanford: Stanford University Press, 1951), 134; and Paul Gates, *Free Homesteads for All Americans: The Homestead Act of 1862* (Washington, D.C.: Civil War Centennial Commission, 1962).

6. Sheryll Patterson-Black found an even wider range in the percentages of claims made by women in the land office records of Douglas, Wyoming, and Lamar, Colorado. In 1891 only 4.8 percent of the claimants at the Douglas land office were women. In contrast, 18.2 percent of the Lamar claimants in 1907 were women. See her "Women Homesteaders on the Great Plains Frontier," *Frontiers* 1 (Summer 1976): 68.

7. Federal Population Census Schedules for 1910 are available on microfilm at the Denver Federal Records Center.

8. The number of land entries reported in the family histories is approximately equivalent to the number of land entrants. This equation, of course, does not hold for the tract book records, where multiple entries for the same individual are common. When calculating the percentages of male and female entrants, I tried to avoid counting the same person twice.

9. Donald J. Bogue, *The Population of the United States* (Glencoe, Ill.: Free Press, 1959), 158, 161.

10. I would hesitate to present the small data samples shown in Tables 2.11 and 2.12 except that the numbers indicate overwhelming majorities in single categories. Because this information is so hard to find anywhere, I think the data are worth presenting despite their shortcomings.

11. I calculated all median ages according to E. A. Wrigley, ed., *An Introduction to English Historical Demography* (New York: Basic Books, 1966), 150.

12. Malin, *Grassland*, 289. In his study of early white settlements in Iowa and Illinois, Allan Bogue described the "typical" (male) pioneer as "a married man between the ages of twenty five and forty five who had started his family before he moved to the ... frontier." See his *From Prairie to Corn Belt: Farming on the Illinois and Iowa Prairies in the Nineteenth Century* (Chicago: The University of Chicago Press, 1963), 22–24.

13. John C. Hudson, "The Study of Western Frontier Populations," in *The American West: New Perspectives, New Dimensions*, ed. Jerome Steffen (Norman: University of Oklahoma Press, 1979), 45. Median ages of all males in the United States at first marriage in 1890, 1900, and 1910 were 26.1, 25.9, and 25.1 years, respectively. Median ages of all females at first marriage were 22.0 in 1890, 21.9 in 1900, and 21.6 in 1910. Bogue, *Population*, 215.

14. By 1900 all white, American-born women bore, on the average, 3.5 children each. Ansley J. Coale and Melvin Zelnik, *New Estimates of Fertility and Population in the United States* (Princeton: Princeton University Press, 1963), 36, cited in Daniel Scott Smith, "Family Limitation, Sexual Control and Domestic Feminism in Victorian America," in *Clio's Consciousness Raised*, ed. Mary Hartman and Lois Banner (New York: Harper Colophon Books, 1974), 122–123.

15. Conrad Taeuber and Irene B. Taeuber, *The Changing Population of the United States* (New York: John Wiley and Sons, 1958), 256. I grouped homesteading wives by age according to whether they lived on homesteads claimed before or after 1900. The precise age groups in the federal census data were impossible to apply to the reminiscences because of the small sample sizes and the irregular reporting of age.

16. For example, Jack E. Eblen, "An Analysis of Nineteenth Century Frontier Populations," *Demography* 2 (1965): 406–407. Hudson ("Western Frontier Populations," 47–48) discusses the complexity of fertility patterns among the early white settlers of Dakota Territory. The territorial census of 1885 showed American-born women of American-born parents having only 3.9 children, while German-Russians and Mormons had very large families.

17. *PBWC II*, 445, 516, 656; FHS, *Memories*, 62, 160, 178, 204; *PBWC*, 222; and Glen R. Durrell, "Homesteading in Colorado," *Colorado Magazine*, Spring 1974, 110.

18. Bureau of the Census, *United States Life Tables: 1890, 1901, 1910, 1901–1910* (Washington, D.C.: GPO, 1921), 104, 118.

19. Bogue, *Population*, 210. The earliest maternal death rate figures in the census date from 1915.

20. The "average expectation of life" for women sixty-five years old in 1967 was 81.5 years. Bureau of the Census, *Statistical Abstract of the United States, 1970* (Washington, D.C.: GPO,1970), 53.

21. Nell Brown Propst, *Those Strenuous Dames of the Colorado Prairie* (Boulder, Colo.: Pruett Publishing Company, 1982), 143–144. Divorces were open and easy to obtain in some western communities. See, for example, Everett Dick, *The Sod-House Frontier, 1854– 1890: A Social History of the Northern Plains From the Creation of Kansas and Nebraska to the Admission of the Dakotas* (Lincoln: University of Nebraska Press, 1979), 505–506;

and Abby T. Mansur, quoted in Christiane Fischer, ed., *Let Them Speak for Themselves: Women in the American West, 1849–1900* (Hamden, Conn.: Archon Books, 1977), 52.

22. Among the entire U.S. population fourteen years of age and older, the percentage of females classified as divorced rose steadily from 0.4 in 1890 to 0.8 in 1920. Values for males are lower because men tended to remarry at a higher rate than women. Bogue, *Population*, 220–221. Statistics on persons who were ever divorced are not available. County divorce statistics are unlikely to accurately reflect local divorce rates; partners to a broken marriage might well move away and obtain their divorce elsewhere.

23. Gates, *Free Homesteads*, 11. Patterson-Black reported that about 37 percent of men and 42 percent of women received patents near Lamar, Colorado, and Douglas, Wyoming. See her "Women Homesteaders," 68.

Chapter 3

1. Ruth Schooley Hall, *Soddie Bride* (Fort Collins, Colo.: Robinson Press, 1973), 11.

2. Emma Burke Conklin, *A Brief History of Logan County, Colorado, With Reminiscences by Pioneers* (Denver: Welch-Haffner Printing Company, 1928), 152–153, 334–335; Washington County Museum Association, *The Pioneer Book of Washington County, Colorado* (Denver: Big Mountain Press, 1959), 30, 42, 194, 312, 328, 343 (hereafter cited as *PBWC*); Washington County Museum Association, *The Pioneer Book II of Washington County, Colorado* (Fort Morgan, Colo.: Print Shop, n.d.; Aurora, Colo.: Rocky Mountain Press, n.d.), 54, 57, 120, 662 (hereafter cited as *PBWC II*); and Fleming Historical Society, *Memories of Our Pioneers* (Iowa Falls, Iowa: General Publishing and Binding, 1971), 79, 214 (hereafter cited as FHS, *Memories*). Although settlers did not recognize a direct connection between mosquitoes and malaria, they did sense that mosqitoes somehow caused disease.

3. FHS, *Memories*, 79, 203; *PBWC II*, 287–289, 463; and *PBWC*, 69.

4. *PBWC II*, 400–401. "Many, possibly the majority (depending on the time and place), of homesteaders never intended to live on their farms." Everett Dick, *The Lure of the Land: A Social History of the Public Lands From the Articles of Confederation to the New Deal,* (Lincoln: University of Nebraska Press, 1970), 151.

5. *PBWC*, 16, 199.

6. Crook Historical Society, *No Fuss and Feathers — Crook: A History of the Crook Community,* ed. Dorothea Safford and Helen Taylor (Fort Collins, Colo.: Economy Printing, 1977), 130; and FHS, *Memories*, 50–51. Mary Clark was a young widow who homesteaded to support her sons, aged seven and eight. She and her husband had earlier failed to prove up on land he had claimed. In 1915 she received a patent and promptly sold out. *PBWC II*, 116–117.

7. *PBWC*, 568–569.

8. Lillian Schlissel argues that the earlier "overland passage played a vital role in the life cycle of men, corresponding to 'breaking away,' improving, or bettering oneself, the stages that mark a man's life." In contrast, women experienced severe "dislocation" because the journey came at a time in their lives when they were pregnant or caring for small children. See Schlissel's *Women's Diaries of the Westward Journey* (New York: Schocken Books, 1982), 14, citing Howard R. Lamar, "Rites of Passage: Young Men and Their Families in the Overland Trail Experience 1843–1869," in *Soul-Butter and Hog Wash and Other Essays on the American West*, Charles Redd Monographs in Western

History, no. 8 (Provo, Utah: Brigham Young University Press, 1978), 51; and Daniel Levinson, "The Mid-Life Transition: A Period in Adult Psychosocial Development," *Psychiatry* 40 (1977): 100. Single women homesteaders obviously did not suffer this dislocation because they were not in the reproductive phase of their lives.

9. *PBWC II*, 176–177.

10. Ibid., 250–251.

11. Ibid., 673.

12. Amy Dickensen Worthley, tape recorded interview with author, at Mrs. Worthley's home near Sterling, June 7, 1980. The National Woman's Party, under the leadership of Alice Paul, drafted the first Equal Rights Amendment to the Constitution. Paul arranged to have the ERA introduced into Congress in 1923. Christine A. Lunardini, *From Equal Rights to Equal Suffrage: Alice Paul and the National Woman's Party, 1910–1928* (New York: New York University Press, 1986), 150–168.

13. Georgia L. McRoberts, "Pioneer Ranch Life Near Sterling," *Colorado Magazine*, January 1934, 64.

14. Conklin, *Logan County*, 82; and FHS, *Memories*, 87.

15. *PBWC*, 197.

16. Ibid., 53, 82, 136, 139; and *PBWC II*, 357, 395.

17. FHS, *Memories*, 172–173; and *PBWC*, 197. On the hazards of the Overland Trail, see, for example, Schlissel, *Women's Diaries*, 15, 23–27.

18. Prior to 1900 tract book records included very few addresses.

19. Stella Sparling, tape recorded interview with Margaret Cooley, Akron, Colo., June 23, 1975; and *PBWC*, 171. Factors influencing settlement patterns in Iowa and Illinois were also complex, although not identical to those in eastern Colorado. See Allan Bogue, *From Prairie to Corn Belt: Farming on the Illinois and Iowa Prairies in the Nineteenth Century* (Chicago: University of Chicago Press, 1963), 10–12.

20. S. S. Worley, interview with M. Armour, Civil Works Administration, *Interviews Collected During 1933–34 for the State Historical Society of Colorado: Logan and Phillips Counties*, Document 27, Pamphlet 341, Colorado Historical Society (hereafter cited as CWA, Doc, Pam, CHS). Worley was a locator in 1886 in an area that later became part of Phillips County. I am indebted to Matthew Downey for supplying this reference to me.

21. Laybourn's daughter provided the quotations. *PBWC*, 213–214, 377.

22. Ibid., 214; and Millard Fillmore Vance, "Pioneering at Akron, Colorado," *Colorado Magazine*, September 1931, 176.

23. Prairie is "that portion of the grassland with forest along the streams lying east of an irregular north-south line falling mostly between the 96 and 98 meridians." West of the line is the beginning of the plains. James C. Malin, *The Grassland of North America: Prolegomena to Its History* (Ann Arbor: Edwards Brothers, 1956), 2.

24. *PBWC*, 117, 224, 362; FHS, *Memories*, 205; and CHS, *No Fuss and Feathers*, 71.

25. Throughout the period of this study, homesteaders lived in sod and adobe houses. Wood houses appeared by the mid-1870s and may have become the predominant dwelling in the years just preceding 1920. This conclusion is speculation based on the fact that many homesteaders were using profits from increased production during World War I to replace their soddies with modern housing. Stone houses were present from the

earliest days of settlement. On stone houses, see PBWC, 213; and FHS, Memories, 111. On cement houses, see PBWC II, 570; and PBWC, 125, 127.

26. Ruth Schooley Hall, *Soddie Bride* (Fort Collins, Colo.: Robinson Press, 1973), 6–7; and FHS, Memories, 174. I found no evidence that homesteaders paid cash to anyone for help in building a sod house.

27. FHS, Memories, 9, 175, 200; Hall, *Soddie Bride*, 6; and PBWC, 33. For a description of sod house construction in Nebraska, see Cass G. Barns, *The Sod House* (Lincoln: University of Nebraska Press, 1970), 59–61.

28. FHS, Memories, 200; and PBWC, 349–350. The year was 1887.

29. PBWC, 33; and PBWC II, 637. For a description of problems associated with sod construction, see Sheryll Patterson-Black and Gene Patterson-Black, *Western Women, in History and Literature* (Crawford, Nebr.: Cottonwood Press, 1978), 27.

30. PBWC, 42; and Hall, *Soddie Bride*, 6.

31. Hall, *Soddie Bride*, 108; and PBWC, 378, 380. Opinions regarding the prevalence of wood floors varied. One source (post-1900) said floors were usually dirt; another (1890s), that most were wood. PBWC II, 206; and PBWC, 218.

32. Hall, *Soddie Bride*, 22; and FHS, Memories, 206.

33. PBWC, 42, 218, 326; and PBWC II, 118, 360.

34. Clara Watson, "Homesteading on the Plains," *Colorado Magazine*, April 1961, 142. Many homes combined dugout and sod construction, sometimes reflecting a later sod addition to the earlier underground dwelling.

35. Sallie J. Cheairs, interview with M. Armour, CWA, Doc 10, Pam 341, CHS.

36. PBWC II, 206; Cheairs interview; and PBWC, 238, 349–350. To make adobe bricks, homesteaders placed a mixture of clay and straw in molds to dry in the sun.

37. PBWC, 82, 213; FHS, Memories, 41, 88, 111; and PBWC II, 125.

38. PBWC, 86, 221, 349–350, 380; and Lois Ervin, interview with author, Sterling, Colo., June 7, 1980.

39. PBWC, 146, 324; FHS, Memories, 30, 88; Hall, *Soddie Bride*, 22, 27, 30–31.

40. PBWC, 216, 380; FHS, Memories, 30, 41; and Hall, *Soddie Bride*, 30. A typical sod house had one room, ten to twelve feet wide and twenty to thirty feet long. PBWC II, 290.

41. The Payne family was exceptionally musical. They formed a band that played "all over eastern Colorado" after the turn of the century. Thomas played the fiddle, and Dorothy performed on the guitar, organ, and banjo. As the children grew, the Paynes added a piano, drums, saxophone, and bull fiddle to their band. PBWC II, 428–429, 443; and PBWC, 151.

42. Lizzie Gordon Buchanan, interview with M. Armour, CWA, Doc 18, Pam 341, CHS.

43. PBWC, 351; and FHS, Memories, 31.

44. FHS, Memories, 169. See also Table 2.3. Few members of the working class could afford the cash investment needed to move west. Murray Kane, "Some Considerations on the Safety Valve Doctrine," *Mississippi Valley Historical Review* 23 (September 1936): 169–188.

45. FHS, Memories, 219; and PBWC, 274.

46. PBWC, 365.

47. Ibid., 249, 333, 367; Alice to Mama, letter dated April 10, 1909, Alice C. Newberry Papers, Colorado Historical Society Library.

48. Hall, *Soddie Bride*, 31.

49. FHS, *Memories*, 31, 41, 157, 162; *PBWC II*, 161, 596; and *PBWC*, 356.

50. Conklin, *Logan County*, 153, quoting M. A. Propst, letter dated June 23, 1874.

51. *PBWC*, 54, 177; *PBWC II*, 672, 675; and Cheairs interview.

52. *PBWC*, 40–41, 64, 162–163, 218; *PBWC II*, 224, 464; FHS, *Memories*, 159, 178; Chet Kincheloe, letter to author, dated March 31, 1980; and Hall, *Soddie Bride*, 30, 69.

53. *PBWC*, 25, 151, 233, 259; and FHS, *Memories*, 31.

54. Hall, *Soddie Bride*, 30; FHS, *Memories*, 200; and *PBWC*, 146, 234, 326, 353, 380.

55. FHS, *Memories*, 89, 159; and *PBWC*, 131, 326, 344–345. By 1917 wheat production in Logan County had begun to equal corn production, but in Washington County corn remained by far the largest crop. Colorado State Board of Immigration, *Year Book of the State of Colorado, 1918* (Denver: Brock-Haffner Press, n.d.), 34–36.

56. *PBWC II*, 351; and *PBWC*, 324–325, 353.

57. Hall, *Soddie Bride*, 120; *PBWC II*, 161, 450; and FHS, *Memories*, 41.

58. *PBWC*, 188, 232; *PBWC II*, 30–31, 517, 622; and FHS, *Memories*, 200.

59. FHS, *Memories*, 38; and *PBWC II*, 622. The first anecdote dates from around 1910; the second, from the late 1880s.

60. Hall, *Soddie Bride*, 10, 123; and Dale Wells, *The Logan County Ledger* (Logan County Historical Society, 1976), 55.

61. *PBWC*, 117, 345, 362. On the Overland Trail, collecting chips was a chore for women and children. Sandra L. Myres, *Westering Women and the Frontier Experience, 1800–1915* (Albuquerque: University of New Mexico Press, 1982), 105.

62. *PBWC II*, 205–206; and FHS, *Memories*, 151.

63. *PBWC*, 146–147, 193; *PBWC II*, 205; and FHS, *Memories*, 201. The richest family was the one with the largest pile of chips. *PBWC*, 227.

64. FHS, *Memories*, 124–125; and *PBWC II*, 143.

65. *PBWC II*, 464; and *PBWC*, 163, 240.

66. *PBWC*, 117, 163, 258, 388; FHS, *Memories*, 159; and Hall, *Soddie Bride*, 22.

67. *PBWC II*, 114, 363–364; CHS, *No Fuss and Feathers*, 124; and *PBWC*, 43, 62, 76.

68. *PBWC II*, 137; and *PBWC*, 169, 191–192, 222.

69. CHS, *No Fuss and Feathers*, 117–118; *PBWC*, 299; and FHS, *Memories*, 178–179.

70. CHS, *No Fuss and Feathers*, 117; and *PBWC II*, 87.

71. *PBWC*, 43, 153–154, 216–217; *PBWC II*, 125, 267, 422; and FHS, *Memories*, 160.

72. FHS, *Memories*, 127, 201, 241; and *PBWC II*, 596.

73. *PBWC*, 57, 193, 390; *PBWC II*, 87, 410, 584, 663, 687; and FHS, *Memories*, 40, 200. For studies of coyote and wolf behavior, see, for example, Dayton O. Hyde, *Don Coyote* (New York: Ballantine Books, 1986); and Farley Mowat, *Never Cry Wolf* (Boston: Little, Brown and Company, 1963). Two sightings of mountain lions are reported in accounts dating from the 1890s in Washington County. *PBWC*, 44–45, 359–360.

74. *PBWC*, 145, 159; and *PBWC II*, 252, 379.

75. *PBWC*, 144, 217; and *PBWC II*, 205.

76. *PBWC*, 45, 55, 63, 196; and Ezra and Helen Alishouse, tape recorded interview with Margaret Cooley, Akron, Colo., November 12, 1975.

77. *PBWC*, 45, 55, 63, 260–261, 327. The Rasmussen family moved from their Washington County homestead because of the abundance of locoweed on their claim. *PBWC*, 301.

78. In 1910 Charlie Nolan rode his bicycle seventy miles on weekly visits to his family from his job in Akron as a blacksmith. *PBWC II*, 400, 194; FHS, *Memories*, 77; *PBWC*, 65; CHS, *No Fuss and Feathers*, 50. For a discussion of the conditions that impaired development of community loyalties among agrarian pioneers, see Robert V. Hine, *Community on the American Frontier: Separate but Not Alone* (Norman: University of Oklahoma Press, 1980), 96–99, 116–126.

79. *PBWC II*, 55.

80. Ibid., 310; and *PBWC*, 110, 146, 173–174.

81. Claim jumpers were most troublesome in the early nineties when many homesteaders were experiencing hard times. I found no evidence of formally organized claim clubs to defend settlers' interests in Washington and Logan counties. Buchanan interview; *PBWC II*, 13; *PBWC*, 190; and FHS, *Memories*, 176, 179, 202.

82. *PBWC II*, 661; FHS, *Memories*, 83; and Chet Kincheloe letter.

83. *PBWC II*, 264; and Hall, *Soddie Bride*, 123.

Chapter 4

An early version of this chapter appeared in *Frontiers* 7 (Special Issue, 1984), 43–49; and in Susan Armitage and Elizabeth Jameson, eds., *The Women's West* (Norman: University of Oklahoma Press, 1987), 165–178. Reprinted with permission.

1. Fleming Historical Society, *Memories of Our Pioneers* (Iowa Falls, Iowa: General Publishing and Binding, 1971), 206–207, 209 (hereafter cited as FHS, *Memories*).

2. On the origins and development of the separate-spheres ideal, see Barbara Welter, "The Cult of True Womanhood, 1820–1860," *American Quarterly* 18 (Summer 1966): 151–174.

3. John Mack Faragher, *Women and Men on the Overland Trail* (New Haven, Conn.: Yale University Press, 1979), n. 5 on 244, 119, 138–140. For more on the patriarchal structure of mid-nineteenth-century midwestern farm families, see Faragher's "History From the Inside-Out: Writing the History of Women in Rural America," *American Quarterly* 33 (Winter 1981): 537–557.

4. Nancy F. Cott, "Passionlessness: An Interpretation of Victorian Sexual Ideology, 1790–1850," *Signs* 4 (1978): 219–236. On nineteenth-century reformers promoting a separate and autonomous domestic sphere for women, see, for example, Kathryn Kish Sklar, *Catharine Beecher: A Study in American Domesticity* (New York: W. W. Norton, 1976); Ann Douglas, *The Feminization of American Culture* (New York: Alfred A. Knopf, 1977); and Ruth Bordin, *Frances Willard* (Chapel Hill: University of North Carolina Press, 1986). On the spread of the separate-spheres ideal among farm families, see Norton Juster, *So Sweet to Labor: Rural Women in America, 1865–1895* (New York: Viking Press, 1979); and Mary P. Ryan, *Womanhood in America From Colonial Times to the Present* (New York: New Viewpoints, 1975), 143. Ryan placed the beginnings of widespread dissemination of the separate-spheres ideal after the invention of low-cost printing technology in 1830.

5. Washington County Museum Association, *The Pioneer Book of Washington County, Colorado* (Denver: Big Mountain Press, 1959), 70, 223, 276, 324, 367, 379 (hereafter

cited as *PBWC*). Around the turn of the century, one Akron family received the *Saturday Evening Post, Youth's Companion, American Boy, Delineator, Ladies Home Journal*, and *Colliers*. Stella Sparling, interview with Margaret Cooley, June 23, 1975, Akron Public Library; Lois Ervin, interview with author, Sterling, Colo., June 7, 1980; Amy Dickensen Worthley, interview with author, Sterling, Colo., June 7, 1980; Crook Historical Society, *No Fuss and Feathers — Crook: A History of the Crook Community*, ed. Dorothea Safford and Helen Taylor (Fort Collins, Colo.: Economy Printing, 1977), 49–50 (hereafter cited as CHS, *No Fuss and Feathers*); Washington County Museum Association, *The Pioneer Book II of Washington County, Colorado* (Fort Morgan, Colo.: Print Shop, n.d.; Aurora, Colo.: Rocky Mountain Press, n.d.), 207 (hereafter cited as *PBWC II*); Alice to Mama, letter dated April 10, 1909, Alice C. Newberry Collection, Colorado Historical Society.

6. *PBWC*, 221.

7. Ervin interview.

8. *PBWC*, 31, 324; *PBWC II*, 426.

9. CHS, *No Fuss and Feathers*, 49; *PBWC*, 387; *PBWC II*, 253, 276, 339, 423.

10. CHS, *No Fuss and Feathers*, 49; FHS, *Memories*, 50–51.

11. *PBWC*, 73, 163; *PBWC II*, 381, 585.

12. *PBWC II*, 126–127, 181, 396, 427.

13. FHS, *Memories*, 112; Opal Covington, tape recorded interview with Margaret Cooley, Akron, Colo., May 15, 1975; and *PBWC*, 163, 190, 222.

14. FHS, *Memories*, 204.

15. *PBWC*, 56; FHS, *Memories*, 76, 238, 242; and *PBWC II*, 49–50, 139–140.

16. FHS, *Memories*, 202; *PBWC II*, 452; Olive Ross, letter to author, dated April 8, 1980; and *PBWC*, 198, 357.

17. FHS, *Memories*, 127–128.

18. *PBWC II*, 30, 254–255, 452.

19. *PBWC*, 379.

20. Ibid., 175, 195–196, 352; and Ezra and Helen Alishouse, interview with Margaret Cooley, November 12, 1975, Akron Public Library.

21. *PBWC*, 27–28, 45, 141, 229, 379; FHS, *Memories*, 180; and *PBWC II*, 355.

22. *PBWC II*, 230, 355, 680.

23. Ibid., 230–231; and *PBWC*, 137. With the introduction of the automobile, the churches' recreational role became less important. One settler credited cars with declining church attendance and, by the early 1920s, the dissolution of some congregations. *PBWC II*, 496, 601; and FHS, *Memories*, 180.

24. *PBWC*, 119, 261, 329; and *PBWC II*, 229.

25. *PBWC*, 27, 91, 138, 151, 172, 218–219; and CHS, *No Fuss and Feathers*, 50. Homesteaders square danced most of the time, but they also waltzed. Fiddles, mouth harps, guitars, organs, and pianos accompanied the dancing.

26. *PBWC*, 66; *PBWC II*, 253.

27. *PBWC*, 27, 34, 58, 358, 381. Every August people gathered from miles around to attend Old Settlers picnics at Cope Grove, Washington County. Planted by Jonathon Calvin Cope in 1890, the five or six acres of surviving trees measured forty to fifty feet high and as much as fifteen inches in diameter by 1900. His was one of the few tree claims

to weather the drought. Alvin T. Steinel, *History of Agriculture in Colorado* (Fort Collins, Colo.: State Agricultural College, 1926), 256.

28. Flinch, rook, pinochle, pitch, and checkers were common adult games. Children played checkers, old maid, carromboard, and authors. *PBWC II*, 132, 183–184, 210, 214, 465, 522; *PBWC*, 120, 137, 261, 324, 341, 380; and FHS, *Memories*, 77, 105.

29. *PBWC II*, 349–350.

30. Glen R. Durrell, "Homesteading in Colorado," *Colorado Magazine*, Spring 1974, 105; FHS, *Memories*, 77; and *PBWC*, 120.

31. *PBWC*, 351.

32. Ibid., 198, 380; and *PBWC II*, 275–276, 425, 451, 515.

33. *PBWC II*, 44, 396, 523.

34. *PBWC*, 354. Logan County voters cast 286 ballots for woman suffrage and 161 against; Washington County voters, 207 in favor and 119 against. Across Colorado, 55 percent of the voters approved woman suffrage. State of Colorado, *Abstract of Votes Cast for State Officers at the General Elections of the Years 1892 to 1900 Inclusive* (Denver: Smith-Brooks Printing Company, 1901), 7.

35. Nell Brown Propst, *Forgotten People: A History of the South Platte Trail* (Boulder, Colo.: Pruett Publishing Company, 1979), 178–179; Georgia L. McRoberts, "Pioneer Ranch Life Near Sterling," *Colorado Magazine*, January 1934, 64; *PBWC*, 67; and Etta Shannon Monroe, interview with M. Armour, Civil Works Administration, *Interviews Collected During 1933–34 for the State Historical Society of Colorado: Logan and Phillips Counties*, Document 23, Pamphlet 341, Colorado Historical Society (hereafter cited as CWA, Doc, Pam, CHS).

36. *PBWC*, 330.

37. *PBWC II*, 196–197, 253, 275, 428; and FHS, *Memories*, 167.

38. *PBWC II*, 424; and FHS, *Memories*, 175.

39. Nell Brown Propst, *Those Strenuous Dames of the Colorado Prairie* (Boulder, Colo.: Pruett Publishing Company, 1982), 61; and *PBWC*, 345.

40. *PBWC*, 322; *PBWC II*, 354, 410, 426, 601; and FHS, *Memories*, 206. A report from Iowa dated 1860 noted that "women never work in the fields — not even milking cows. We men must do that." John Z. Sandahl, Henry County, Iowa, letter to Jonas P. Zachrison, in Swedish Historical Society of America, *Year-Book, VII, 1921–1922* (Chicago, 1922), 60, cited in Allan G. Bogue, *From Prairie to Corn Belt: Farming of the Illinois and Iowa Prairies in the Nineteenth Century* (Chicago: University of Chicago Press, 1963), 238.

41. *PBWC II*, 252, 515, 601; *PBWC*, 43, 64, 169–170; and FHS, *Memories*, 159. Others have noted the importance of women's butter and egg money. See Glenda Riley, *Frontierswomen: The Iowa Experience* (Ames, Iowa: The Iowa State University Press, 1981), 86–87; and Gilbert C. Fite, *The Farmers' Frontier, 1865–1900* (New York: Holt, Rinehart and Winston, 1966), 47.

42. *PBWC*, 151, 353; and *PBWC II*, 325, 529. Some women living on the dry lands did not attempt to maintain a garden. FHS, *Memories*, 31.

43. *PBWC II*, 111, 353, 553; *PBWC*, 131, 382. For a description of wash day on the Overland Trail, see Sandra L. Myres, *Westering Women and the Frontier Experience, 1800–1915* (Albuquerque: University of New Mexico Press, 1982), 151–153. The method was essentially the same.

44. *Diaries of Ruth and Clark Woodis: The Story of a Colorado Homestead, 1913–1928* (n.p., 1976). Ruth and Clark Woodis homesteaded near Deertrail. Ruth's chores appear to have been much more varied than Clark's.

45. *PBWC*, 31, 42–43, 117, 322; and FHS, *Memories*, 104, 216.

46. Teresa Jordan's oral history of modern ranch women supports this conclusion. See her *Cowgirls: Women of the American West* (New York: Anchor Press, Doubleday and Company, 1982), 24–25, 39–41, 50–51, 66–67. See also Elliott West, *Growing Up With the Country: Childhood on the Far Western Frontier* (Albuquerque: University of New Mexico Press, 1989), 257.

47. *PBWC II*, 66, 197; *PBWC*, 149, 173, 342; and FHS, *Memories*, 246.

48. Eva was born in 1898. FHS, *Memories*, 195–196, 204; and *PBWC*, 259.

49. *PBWC II*, 256.

50. Ibid., 49, 58, 231; *PBWC*, 130, 145, 252, 313; and FHS, *Memories*, 181.

51. Christine Stansell, "Women on the Great Plains, 1865–1890," *Women's Studies* 4 (1976): 87–98.

52. *Diaries of Ruth and Clark Woodis*, May 5, 1918, and March 5, 1919; and *PBWC*, 382.

53. Ruth Schooley Hall, *Soddie Bride* (Fort Collins, Colo.: Robinson Press, 1973), 34, 70, 80; and FHS, *Memories*, 56–57.

54. Alishouse interview; and *PBWC*, 138, 147–148, 160, 163, 170, 192, 350; *PBWC II*, 20, 125–126, 231, 354–355, 426, 695; and FHS, *Memories*, 167.

55. *PBWC*, 87, 173, 248, 264.

56. Elva Bowles, tape recorded interview with author, Longmont, Colo., July 18, 1980; Ervin interview; Worthley interview; and Ross letter.

57. *PBWC*, 49, 88, 265; and *PBWC II*, 183. Mary Clark Peterson's reminiscences indicate the gender and marital status of teachers in Hyde before the turn of the century. She recalled eight teachers. Seven were women, of whom one was married. *PBWC*, 60.

58. Edwin A. Curley, *Nebraska, Its Advantages, Resources, and Drawbacks* (New York: American and Foreign Publications Company, 1875), 428–429, cited in William Forrest Sprague, *Women and the West: A Short Social History* (Boston: Christopher Publishing House, 1940), 116–117.

59. FHS, *Memories*, 126–127, 161, 175, 194–195, 201, 207; *PBWC*, 162, 177, 192, 258, 284–285, 321, 359–360; *PBWC II*, 125–126, 348–349, 449; and Propst, *Those Strenuous Dames*, 77–78.

60. *PBWC*, 160, 359–360; and *PBWC II*, 18, 101, 396, 588.

61. *PBWC*, 150, 380.

62. See, for example, Stansell, "Women on the Great Plains," 91; and Mary Wilma M. Hargreaves, "Women in the Agricultural Settlement of the Northern Plains," *Agricultural History* 50 (January 1976): 187.

63. *PBWC*, 176; and FHS, *Memories*, 216.

64. Hall, *Soddie Bride*, 122–123; FHS, *Memories*, 30; and Worthley interview.

65. *PBWC*, 157, 163, 353.

66. FHS, *Memories*, 209.

67. Ibid., 131; and Hall, *Soddie Bride*, 95.

68. Propst, *Forgotten People*, 154; and FHS, *Memories*, 214.

69. Clara Watson and her family came to Colorado in 1915. Clara Watson, "Homesteading on the Plains," *Colorado Magazine*, April 1961, 142–143; and *PBWC II*, 175, 201, 585, 596. Dorothy Schwieder noted a similar sense of isolation among Iowa women, though they too had many contacts with family and neighbors. See her "Labor and Economic Roles of Iowa Farm Wives, 1840–80," in *Farmers, Bureaucrats, and Middlemen: Historical Perspectives on American Agriculture*, ed. Trudy Huskamp Peterson (Washington, D.C.: Howard University Press, 1980), 165.

70. FHS, *Memories*, 123; and Hall, *Soddie Bride*, 69.

71. FHS, *Memories*, 31; and *PBWC II*, 398.

72. *PBWC*, 159–160.

73. Refer to my discussion of women's homestead entry rates in Chapter 2, and see Tables 2.6 and 2.7.

74. *PBWC II*, 673.

Chapter 5

An early version of this chapter appeared in the *Nebraska Humanist* 9 (1986): 32–38. Reprinted with permission.

1. Two published collections of women homesteaders' letters are Elinore Pruitt Stewart's well-known *Letters of a Woman Homesteader* (Lincoln: University of Nebraska Press, 1961); and Enid Bern, ed., "They Had a Wonderful Time: The Homesteading Letters of Anna and Ethel Erickson," *North Dakota History* 45 (Fall 1978): 4–31. In the same enthusiastic vein are the letters of Cecilia Hennel Hendricks, *Letters From Honeyhill: A Woman's View of Homesteading, 1914–1931*, comp. and ed. Cecilia Hendricks Wahl (Boulder, Colo.: Pruett Publishing Company, 1986).

2. Alice to Mama, letter dated June 30, 1907, Alice C. Newberry Papers, Colorado Historical Society Library, Denver; and Bureau of Land Management, Land Office Records for Kit Carson County, Section 20, Township 9, Range 46.

3. Edna to Alice, letter dated November 3, 1894; Aunt Lizzie to Alice, letter dated May 16, 1893; and Alice to Edna, letter dated July 20, 1902.

4. Grover Blake to Eldon Newberry, letter dated February 19, 1955.

5. Florence to Alice, letter dated June 3, 1894; Mama to Alice, letter dated June 3, (1894?); Alice to Family, letter dated December 8, 1895; and Alice to Mama, letters dated October 24, 1897, and August 31, 1900.

6. Alice to Eldon, letter dated September 20, 1906.

7. Alice to Mama, letter dated June 30, 1907.

8. Alice to Eldon, letters dated September 20, 1906, and January 7, 1907; Alice to Mama, letter dated April 21, 1907; and Alice to Mother, letter dated June 25, 1908.

9. Alice to Mama, letter dated March 7, 1909.

10. Ibid., letter dated April 10, 1909.

11. Ibid., letters dated June 4, 1907, and June 30, 1907.

12. Ibid., letters dated March 11, 1909, and June 30, 1907.

13. Alice to Edna, letter dated February 21, 1911.

14. Ibid., letters dated December 14, 1938, and January 3, 1939; Eldon to Edna, letter dated January 4, 1939.

15. File folder 271; and Alice to Edna, letter dated December 14, 1938. Ethel F. Yergen to author, letter dated June 28, 1985.

16. Alice to Edna, letters dated February 21, 1911, December 14, 1938, and January 16, 1939.

17. Alice to Henry Weingardt, letter dated February 17, 1938.

18. Edna to Alice, letter dated March 16, 1938.

19. Yergen letter.

Chapter 6

1. Although class distinctions came west with the settlers, western society often offered more flexibility in social relations than did established eastern communities. Burton Harris, who grew up in a small Wyoming town in the early twentieth century, once explained to me a cardinal rule of western etiquette: Never ask anyone about his or her past. Questioning an outlaw might prove dangerous and questioning ordinary citizens might subject them to embarrassing exposure. The local population generally agreed that it was better to have neighbors relate to each other on more or less the same social level than to risk trouble by making judgments about people based on their past lives.

   For two studies that deal with class issues in the West, see Lewis Atherton, *The Cattle Kings* (Bloomington: Indiana University Press, 1967); and Ralph Mann, *After the Gold Rush: Society in Grass Valley and Nevada City, California, 1849–1870* (Stanford: Stanford University Press, 1982).

2. General Land Office, *Suggestions to Homesteaders and Persons Desiring to Make Homestead Entries* (Washington, D.C.: GPO, 1906); General Land Office, *The Manner of Proceeding to Obtain Title to Public Lands Under the Preemption, Homestead, and Other Laws* (Washington, D.C.: GPO, 1884), cited in Jill Thorley Warnick, "Women Homesteaders in Utah, 1869–1934" (M.A. thesis, Brigham Young University, 1984), 66.

3. John Mack Faragher, *Women and Men on the Overland Trail* (New Haven, Conn.: Yale University Press, 1979); Joan Jensen, *With These Hands: Women Working on the Land* (New York: Feminist Press, 1981); Julie Roy Jeffrey, *Frontier Women: The Trans-Mississippi West, 1840–1880* (New York: Hill and Wang, 1979); Lillian Schlissel, *Women's Diaries of the Westward Journey* (New York: Schocken Books, 1982); Christine Stansell, "Women on the Great Plains, 1865–1890," *Women's Studies* 4 (1976): 87–98. Antebellum homestead laws in Oregon and Texas allowed women to claim land.

4. Women reformers argued that women's moral superiority gave them a mandate to reform society. William O'Neill identified these women as "social" feminists to distinguish them from "hard core or extreme" feminists who entered public life as a means of claiming their individual rights as citizens. William O'Neill, ed., *The Woman Movement* (Chicago: Quadrangle Books, 1971), 33.

5. Philip J. Greven, *The Protestant Temperament: Patterns of Child-Rearing, Religious Experience, and the Self in Early America* (New York: Alfred A. Knopf, 1977), 12–18, 25–28, 124–140.

6. Variation occurred within companionate families. A few homesteading families among the many I studied rigidly adhered to the concept of separate spheres. Others accepted the ideal but did not practice it.

7. Schlissel, *Women's Diaries*, 78. For another critical view of Missouri men and their treatment of women, see Faye Cashatt Lewis, *Nothing to Make a Shadow* (Ames, Iowa: The Iowa State University Press, 1971), 58–62.

8. Ruth Barnes Moynihan, *Rebel for Rights: Abigail Scott Duniway* (New Haven, Conn.: Yale University Press, 1983), 15–22.

9. Willa Cather, *My Antonia* (Boston: Houghton Mifflin Company, 1918); and *O Pioneers!* (Boston: Houghton Mifflin Company, 1913). Linda Rasmussen et al., *A Harvest Yet to Reap: A History of Prairie Women* (Toronto: Women's Press, 1976); and Carol Fairbanks, "Lives of Girls and Women on the Canadian and American Prairies," *International Journal of Women's Studies* 2 (September/October 1979): 452–472.

10. Fleming Historical Society, *Memories of Our Pioneers* (Iowa Falls: General Publishing and Binding, 1971), 116, 118–119 (hereafter cited as FHS, *Memories*).

11. Norma Milton, "Essential Servants: Immigrant Domestics on the Canadian Prairies" (paper presented at the Women's West Conference, Institute of the American West, Sun Valley, Idaho, August 12, 1983).

12. Warnick, "Women Homesteaders in Utah," 55–56. The percentages of young and single women claimants are my calculations based on Warnick's figures in Appendix A, 125–126.

13. Jessie L. Embry, *Mormon Polygamous Families: Life in the Principle* (Salt Lake City: University of Utah Press, 1987), 32.

14. Warnick, "Women Homesteaders in Utah," 24, 32–41.

15. Elizabeth Pleck, *Domestic Tyranny: The Making of Social Policy Against Family Violence From Colonial Times to the Present* (New York: Oxford University Press, 1987), 23–24; and Nancy F. Cott, "Divorce and the Changing Status of Women in Eighteenth-Century Massachusetts," in *The American Family in Social-Historical Perspective*, ed. Michael Gordon (New York: St. Martin's Press, 1978), 130.

16. Warnick, "Women Homesteaders in Utah," 38.

17. Ibid., 15, citing *Women's Exponent*, December 1, 1895.

18. My analysis of Warnick's data differs from hers. She concluded that there existed in Utah "an atmosphere that was as open as other frontiers for participation of women in the homestead movement." "Women Homesteaders in Utah," 89.

19. Florence C. Gould and Patricia N. Pando, *Claiming Their Land: Women Homesteaders in Texas* (El Paso: Texas Western Press, 1990), 8–13, 34.

20. Paula Marie Nelson, "No Place for Clinging Vines: Women Homesteaders on the South Dakota Frontier, 1900–1915" (M.A. thesis, University of South Dakota, 1978), 4–6, 19, 42, 59–61. See also chapters 3, 4, and 5 in Nelson's *After the West Was Won: Homesteaders and Town-Builders in Western South Dakota, 1900–1917* (Iowa City: University of Iowa Press, 1986).

21. Paula M. Bauman, "Single Women Homesteaders in Wyoming, 1880–1930," *Annals of Wyoming* 58 (Spring 1986): 41, citing Peggy Kirkbride, *From These Roots* (Cheyenne: Pioneer Printing Co., 1972), 121. Sheryll Patterson-Black, "Women Homesteaders on the Great Plains Frontier," *Frontiers* 1 (Summer 1976): 68.

22. H. Elaine Lindgren, "Ethnic Women Homesteading on the Plains of North Dakota," *Great Plains Quarterly* 9 (Summer 1989): 157–173. See also Lindgren's *Land in Her Own Name: Women as Homesteaders in North Dakota* (Fargo: The North Dakota Institute for Regional Studies, 1991), 51–55.

23. Schlissel, *Women's Diaries*; and Faragher, *Women and Men on the Overland Trail.*

24. In 1924, 44 percent of Logan County farmers and 53 percent of Washington County farmers owned all the land they worked. In 1933 those percentages had dropped to 26 and 24, respectively. Colorado State Board of Immigration, *Year Book of the State of Colorado, 1925*, ed. Tolbert R. Ingram (Denver: Bradford-Robinson Printing Company, n.d.), 84; and Colorado State Board of Immigration, *Year Book of the State of Colorado, 1933–1934*, ed. Tolbert R. Ingram (Denver: Bradford-Robinson Printing Company, n.d.), 124. FHS, *Memories*, 128–129.

25. Washington County Museum Association, *The Pioneer Book II of Washington County, Colorado* (Fort Morgan, Colo.: Print Shop, n.d.; Aurora, Colo.: Rocky Mountain Press, n.d.) (hereafter cited as *PBWC II*).

26. Jensen, *With These Hands*, 148–149.

27. Department of Agriculture, *Social and Labor Needs of Farm Women* (Washington, D.C.: GPO, 1915), 89; Amy DickensenWorthley, interview with author, Sterling, Colo., June 7, 1980.

28. Jensen, *With These Hands*, 150.

29. *PBWC II*, 466, 624. Nancy Grey Osterud's study of farm women in nineteenth-century New York showed a similar connection between women's inability to own land and their inferior negotiating position in relationships with men. See her "Strategies of Mutuality: Relations Among Women and Men in an Agricultural Community" (Ph.D. diss., Brown University, 1984), 15, 295–297.

30. Ruth Schooley Hall, *Soddy Bride* (Fort Collins, Colo.: Robinson Press, 1973), 123.

31. Most citizens of the city and county of Denver had telephone and electric service by 1940. Among all Colorado farm dwellings, 38.4 percent had electric lighting and 32.7 percent had telephones. Colorado State Planning Commission, *Year Book of the State of Colorado, 1941–1942*, ed. Tolbert R. Ingram (Denver: Bradford-Robinson Printing Company, n.d.), 19, 87, 266; and Bureau of the Census, *Sixteenth Census of the United States: 1940, Agriculture*, vol. 1, part 6, *Statistics for Counties* (Washington, D.C.: GPO, 1942), 284–285.

32. For a discussion of jokes at farmers' expense and their origins in conservatives' fears of agrarian radicalism and in reformers' fears of rural fundamentalism, see Jensen, *With These Hands*, 153.

33. The average size of Logan County farms in 1925 was 312 acres; of Washington County farms, 437 acres. By 1940 these averages had risen to 661 acres and 904 acres, respectively. By 1978 the average farm size in Logan County had risen to 1,118 acres; and in Washington County, to 1,534 acres. *Year Book of the State of Colorado, 1925*, 84; Colorado State Planning Division, *Colorado, 1959–1961: Year Book of the State of Colorado* (n.p., n.d.), 500 fold-in; and Bureau of the Census, *1978 Census of Agriculture*, vol. 1, part 6, *Colorado: State and County Data* (Washington, D.C.: GPO, 1981), 360, 470. In 1945 land in Logan County cost on average $19 per acre; in Washington County, $9 per acre. In 1930 land prices per acre in each county averaged $27 and $12, respectively. Colorado State Planning Commission, *Year Book of the State of Colorado, 1948–1950* (Denver: Bradford-Robinson Printing Company, n.d.), 239.

34. Maureen Honey, "The 'Womanpower' Campaign: Advertising and Recruitment Propaganda During World War II," *Frontiers* 6 (Spring/Summer 1981): 50–56; Scott G. McNall and Sally Allen McNall, *Plains Families* (New York: St. Martin's Press, 1982), 274.

35. Teresa Jordan, *Cowgirls: Women of the American West* (New York: Anchor Press, Doubleday and Company, 1982), 57.

36. Comparisons between the ratios of women to men operating farms today and in the post-1900 homesteading years are difficult to make. Only recently has the federal census tabulated tenancy by gender, and even so, it does not distinguish between operators, owners, and tenants, by county. In 1987 women operated 6.8 percent of family or individually owned farms in Washington County; in Logan County, women operated 3.4 percent of such farms. Between 1900 and 1920, about 18 percent of homestead entrants were women. These data do not reflect sales to men of land patented by women or sales to women of land patented by men. Nor do they include government land patented by means other than homesteading. Bureau of the Census, *1987 Census of Agriculture*, vol. 1, part 6, *Colorado: State and County Data* (Washington, D.C.: GPO, 1989), 144, 147, 236, 239.

37. The Reverend Gertrude Horn, tape recorded interview with Kathryn Nelson, Grover, Colo., June 30, 1982, for "Grassland Women," produced and photographed by Kathryn Nelson for the Colorado Humanities Program.

38. Debbie Bauman Idler, tape recorded interview with Kathryn Nelson, Grover, Colo., 1982, for "Grassland Women"; and Jordan, *Cowgirls*, xxix, 57, 72, 133.

39. Idler, interview; and Jordan, *Cowgirls*, 63–64, 88.

40. Jordan, *Cowgirls*, 62–63. Kathryn Nelson shared with me her insights regarding ranch women and their sometimes conflicted feelings about their femininity.

41. Jordan, *Cowgirls*, 89.

42. Ibid., 35.

Bibliography

Unpublished Sources

Alishouse, Ezra and Helen. Interview with Margaret Cooley. November 12, 1975. Akron Public Library.

Bowles, Elva. Interview with author. Longmont, Colorado. July 18, 1980.

Covington, Opal. Interview with Margaret Cooley. May 15, 1975. Akron Public Library.

Ervin, Lois. Interview with author. Sterling, Colorado. June 7, 1980.

Horn, Rev. Gertrude. Interview with Kathryn Nelson. Grover, Colorado. June 30, 1982.

Idler, Debbie Bauman. Interview with Kathryn Nelson. Grover, Colorado.

Kennedy, Sister Patricia. "The Pioneer Woman in Middle Western Fiction." Ph.D. diss., University of Illinois, 1968.

McElhiney, Annette Bennington. "The Image of the Pioneer Woman in the American Novel." Ph.D. diss., University of Denver, 1978.

Markoff, Dena Sabin. "The Beet Sugar Industry in Microcosm: The National Sugar Manufacturing Company, 1899 to 1967." Ph.D. diss., University of Colorado, 1980.

Mehls, Steven F. "The New Empire of the Rockies: A History of Northeastern Colorado." Draft prepared for the Bureau of Land Management, Colorado State Office, 1981.

Milton, Norma. "Essential Servants: Immigrant Domestics on the Canadian Prairies." Paper presented at the Women's West Conference, Institute of the American West, Sun Valley, Idaho, August 2, 1983.

Nelson, Paula Marie. "No Place for Clinging Vines: Women Homesteaders on the South Dakota Frontier, 1900–1915." Master's thesis, University of South Dakota, 1978.

Newberry, Alice C. Papers. Colorado Historical Society Library, Denver.

Osterud, Nancy Grey. "Strategies of Mutuality: Relations Among Women and Men in an Agricultural Community." Ph.D. diss., Brown University, 1984.

Sparling, Stella. Interview with Margaret Cooley. June 23, 1975. Akron Public Library.

U.S. Bureau of the Census. Federal Population Census Schedules for 1910. Record Group 29, microfilm publication T624. Available at the Denver Federal Records Center.

U.S. Bureau of Land Management. Land Office Records for Kit Carson, Logan, and Washington Counties. Available on microfilm at the BLM Denver office.

Warnick, Jill Thorley. "Women Homesteaders in Utah, 1869–1934." Master's thesis, Brigham Young University, 1984.

Worthley, Amy Dickensen. Interview with author. Sterling, Colorado. June 7, 1980.

Published Sources

Allen, Barbara. *Homesteading the High Desert*. Salt Lake City: University of Utah Press, 1987.

Armour, M., interviewer for Civil Works Administration. *Interviews Collected During 1933–34 for the State Historical Society of Colorado: Logan and Phillips Counties*. Pamphlet 341, Docs. 1–52 (inclusive). Denver: Colorado State Historical Society.

Arnett, R. E. "Ranching in Northeastern Colorado in the Early Eighties." *Colorado Magazine*, November 1943, 201–213.

Athearn, Robert G. *The Coloradans*. Albuquerque: University of New Mexico Press, 1976.

———. *Union Pacific Country*. Chicago: Rand McNally and Company, 1971.

Atherton, Lewis. *The Cattle Kings*. Bloomington: Indiana University Press, 1967.

Barker, Roger G. "Influence of the Frontier Environment on Behavior." In *The American West: New Perspectives, New Dimensions*, edited by Jerome Steffen. Norman: University of Oklahoma Press, 1979.

Barns, Cass G. *The Sod House*. Lincoln: University of Nebraska Press, 1970.

Bauman, Paula M. "Single Women Homesteaders in Wyoming, 1880–1930." *Annals of Wyoming* 58 (Spring 1986): 40–53.

Bern, Enid, ed. "They Had a Wonderful Time: The Homesteading Letters of Anna and Ethel Erickson." *North Dakota History* 45 (Fall 1978): 4–31.

Billington, Ray Allen. *America's Frontier Heritage*. New York: Holt, Rinehart and Winston, 1966.

———. *Westward Expansion*. New York: Macmillan Publishing Company, 1974.

Blouet, Brian W., and Frederick C. Luebke, eds. *The Great Plains: Environment and Culture*. Lincoln: University of Nebraska Press, 1979.

Bogue, Allan G. *From Prairie to Corn Belt: Farming on the Illinois and Iowa Prairies in the Nineteenth Century*. Chicago: University of Chicago Press, 1963.

Bogue, Donald J. *The Population of the United States*. Glencoe, Ill.: Free Press, 1959.

Bordin, Ruth. *Frances Willard*. Chapel Hill: University of North Carolina Press, 1986.

———. *Woman and Temperance: The Quest for Power and Liberty, 1873–1900*. Philadelphia: Temple University Press, 1981.

Brad, Jacoba Boothman. *Homestead on the Kootenai*. Caldwell, Idaho: Caxton Printers, 1960.

Brown, Dee. *The Gentle Tamers: Women of the Old Wild West*. New York: Bantam Pathfinder Editions, 1974.

Calhoun, Arthur. *A Social History of the American Family*. 3 vols. New York: Barnes and Noble, 1945.

Cather, Willa. *My Antonia*. Boston: Houghton Mifflin Company, 1918.

———. *O Pioneers!* Boston: Houghton Mifflin Company, 1913.

Coale, Ansley J., and Melvin Zelnik. *New Estimates of Fertility and Population in the United States*. Princeton: Princeton University Press, 1963.

Colorado, State of. *Abstract of Votes Cast for State Officers at the General Elections of the Years 1892 to 1900 Inclusive*. Denver: Smith-Brooks Printing Company, 1901.

Colorado State Board of Immigration. *Year Book of the State of Colorado, 1918.* Denver: Brock-Haffner Press, n.d.

———. *Year Book of the State of Colorado, 1920.* Denver: Welch-Haffner Printing Company, n.d.

———. *Year Book of the State of Colorado, 1921.* Denver: Welch-Haffner Printing Company, n.d.

———. *Year Book of the State of Colorado, 1925.* Compiled and edited by Tolbert R. Ingram. Denver: Bradford-Robinson Printing Company, n.d.

———. *Year Book of the State of Colorado, 1933–1934.* Compiled and edited by Tolbert R. Ingram. Denver: Bradford-Robinson Printing Company, n.d.

Colorado State Planning Commission. *Year Book of the State of Colorado, 1941–1942.* Compiled and edited by Tolbert R. Ingram. Denver: Bradford-Robinson Printing Company, n.d.

———. *Year Book of the State of Colorado, 1948–1950.* Denver: Bradford-Robinson Printing Company, n.d.

Colorado State Planning Division. *Colorado, 1959–1961: Year Book of the State of Colorado.* Edited by Salma A. Waters. n.p., n.d.

Conklin, Emma Burke. *A Brief History of Logan County, Colorado, With Reminiscences by Pioneers.* Denver: Welch-Haffner Printing Company, 1928.

Corsberg, Inez S. *Remembering 1916: Some Recollections of a One-Room School Teacher.* Sterling, Colo.: Royal Printing Company, 1969.

Cott, Nancy F. "Divorce and the Changing Status of Women in Eighteenth-Century Massachusetts." In *The American Family in Social-Historical Perspective,* edited by Michael Gordon. New York: St. Martin's Press, 1978.

———. "Passionlessness: An Interpretation of Victorian Sexual Ideology, 1790–1850." *Signs* 4 (1978): 219–236.

Crook Historical Society. *No Fuss and Feathers — Crook: A History of the Crook Community.* Edited by Dorothea Safford and Helen Taylor. Fort Collins, Colo.: Economy Printing, 1977.

Curley, Edwin A. *Nebraska, Its Advantages, Resources, and Drawbacks.* New York: American and Foreign Publications Company, 1875.

Degler, Carl. *At Odds: Women and the Family in America From the Revolution to the Present.* New York: Oxford University Press, 1980.

Deutsch, Sarah. *No Separate Refuge: Culture, Class, and Gender on an Anglo-Hispanic Frontier in the American Southwest, 1880–1940.* New York: Oxford University Press, 1987.

Diaries of Ruth and Clark Woodis: The Story of a Colorado Homestead, 1913–1928. N.p., 1976.

Dick, Everett. *The Lure of the Land: A Social History of the Public Lands From the Articles of Confederation to the New Deal.* Lincoln: University of Nebraska Press, 1970.

———. *The Sod-House Frontier, 1854–1890: A Social History of the Northern Plains From the Creation of Kansas and Nebraska to the Admission of the Dakotas.* Lincoln: University of Nebraska Press, 1979.

Douglas, Ann. *Feminization of American Culture.* New York: Alfred A. Knopf, 1977.

Dunbar, Robert G. "History of Agriculture." In *Colorado and Its People*, edited by LeRoy R. Hafen, vol. 2, 121–157. New York: Lewis Historical Publishing Company, 1948.

Durrell, Glen R. "Homesteading in Colorado." *Colorado Magazine*, Spring 1974, 93–114.

Eblen, Jack E. "An Analysis of Nineteenth Century Frontier Populations." *Demography* 2 (1965): 399–413.

Embry, Jessie L. *Mormon Polygamous Families: Life in the Principle*. Salt Lake City: University of Utah Press, 1987.

Fairbanks, Carol. "Lives of Girls and Women on the Canadian and American Prairies." *International Journal of Women's Studies* 2 (September/October 1979): 452–472.

Faragher, John Mack. "History From the Inside-Out: Writing the History of Women in Rural America." *American Quarterly* 33 (Winter 1981): 537–557.

———. *Women and Men on the Overland Trail*. New Haven, Conn.: Yale University Press, 1979.

Fehrenbacher, Don E., ed. *History and American Society: Essays of David M. Potter*. New York: Oxford University Press, 1973.

Fischer, Christiane, ed. *Let Them Speak for Themselves: Women in the American West, 1849–1900*. Hamden, Conn.: Archon Books, 1977.

Fite, Gilbert C. *The Farmers' Frontier, 1865–1900*. New York: Holt, Rinehart and Winston, 1966.

Fleming Historical Society. *Memories of Our Pioneers*. Iowa Falls, Iowa: General Publishing and Binding, 1971.

Fowler, William W. *Woman on the American Frontier*. Hartford, Conn.: S. S. Scranton & Company, 1880.

Garland, Hamlin. *Main-Travelled Roads*. New York: Harper and Brothers, 1899.

———. *Other Main-Travelled Roads*. New York: Harper and Brothers, 1910.

———. *A Son of the Middle Border*. New York: Macmillan Company, 1938.

Gates, Paul. *Free Homesteads for All Americans: The Homestead Act of 1862*. Washington, D.C.: Civil War Centennial Commission, 1962.

Gould, Florence C., and Patricia N. Pando. *Claiming Their Land: Women Homesteaders in Texas*. El Paso: Texas Western Press, 1990.

Greven, Philip J. *The Protestant Temperament: Patterns of Child-Rearing, Religious Experience, and the Self in Early America*. New York: Alfred A. Knopf, 1977.

Hafen, LeRoy R. "The Counties of Colorado: A History of Their Creation and the Origin of Their Names." *Colorado Magazine*, March 1931, 48–60.

Hall, Ruth Schooley. *Soddie Bride*. Fort Collins, Colo.: Robinson Press, 1973.

Hargreaves, Mary Wilma M. *Dry Farming in the Northern Great Plains, 1900–1925*. Cambridge: Harvard University Press, 1957.

———. "Women in the Agricultural Settlement of the Northern Plains." *Agricultural History* 50 (January 1976): 179–189.

Haugen, Einar. *Ole Edvart Rolvaag*. Boston: Twayne Publishers, 1983.

Hendricks, Cecilia Hennel. *Letters From Honeyhill: A Woman's View of Homesteading, 1914–1931*. Compiled and edited by Cecilia Hendricks Wahl. Boulder, Colo.: Pruett Publishing Company, 1986.

Hine, Robert V. *Community on the American Frontier: Separate but Not Alone*. Norman: University of Oklahoma Press, 1980.

Hoig, Stan. *The Sand Creek Massacre*. Norman: University of Oklahoma Press, 1961.

Honey, Maureen. "The 'Womanpower' Campaign: Advertising and Recruitment Propaganda During World War." *Frontiers* 6 (Spring/Summer 1981): 50–56.

Hudson, John C. "The Study of Western Frontier Populations." In *The American West: New Perspectives, New Dimensions*, edited by Jerome Steffen. Norman: University of Oklahoma Press, 1979.

Hughes, J. Donald. *American Indians in Colorado*. Boulder, Colo.: Pruett Publishing Company, 1977.

Humphrey, Seth K. *Following the Prairie Frontier*. Minneapolis: University of Minnesota Press, 1931.

Hyde, Dayton O. *Don Coyote*. New York: Ballantine Books, 1986.

Jeffrey, Julie Roy. *Frontier Women: The Trans-Mississippi West, 1840–1880*. New York: Hill and Wang, 1979.

Jensen, Joan. *With These Hands: Women Working on the Land*. New York: The Feminist Press, 1981.

Jensen, Joan, and Darlis A. Miller. "The Gentle Tamers Revisited: New Approaches to the History of Women in the American West." *Pacific Historical Review* 49 (May 1980): 173–213.

Jones, Daryl. *The Dime Novel Western*. Bowling Green, Ohio: Bowling Green University Popular Press, 1978.

Jordan, Teresa. *Cowgirls: Women of the American West*. New York: Anchor Press, Doubleday and Company, 1982.

Juster, Norton. *So Sweet to Labor: Rural Women in America, 1865–1895*. New York: Viking Press, 1979.

Kane, Murray. "Some Considerations on the Safety Valve Doctrine." *Mississippi Valley Historical Review* 23 (September 1936): 169–188.

Kelly, Joan. "The Doubled Vision of Feminist Theory: A Postscript to the Women and Power Conference." *Feminist Studies* 5 (Spring 1979): 216–227.

Kirkbride, Peggy. *From These Roots*. Cheyenne: Pioneer Printing Co., 1972.

Kloberdanz, Timothy J. "People Without a Country: The Russian Germans of Logan County, Colorado." In Dale Wells, *The Logan County Ledger*, 225–247. The Logan County Historical Society, 1976.

Kohl, Edith Eudora. *Land of the Burnt Thigh*. New York: Funk and Wagnalls Company, 1938.

Kolodny, Annette. *The Lay of the Land: Metaphor as Experience and History in American Life and Letters*. Chapel Hill: University of North Carolina Press, 1975.

Krakel, Dean. *South Platte Country: A History of Old Weld County, Colorado, 1739–1900*. Laramie: Powder River Publishers, 1954.

Lamar, Howard R. "Rites of Passage: Young Men and Their Families in the Overland Trail Experience, 1843–1869." In *Soul-Butter and Hog Wash and Other Essays on the American West.* Charles Redd Monographs in Western History, no. 8. Provo, Utah: Brigham Young University Press, 1978.

Levinson, Daniel. "The Mid-Life Transition: A Period in Adult Psychosocial Development." *Psychiatry* 40 (1977): 99–112.

Lewis, Faye Cashatt. *Nothing to Make a Shadow.* Ames, Iowa: Iowa State University Press, 1971.

Lindgren, H. Elaine. "Ethnic Women Homesteading on the Plains of North Dakota." *Great Plains Quarterly* 9 (Summer 1989): 157–173.

———. *Land in Her Own Name: Women as Homesteaders in North Dakota.* Fargo: The North Dakota Institute for Regional Studies, 1991.

Lunardini, Christine A. *From Equal Rights to Equal Suffrage: Alice Paul and the National Woman's Party, 1910–1928.* New York: New York University Press, 1986.

McNall, Scott G., and Sally Allen McNall. *Plains Families.* New York: St. Martin's Press, 1982.

McRoberts, Georgia L. "Pioneer Ranch Life Near Sterling." *Colorado Magazine,* January 1934, 64–68.

Malin, James C. *The Grassland of North America: Prolegomena to Its History.* Ann Arbor: Edwards Brothers, 1956.

Mann, Ralph. *After the Gold Rush: Society in Grass Valley and Nevada City, California, 1849–1870.* Stanford: Stanford University Press, 1982.

Mowat, Farley. *Never Cry Wolf.* Boston: Little, Brown and Company, 1963.

Moynihan, Ruth Barnes. *Rebel for Rights: Abigail Scott Duniway.* New Haven, Conn.: Yale University Press, 1983.

Myres, Sandra L. *Westering Women and the Frontier Experience, 1800–1915.* Albuquerque: University of New Mexico Press, 1982.

Nelson, Paula Marie. *After the West Was Won: Homesteaders and Town-Builders in Western South Dakota, 1900–1917.* Iowa City: University of Iowa Press, 1986.

Norton, Mary Beth. *Liberty's Daughters: The Revolutionary Experience of American Women, 1750–1800.* Boston: Little, Brown and Company, 1980.

O'Kieffe, Charley. *Western Story: The Recollections of Charley O'Kieffe, 1884–1898.* Pioneer Heritage Series, no. 8. Lincoln: University of Nebraska Press, 1960.

O'Neill, William, ed. *The Woman Movement.* Chicago: Quadrangle Books, 1971.

Osgood, Ernest Staples. *The Day of the Cattleman.* Chicago: University of Chicago Press, 1929.

Patterson-Black, Sheryll. "Women Homesteaders on the Great Plains Frontier." *Frontiers* 1 (Summer 1976): 67–88.

Patterson-Black, Sheryll, and Gene Patterson-Black. *Western Women, in History and Literature.* Crawford, Nebr.: Cottonwood Press, 1978.

Peffer, Louise E. *The Closing of the Public Domain.* Stanford: Stanford University Press, 1951.

Petrik, Paula. *No Step Backward: Women and Family on the Rocky Mountain Mining Frontier, Helena, Montana, 1865–1900.* Helena: Montana Historical Society Press, 1987.

Pleck, Elizabeth. *Domestic Tyranny: The Making of Social Policy Against Family Violence From Colonial Times to the Present.* New York: Oxford University Press, 1987.

Propst, Nell Brown. *Forgotten People: A History of the South Platte Trail.* Boulder, Colo.: Pruett Publishing Company, 1979.

———. "The New Americans: A History of the Ethnic Groups Who Settled Logan County: The Mexicans." In Dale Wells, *The Logan County Ledger*, 217–223. Logan County Historical Society, 1976.

———. *Those Strenuous Dames of the Colorado Prairie.* Boulder, Colo.: Pruett Publishing Company, 1982.

Rasmussen, Linda, Lorna Rasmussen, Candace Savage, and Anne Wheeler. *A Harvest Yet to Reap: A History of Prairie Women.* Toronto: Women's Press, 1979.

Riley, Glenda. *The Female Frontier: A Comparative View of Women on the Prairie and Plains.* Lawrence, Kans.: University Press of Kansas, 1988.

———. *Frontierswomen: The Iowa Experience.* Ames, Iowa: Iowa State University Press, 1981.

———. *Inventing the American Woman: A Perspective on Women's History.* Arlington Heights, Ill.: Harlan Davidson, 1987.

———. "Women in the West." *Journal of American Culture* 3 (Summer 1980): 311–329.

Robbins, Roy. *Our Landed Heritage: The Public Domain, 1776–1936.* Gloucester, Mass.: Peter Smith, 1960.

Rock, Kenneth W. " 'Unsere Leute': The Germans From Russia in Colorado." *Colorado Magazine*, Spring 1977, 155–183.

Rolvaag, O. E. *Giants in the Earth: A Saga of the Prairie.* New York: Harper and Brothers Publishers, 1927.

Ruede, Howard. *Sod-House Days: Letters From a Kansas Homesteader, 1877–1878.* Edited by John Ise. New York: Cooper Square Publishers, 1966.

Russell, Don. "Foreword." In *The Life of Hon. William F. Cody Known as Buffalo Bill.* Lincoln: University of Nebraska Press, 1978.

Ryan, Mary P. *Womanhood in America From Colonial Times to the Present.* New York: New Viewpoints, 1975.

Sallet, Richard. *Russian-German Settlements in the United States.* Translated by LaVern J. Rippley and Armand Bauer. Fargo: North Dakota Institute for Regional Studies, 1974.

Sandoz, Mari. *Old Jules.* New York: Hastings House Publishers, 1935.

———. *Sandhill Sundays and Other Recollections.* Lincoln: University of Nebraska Press, 1970.

———. *Slogum House.* Boston: Little, Brown and Company, 1937.

Schlissel, Lillian. "Mothers and Daughters on the Western Frontier." *Frontiers* 3 (Summer 1978): 29–33.

———. *Women's Diaries of the Westward Journey.* New York: Schocken Books, 1982.

Schwieder, Dorothy. "Labor and Economic Roles of Iowa Farm Wives, 1840–80." In *Farmers, Bureaucrats, and Middlemen: Historical Perspectives on American Agriculture,* edited by Trudy Huskamp Peterson. Washington, D.C.: Howard University Press, 1980.

Sklar, Kathryn Kish. *Catherine Beecher: A Study in American Domesticity*. New York: W. W. Norton and Company, 1976.

Smith, Daniel Scott. "Family Limitation, Sexual Control and Domestic Feminism in Victorian America." In *Clio's Consciousness Raised*, edited by Mary Hartman and Lois W. Banner. New York: Harper Colophon Books, 1974.

Smith, Henry Nash. *Virgin Land: The American West as Symbol and Myth*. Cambridge: Harvard University Press, 1978.

Smith, Page. *Daughters of the Promised Land: Women in American History*. Boston: Little, Brown and Company, 1970.

Smithwick, Noah. *The Evolution of a State or Recollections of Old Texas Days*. Austin: Gammel Book Company, 1900.

Sprague, William Forrest. *Women and the West: A Short Social History*. Boston: Christopher Publishing House, 1940.

Stansell, Christine. "Women on the Great Plains, 1865–1890." *Women's Studies* 4 (1976): 87–98.

Steffen, Jerome, ed. *The American West: New Perspectives, New Dimensions*. Norman: University of Oklahoma Press, 1979.

Steinel, Alvin T. *History of Agriculture in Colorado*. Fort Collins, Colo.: State Agricultural College, 1926.

Stewart, Elinore Pruitt [Rupert]. *Letters of a Woman Homesteader*. Lincoln: University of Nebraska Press, 1961.

Stoeltje, Beverly J. "A Helpmate for Man Indeed: The Image of the Frontier Woman." *Journal of American Folklore* 88 (January–March 1975): 25–41.

Stratton, Joanna L. *Pioneer Women: Voices From the Kansas Frontier*. New York: Simon and Schuster, 1981.

Swedish Historical Society of America. *Year-Book, VII, 1921–1922*. Chicago, 1922.

Taeuber, Conrad, and Irene B. Taeuber. *The Changing Population of the United States*. New York: John Wiley and Sons, 1958.

Turner, Frederick Jackson. *The Frontier in American History*. New York: Henry Holt and Company, 1920.

————. *The Significance of the Frontier in American History*. Edited by Harold P. Simonson. New York: Frederick Ungar Publishing Company, 1963.

U.S. Bureau of the Census. *Fourteenth Census of the United States, Taken in the Year 1920: Agriculture*. Vol. 6, part 3. Washington, D.C.: GPO, 1922.

————. *Fourteenth Census of the United States Taken in the Year 1920*. Vols. 1, 2, and 3, *Population, 1920*. Washington, D.C.: GPO, 1922.

————. *1987 Census of Agriculture*. Vol. 1, part 6. *Colorado: State and County Data*. Washington, D.C.: GPO, 1989.

————. *1978 Census of Agriculture*. Vol. 1, part 6. *Colorado: State and County Data*. Washington, D.C.: GPO, 1981.

———. *Sixteenth Census of the United States: 1940, Agriculture.* Vol. 1, part 6, *Statistics for Counties.* Washington, D.C.: GPO, 1942.

———. *Statistical Abstract of the United States, 1970.* Washington, D.C.: GPO, 1970.

———. *Thirteenth Census of the United States, Taken in the Year 1910: Abstract of the Census With Supplement for Colorado.* Washington, D.C.: GPO, 1913.

———. *United States Life Tables: 1890, 1901, 1910, 1901–1910.* Washington, D.C.: GPO, 1921.

U.S. Census Office. *Compendium of the Eleventh Census: 1890.* Parts 1 and 2. Washington, D.C.: GPO, 1894.

———. *Report on Agriculture by Irrigation in the Western Part of the United States at the Eleventh Census, 1890.* Washington, D.C.: GPO, 1894.

———. *Report on the Statistics of Agriculture in the United States at the Eleventh Census: 1890.* Washington, D.C.: GPO, 1895.

———. *Twelfth Census of the United States, Taken in the Year 1900: Agriculture.* Part 1. Washington, D.C.: GPO, 1902.

———. *Twelfth Census of the United States, Taken in the Year 1900: Population.* Part 1. Washington, D.C.: GPO, 1901.

U.S. Department of Agriculture. *Social and Labor Needs of Farm Women.* Washington, D.C.: GPO, 1915.

U.S. General Land Office. *The Manner of Proceeding to Obtain Title to Public Lands Under the Preemption, Homestead and Other Laws.* Washington, D.C.: GPO, 1884.

———. *Suggestions to Homesteaders and Persons Desiring to Make Homestead Entries.* Washington, D.C.: GPO, 1906.

Vance, Millard Fillmore. "Pioneering at Akron, Colorado." *Colorado Magazine*, September 1931, 173–177.

Washington County Museum Association. *The Pioneer Book of Washington County, Colorado.* Denver: Big Mountain Press, 1959.

———. *The Pioneer Book II of Washington County, Colorado.* Fort Morgan, Colo.: Print Shop, n.d.; and Aurora, Colo.: The Rocky Mountain Press, n.d.

Watson, Clara. "Homesteading on the Plains." *Colorado Magazine*, April 1961, 142–143.

Webb, Walter Prescott. *The Great Plains: A Study in Institutions and Environment.* Boston: Ginn and Company, 1931.

Wells, Dale. *The Logan County Ledger.* Logan County Historical Society, 1976.

Welter, Barbara. "The Cult of True Womanhood, 1820–1860." *American Quarterly* 18 (Summer 1966): 151–174.

West, Elliott. *Growing Up With the Country: Childhood on the Far Western Frontier.* Albuquerque: University of New Mexico Press, 1989.

Westbrook, Melva Cummins. *Mom and Me.* Worland, Wyo.: Worland Press, 1971.

Westermeier, Clifford P. "The Legal Status of the Colorado Cattleman, 1867–1887." *Colorado Magazine*, May 1948, 109–118.

Williams, Blaine T. "The Frontier Family: Demographic Fact and Historical Myth." In *Essays on the American West*, edited by Harold M. Hollingsworth and Sandra Myres. Austin: University of Texas Press, 1969.

Wrigley, E. A., ed. *An Introduction to English Historical Demography*. New York: Basic Books, 1966.

Wyman, Walker D. *Frontier Woman: The Life of a Woman Homesteader on the Dakota Frontier*. River Falls, Wis.: University of Wisconsin Press, 1972.

Zaretsky, Eli. *Capitalism, the Family and Personal Life*. New York: Harper Colophon Books, 1976.

Index